THE TROUBLE WITH BLAME

THE TROUBLE WITH BLAME

VICTIMS, PERPETRATORS, AND RESPONSIBILITY

Sharon Lamb

HARVARD UNIVERSITY PRESS
Cambridge, Massachusetts
London, England

Copyright © 1996 by the President and Fellows of Harvard College
Printed in the United States of America
First Harvard University Press paperback edition, 1999
Library of Congress Cataloging-in-Publication Data
Lamb, Sharon.
   The trouble with blame : victims, perpetrators, and
responsibility / Sharon Lamb.
      p. cm.
   Includes bibliographical references and index.
   ISBN 0-674-91010-9 (cloth)
   ISBN 0-674-91011-7 (pbk.)

   1. Attribution (Social psychology)   2. Blame—Moral and ethical
aspects.   3. Victims—Psychology.   I. Title.
HM291.L235   1996
302'.12—dc20   95-47457
                     CIP

To my mother and father, Martha and Tracy Lamb

CONTENTS

NOTE ON TERMINOLOGY

Throughout this book I have used the male pronoun for perpetrators and the female pronoun for victims, counter to the practice of some of my colleagues who strive to remain gender neutral. The overwhelming preponderance of perpetrators of abuse are male, whereas the majority of victims are female. I have therefore decided that it is less ambiguous and more accurate to use the gendered pronoun throughout. This should in no way diminish the very real experiences of the large number of male victims of sexual abuse.

THE TROUBLE WITH BLAME

Try to imagine a man who is abusive, but imagine him in some detail, carrying out an abusive act, whether it be punching his pregnant wife or fondling his eight-year-old daughter. Picture whatever crime you can conjure up against the defenses that will urge you to shut out the picture, to "change the channel." Then, as you keep the picture in your mind, try to imagine some possible causal links between the explicit act that you imagined and the conditions of the man's life, for example, the poverty he lives in or the stress he is undergoing. Be specific: maybe he can't find work or maybe he was drunk when it happened. Perhaps you'll want to include in your scenario the alcoholism of the man's father or his own drinking problem. Consider a possible history of abuse, beatings from his mother or father. You might add to the picture his own rape as a child. Include any and all circumstances that you believe may make this person act in the way he does. Then try to visualize these links in action. Envision what might be going through his conscious or unconscious mind at the time of the act, and try to relate it to any and all of these imagined circumstances.

Now ask yourself, is the man a puppet? an automaton? Is he an addict? You are asking to what extent he is compelled to do what he is doing. To what extent does he have a choice? Is it fair to say that something inside of him presses so many angry buttons that he is no longer in control? And if we can say that, then who is responsible for what is inside of him?

Next, imagine the feedback this man receives for his actions. Begin with the immediate response. His wife screams or cringes, or she puts her arms in front of her to protect herself. Or maybe his hand stings or the softness giving way registers; he hears an involuntary gasp. And now consider the little girl, surely frightened; she may tremble, her eyes searching around the room, she tries to wriggle away. These are the immediate reactions he can perceive, but there are always later consequences too, not only for the wife or daughter, but also for him. His wife may become depressed, lacking in energy; his daughter may avoid him or wet the bed. She has nightmares. Let's say he's been arrested. To what extent is he responsible for changing his behavior? And when did this responsibility begin? before the act? as the responses took place? after the feedback?

These questions are crucial to our understanding of the responsibility of perpetrators for their abusive acts. If our actions define who we are (and there is some reason to argue that they do not or that under certain circumstances they do not, although this is not a view I generally support), then questions of responsibility and blame are indeed the most important questions of our time. But they are difficult to answer, for though we want to believe in the influence of cultural and historical factors on human beings and their behavior, we also want to believe that the actor has a choice, or, if he didn't really have a choice when he committed the act, that once he recognizes the consequences of his acts (or when authorities "recognize" him through the consequences society can impose), he *then* has a choice.

In the chapters that follow I will explore not only the issues of blame and responsibility but also the kinds of free will we can expect of perpetrators and victims. I will address the question of why victims tend to blame themselves and why perpetrators tend to blame others, and whether any aspect of their self-blame or other-blame is valid. Too many books have examined victims or perpetrators alone and so have not been challenged to commit to a consistent view of people and apply the arguments they make for one (in terms of determinism, choice, and responsibility) to the other. Here I wish to address the question of whether we use external justifications of behavior fairly in our judgments of victims and perpetrators.

If we reject two extreme positions, one that holds that our behavior is totally determined, and the libertarian view that sees our acts as being entirely a product of free will, we face the question of where to draw the line in assigning responsibility to perpetrators or in absolving victims of their guilt. Are these lines drawn rationally, in a way that makes sense? I will also address the increasing tendency in our culture to avoid assigning blame and how this can create difficulties if we are to stop the perpetration of abuse. In so doing, I will enter the territory of cultural criticism.

In the past, cultural criticism seems to have asked that the critic transcend the culture and make observations from that external position. Cultural criticism of the present, influenced by feminism, has shown that there can be no transcendent position with regard to criticism. And so, in thinking about issues of blame and responsibility, we can get caught between these paradigms. In one respect, I cite empirical research, knowing that the scientific endeavor is anything but objective. In another respect, as a psychologist who advocates self-reflection, I see that the very same urges to mute blame and diffuse responsibility that are increasingly present in our culture exist in my own thinking about the people I am, to some extent, blaming. That is, I am continually questioning the answers I have arrived at regarding the responsibility of victims and perpetrators.

Throughout the book I grapple with this uncertainty, because it is at the core of our present-day confusion about how to deal with perpetrators and whether or not to blame the victims. Perhaps my readers will agree with Giles Gunn's assertion that "a divided mind is more illuminating than a settled one."

It is my hope that by asking more pragmatic questions such as, what difference does it make, cognitively, emotionally, or in larger social terms, to believe that a person is or isn't to blame? I can contribute something to the effort to cope with life in a violent world. As a psychologist, I take most of my examples from the field and literature of psychology. From this standpoint I ask, whom can we blame when a person is harmed, and to what extent is blaming useful?

I speak from another, more personal standpoint also, as a person who has had some experience with abuse and victimization. There was the teenage boy who, when I was only six, carried me away to his cellar by tickling me, and there put his hand in my underpants. There was also the boyfriend who once tried to choke me and who sometime later grabbed me by the hair and threatened to crack my head open. These were terrifying experiences at the time, but, in the world of violence against women, minimal and not so difficult for me to overcome. I want to extend my support and gratitude to the victims of abuse who are still struggling with the issues I discuss, and who have had the courage to come forward with the stories of their molestations, rapes, and batterings. I hope this book will be of help to them.

WHO IS TO BLAME?

1

When an act of abuse "happens," who are the victims and who are the perpetrators? Who is to be pitied, and who is to be blamed? Reading a newspaper story about abuse, or hearing an account of battering, we search for representatives of two extremes, perpetrator and victim, two archetypes who will represent for us evil and innocence, a hero and an antihero for our modern-day sagas of woe.

But these contemporary tales of sexual abuse, incest, rape, and battering no longer fit the usual distinctions we make between good and evil. And as much as we might wish to return with clarity of vision to this simple duality, it may be impossible to do so.

The public has recently argued over quite a few victim / perpetrator dilemmas: whether O. J. Simpson was a tragic fallen hero or a deluded, brutal husband, and whether the Menendez brothers were victims as well as murderers, incapacitated by years of excessive verbal and physical abuse.[1] We wondered how it was possible for Lorena Bobbitt to cut off her husband's penis and escape punishment for the crime.[2] We asked whether Tonya Harding was a battered wife forced to go along with a domineering husband's scheme or a schemer herself.[3] We took a second look at battered women who kill (not those who kill in the heat of their battering, but those who hire killers or kill their sleeping husbands) and asked if they should be released from prison and whether or not their acts were understandable, excusable, or even commendable.

But just because it is harder to ascertain absolute guilt and absolute innocence doesn't mean that wrongs haven't been committed. Nor does it mean that, in the end of our analysis, there will be no perpetrator and no victim. Just because we have to revise some former beliefs about what it means to be a victim or a perpetrator doesn't mean that no one will be responsible for the wrongs he or she commits. We might and can still blame; we just can't do it as easily as we used to.

Historically, victims have been blamed much too readily for the crimes of perpetrators, and since William Ryan's seminal book *Blaming the Victim,* the public has become much more aware of our tendency to believe that most abuse is deserved.[4] Female victims of sexual violence, abuse, and battering, along with their advocates, have struggled hard to dispute the automatic victim-blaming that used to occur so frequently, for example, in courtroom rape or battering trials. It used to be that a woman's sexual history was allowed as testimony in the courtroom. Medical and psychological journals intimated that children, because of their sexual fantasy life, desired and provoked sexual advances. Women who had been severely beaten but stayed with the men who abused them and even protected them from the law were seen as "asking for it."

Public opinion has changed dramatically, mainly as a result of consistent efforts by feminists and others who work with abused women in legal, mental health, and social services capacities. In cases like the Big Dan gang-rape trial, for example, where a woman in New Bedford, Massachusetts, was raped on a pool table by several men while other men in the bar watched, some cheering the rapists on, feminists fought hard to ensure that the victim was not blamed for her behavior that night in the bar or judged for her prior sexual history. Their analyses appeared on TV, radio, and in the popular press. Feminists have also fought hard and provided research to change public opinion about battering, showing that women stay not because they like it but for complicated reasons that suggest psychological, physical, and economic coercion. And the public outcry against child sexual abuse has grown to the point where it has fostered a backlash movement.[5]

Today, women are not blamed quite as often for being abused. Rarely do we hear children referred to as "provocative"; nor do we often hear casual statements that a woman deserves to be beaten or raped.[6] One might even say that there is now general public acknowledgment (if one can judge by the surfeit of made-for-TV movies, talk-show topics, and popular-magazine articles) that battering, sexual abuse, and rape are terrible crimes. The suffering of victims has been a cultural focus for at least the last decade, and the public understanding that has developed (and, I might add, could probably be articulated by almost any American adult), is that victims are not to be blamed for their abuse, that men who batter and abuse have absolutely no right to do so, that battering, rape, sexual abuse, and incest are crimes, and that coerced sexual acts are not sexual acts at all but acts of violence. These are powerful beliefs, and empowering words, too—they are, indeed, an ideology, the pronouncing of which can invoke a swell of righteous indignation on behalf of victims, and pride and certainty in the speaker who thus defines an ethic of women's and children's rights so clearly.

But it isn't really so easy as all that. Those of us who have seen and fought against the absurd blaming of victims have, at times, gone too far in the other direction, thereby denying victims any responsibility for their behavior and for their reactions to their abuse, which often include depression, anxiety, anger, and other post-traumatic stress symptoms. Although we have created a context in which victims' rights and injuries are now acknowledged, we have also cost victims some modicum of respect and personhood. More important, the focus on victims has not had a perceptible effect on our treatment of perpetrators and the arguably more important goal of increasing male responsibility for the harm done.

The current overemphasis on victimization and the concomitant overpurification of victims have actually been helpful to perpetrators looking to escape responsibility. Through the all-embracing victims' rights movement, where victims can be rendered into passive, incapacitated shells of people whose acts are seen not as emanating from any self within, but as mere reactions to the abuse and victimization suffered, perpetrators who were once victims themselves can now escape blame.

A premise of this book is that we do not hold perpetrators responsible enough for the harms they inflict. Perpetrators are masters at self-deception, blaming themselves too little; victims blame themselves too much. In our present focus on the pathology of victims' self-blame, we ignore the problem of perpetrators' self-deception, and give little direction that might enable them to take responsibility for the acts they have committed, for the consequences of their actions, and for who they have become. When we begin to hold perpetrators responsible for their actions (and when they begin to hold themselves responsible), victims can then take a realistic look at themselves, and we can feel free to acknowledge some of the assertion, free will, and yes, blame, that also belong to victims.

But if we are to hold perpetrators more accountable for their actions, we need to think about issues of character and excuses. That is, we need to have an adequate account of what constitutes character and what power we may have to shape it, as well as what kinds of explanations might truly excuse harm and cruelty. Once we accept some definition of what character is and which excuses for violence and abuse are in any way acceptable, we need to apply these notions in a fair and equal way to the analysis of *both* victims and perpetrators. In other words, if there is an excuse that we won't allow a perpetrator to make in his attempt to disclaim responsibility for his actions, then we surely can't allow a victim to use this same excuse to disclaim responsibility for her reactions.

CHARACTER AND EXCUSE

To talk about a person's character is to accept the idea that there is a self, a "willing" self, which I am happy to do despite postmodern attempts to discredit this notion.[7] Responsibility presupposes a self, and we have to begin with that premise, as pragmatic as it might seem.

Legally speaking, a person's character is the embodiment of his or her moral self, the sum total of his or her deeds. When a person has committed a crime, his character is examined as an indication of whether this act was representative of who he really is or whether the act was out of character. Traditional ethical theory has examined conduct independent of character, formulating objective rules rather than subjective virtues to guide conduct. According to this tradition, moral judgments are to be made on the basis of rules, through, for example, the Kantian rule of never treating another person as only a means to an end, or the rule that we must always act on principles that can be universalized, or from behind Rawls's "veil of ignorance," which claims that if one were ignorant of one's position in a society, the color of one's skin, one's natural endowments, or access to opportunity, one would of course want to create and live by rules that would guarantee equality.

Modern ethical theory has recently turned away from rule-based or rights-based theories to reexamine Aristotelian ethics and what have been called moral virtues. Virtues have been described as good habits or dispositions of character acquired through actions. To be a good person, one must make a conscious effort to do good deeds, and to be a sympathetic person, one must express sympathy. A person must seek out these virtues—they do not descend upon one. A virtue-ethics view of emotions is incompatible with Western culture's general view of emotion as disruptive of reason; feelings and passions are seen as controllable, and as much reflective of character as one's thoughts. Indeed, emotions are viewed as reflecting a person's thoughts and desires, as well as his or her moral values.[8]

For Aristotle, those who possessed the best character were those who searched for the mean, for moderation in their actions and reactions. So for any given virtue there will be two associated evils, the evil of too much and the evil of too little. If we were to agree that responsibility is a virtue, then victims would err on the side of too much, perpetrators on the side of too little.

The modern view of the perpetrator as a good person who does bad things would not hold up under an Aristotelian analysis of character. For within a virtue-ethics examination of character, behavior cannot be so easily separated from who one is or who one has become. According to Aristotelian ethics, we need hold a person responsible not only for what he does but for who he has become. In most cases of ruined character, Aristotle argued, the person had a choice at an earlier point in time to take a different road, to make a different decision.

Excuses separate acts from character. An excuse not only explains bad behavior but also removes responsibility fully or in part, leaving the character generally unmarked. The most common excuses are legal ones of incapacitation, such as mental retardation, a troubled childhood, insanity, or extreme coercion.

And so from a virtue-ethics perspective, responsibility, along with self-awareness applied to acquiring responsibility, is a virtue to be sought by victims and perpetrators alike. A perpetrator may not be excused by circumstances or prior history or natural constraints that could in some sense be seen as leading to his victimizing behavior, because he has the capacity to be responsible for his character. He cannot separate his self from his act, for his actions reflect his character. As he can aspire to be virtuous, so too can he be blamed when he is not. The victim is, by the same reasoning, responsible for her behavior, depending on varying degrees of incapacitation (coercion as the prime example) and the character that influences her reactions to the abuse. In Chapters 2 and 3 I will address the relative coercion and responsibility of victims and perpetrators of abuse.

WHAT HAPPENS WHEN WE BLAME

We encounter several problems when we start to blame. One kind of problem is pragmatic. First, it seems hypocritical to be advocating a *self-reflective* stance for others, say, perpetrators, through our *other-directed* stance. To set an example of looking inward and apportioning blame to oneself accordingly, one does not want to be in the position of pointing the finger. When any of us blames a perpetrator with the full force of our glare, we are modeling an other-directed stance.

The second pragmatic difficulty with blaming is that it does not, in reality, seem to help. You point the finger, and usually the accused points back. The more you blame a person, the more ashamed he feels and the greater his tendency will be to hide his head, deny his wrongdoing, or look outward for causality. There does not seem to be any easy way to both blame and encourage another to take responsibility for his actions.

Another problem with blame is not pragmatic but philosophical. It has to do with free will. (In this book, I intend not to address the centuries-long debate over free will and determinism but merely to think about free will in the simple sense of whether or not a person committing an act of abuse had the ability to do otherwise.)[9] As soon as we blame someone, and especially if we blame him to his face, many excusing conditions and constraints on free will surface. We can think of these excusing conditions as "natural constraints,"[10] or even the unequal distribution of "up-to-usness" (free choice),[11] rather than extreme constraints such as insanity or infancy. Natural constraints include such things as a prior history of abuse, or living in conditions so brutal that it is difficult to maintain a clear sense of human priorities. The problem is one not of black or white, whether or not a person was incapacitated at the time the abuse occurred, but of how incapacitated a person must be before he or she is excused, and how much free choice is required of a person to be held responsible for his or her acts.

The trouble with blame is this all or nothingness, this black or whiteness. People are drawn to extremes. As soon as we have to study the gray areas, we lean to one side. In this book I argue that the large majority of perpetrators had enough free will not to do what they did, and, more controversially, that more than a few victims also had enough free choice to make their self-blame, at times, reasonable.

Let us return to the trials of Lorena Bobbitt and the Menendez brothers. In these and similar cases juries seem to view abuse or prior abuse as an important, extenuating circumstance and excuse for violent behavior. One might expect that the jury members think this way not only because the victims (murdered father and mother, castrated husband) seemed to deserve their punishment, but because, in a very important way, the perpetrators did not have free will, they were not making choices, and they were controlled or moved by the conditions of their lives.[12]

We would hope in general for the most sincere compassion for all victims. It could be argued that the trend toward relieving victims-turned-perpetrators of moral culpability for their acts is a positive one, founded in compassion, true perspective-taking, and the humility of moral relativism. But then we must also ask ourselves whether we can promote moral responsibility without blame, and what kinds of communities and relationships within those communities can be preserved when it is increasingly difficult to hold others morally accountable for the harm they do.

Feeling compassion for victims is often accompanied by a deep-felt hatred of cruelty. It seems to me that one cannot hate cruelty adequately if one cannot find a cruel person. Moral condemnation of violence and cruelty seems rather empty if there is no agent.

WHY DO WE BLAME?

The question of blame is, in essence, a question of who is "bad." Because in recent history concepts of "bad" and "good" have become so complicated, and so removed from religious authority, it is harder to answer the question, why do we blame?[13]

When we blame, we sometimes succeed in forcing the guilty party to hang his head in shame. We sometimes blame people out of a desire for vengeance, in order to shame them, and not because we think that shame will help them to reform. Occasionally we blame in order to motivate the wrongdoer to make amends or do other good to erase his mark and improve his moral character. But shame does not necessarily motivate reform and encourage good acts.[14]

The root meaning of the word "shame" is related to uncovering, exposing, and wounding.[15] The urge to hide one's face that is associated both literally and metaphorically with shame would seem never to lead to the impulse to make amends. Take, for example, these diverse subjects of shame: Arthur Dimmesdale in *The Scarlet Letter*, and the modern-day alcoholic.

Dimmesdale, heavy with shame, leads a tortured life. He is unable to forgive himself for having engaged in an adulterous affair, but also unable to lead an honest life in his community, to join his lover and daughter on the scaffold during the light of day, thus making amends for his actions to the community, to his daughter, Pearl, and to Hester Prynne. The alcoholic, it has long been argued, is stuck in his alcoholism because of the shame and self-disgust that perpetuate his escape into drinking. Advocates of the disease model of alcoholism argue that if the alcoholic believes that his drinking is not his fault and not a product of a deep-rooted defect in his character, he can avoid the shame associated with his behavior and will be more likely to seek help. Paradoxically, it is the belief that it is *not* his character that is impugned that supposedly leads to a change in character.

So unbearable is shame that those who experience it are often motivated consciously or unconsciously to defend themselves against recognition of their wrongdoing. It is the exposure of oneself to oneself, as Helen Merrill Lynd writes, that underlies all feelings of shame: "In this moment of self-consciousness, the self stands revealed."[16] The impulse, then, when one cannot hide, is to deny any wrongdoing or to point the finger at someone else. This is common behavior in perpetrators of abuse.

Some perpetrators blame others to guard against their feelings of shame. The wife-beater blames his wife for that one last sarcastic comment that sent him over the edge. Sexually offending teenage boys will blame their little-girl victims for not saying no to them. The blaming of others for perpetrators' own sins is not only a defense against shame but also a defense against thinking of themselves as "bad," or as "bad" people. But in this way, blaming becomes an endless chain linked to prior events.

SELF-BLAME

In a very pragmatic sense, we might prefer a world in which everyone took some responsibility for mishaps or harm to a world in which no one did. Richard Shweder writes about society in Orissa, India, where self-blame is taken to such an extreme that people consider their misfortunes in this life to be repayment for bad deeds done in a former one.[17] Victims of abuse tend to take a similarly extreme attitude, and some psychologists have generally held that their unrealistic self-blame is unhealthy.

Such psychologists are admittedly working within a belief system that equates health and happiness, that assumes a happy individual is the most successful, adaptive, and appropriate goal of psychology. Rarely do psychologists ask what is best for the community and rarely do they acknowledge that what might be adaptive for individual happiness may not be useful for the happiness of a community.

Some of the most influential work on self-blame was conducted by Martin Seligman and expanded in his research with Lyn Abramson and other colleagues.[18] Originally, Seligman discovered a phenomenon in dogs that he called "learned helplessness." Some dogs were put into a situation in which there was no escape from an electric shock; after time, they stopped trying to escape. Even when there was an opportunity to escape later, and even after they had been shown the opportunity, they lay "helpless," unable to use this new information. This phenomenon also held true for humans who were put in a situation where they could not initially control the cessation of a noxious sound.

The phenomenon of learned helplessness has since been used by those who present a case for Battered Woman's Syndrome, explaining why women don't leave their abusers.[19]

But Seligman and Abramson could not consistently find learned helplessness in humans. They found instead that certain patterns of thinking were associated with a passive reaction while different patterns were associated with an active reaction. That is, some people kept trying in the face of failure. This was an important discovery. What was once thought to be a purely behavioral response, a stimulus-response kind of phenomenon, a knee-jerk reaction, if you will, was found to be influenced by the mind, by a pattern of thinking, by something connected to what we might call the self, or one's character, or even, but arguably to a lesser extent, one's will.

Thus, "attribution" theorists like Seligman and Abramson claim that when bad things happen to some people they blame themselves, view their characters as flawed, and believe that their misfortune will be long-lasting and will extend to all aspects of their lives. These people are the pessimists, and they are more vulnerable than others to depression.

Two characters, Wavey and Quoyle, in E. Annie Proulx's novel *The Shipping News* show this kind of response to hardship. Both Wavey and Quoyle, widow and widower, are inexplicably attached to the dead spouses who had abused them in word and deed. Wavey says to Quoyle: "It's like you feel to yourself that's all you deserve. And the worse it gets the more it seems true, that you got it coming to you or it wouldn't be that way."[20] These two can be seen as overly responsible, pessimistic, and possibly depressed, but, according to attribution theory, if they can learn to stop blaming themselves excessively for their failings and stop seeing bad events as pervasive and permanent, they could be considerably happier. Seligman also argues more specifically (and paradoxically) that if we want people to be responsible for their actions, they must see their own mistakes and bad deeds as deriving from a temporary condition and not from something long-lasting or fixed (such as character).

Let us apply this theory not to one who has been beaten or who is depressed but to one who perpetrates some harm. Before considering the child molester or the batterer, let us consider momentarily the man who is spending the night in jail for drunk driving. According to this theory he is better off psychologically if he believes (1) that it was bad luck that caused him to get caught, and not the fact that he deserved to get caught; (2) that he isn't a no-good person but just someone who made a mistake; (3) that it won't happen again (no matter if he is deluding himself in this thought); and (4) that his getting drunk that particular night or getting caught was not his fault (perhaps his friend made him drink too much). This man is less likely to be depressed, but also, we are told, more likely to do something about his behavior. If he were to blame himself (correctly, we might add), he might become depressed and might be less likely to act to change his behavior. But would we want to encourage him *not* to blame himself?

Now consider a father who has been sexually abusing his daughter over several years. This man, now facing a prison sentence, might believe that he doesn't deserve to be punished so severely (thus minimizing his crime), that he made a big mistake, that this mistake doesn't really reflect upon his character, and that he did it because he himself had been abused as a child, or because he was drunk, or because his wife won't have sex with him, or because his job was too stressful, and so on. This kind of thinking might ensure his happiness, but wouldn't we want him to blame himself, and to become to some extent depressed?[21] Shouldn't he be depressed when he faces what he has done?

The point is not that Seligman and other cognitive attributionists are wrong. Clearly self-blame is associated with depression and passivity and hopelessness. No wonder perpetrators blame others and focus outward—it allows them to remain optimistic! The theory is meant, however, to address only one side of the virtue responsibility, to address those survivors of rape, incest, battering, and other violent crimes who are overly responsible, who are like depressives who tend to take on too much guilt. Many therapists work to stop victims from blaming themselves and believe that the self-blame victims express in therapy is self-destructive and that they would do better to turn that blame into rage at their perpetrators. It has been said that these victims have introjected their oppressors; they have identified with their abusers and continue to abuse themselves. Herbert Fingarette calls this kind of self-blame "misassigned guilt."[22]

There have also been psychologists and sociologists who have argued for the adaptive quality of certain kinds of self-blame: "I shouldn't have been there at the time," or "I should have run." But research has not clearly shown such thinking to be adaptive. The clearest finding to come out of the immense body of research on this topic has been that only some victims improve by blaming themselves in this behavioral way, but that most of them fare worse psychologically if they blame someone else.[23]

Rare is the perpetrator whose guilt weighs as heavily as the guilt of an Arthur Dimmesdale. And we would expect that deathbed confessions of abuse and rape are rare. More likely the typical rapist separates himself from his behavior in his mind and through his actions: "I went home, watched a little t.v., and got a beer."[24] Why do victims do so poorly when they blame others, but perpetrators do so well?

The researchers who claim that other-blaming and poor functioning do not go very well together are looking at victims, not perpetrators, and thus probably confounding other-blaming with anger, and not just any anger, but pent-up rage, rage that has little social outlet and that finds little social support. Living with anger for which one has no constructive release is debilitating; the rapist, by contrast, has spent his anger, and more than likely feels "refreshed."

IS EVERYONE A VICTIM?

In *The Shipping News*, a small Newfoundland paper with a staff of four or five reporters assigns one special reporter, Nutbeem, to all the sexual abuse cases. On one occasion, he reports to his coworkers:

> More priests connected with the orphanage. It's up to nineteen awaiting trial now. Here's a doctor at the No Name Medical Clinic charged with sexual assault against fourteen female patients—"provocative fondling of breasts and genitals" is how they put it. The choirmaster in Misky Bay pled guilty on Monday to sexual assault and molestation of more than a hundred boys over the past twelve years. Also in Misky Bay an American tourist arrested for fondling young boys at the municipal swimming pool. "He kept feeling my bum and my front," said a ten-year-old victim. And here in Killick-Claw a loving dad is charged with sexually assaulting two of his sons and his teenage daughter in innumerable incidents between 1962 and the present. Buggery, indecent assault and sexual intercourse. Here's another family lover, big strapping thirty-five-year-old fisherman spends his hours ashore teaching his little four-year-old daughter to perform oral sex and masturbate him.
>
> "For Christ's sake," said Quoyle, appalled. "This can't be all in one week."

"One week?" said Nutbeem. "I've got another bloody page of them."

"That's what sells this paper," said Tert Card.[25]

As in this fictionalized, small Newfoundland community, we too are inundated with reports of sexual abuse of children, rape, and battering. Accounts of sexual abuse are of such extreme interest to the families of Killick-Claw because in reading these stories they, like the reporter who tells them, relive and work through their own victimizations. The readers of the paper, inhabitants of Newfoundland, are indeed all victims: they are victims of the cruel climate where ice and snow can be fatal as early as October; victims of the sea that regularly delivers men lifeless and sometimes even headless up onto the rocks of the shore; victims of other people: the cruel husband who slept with other women and "rubbed 'er nose in it," the wife who ran around with other men, the mother who sold her daughters to a pornographer, the father who doesn't love his son, the brother who repeatedly raped his sister in their youth and who in dying entrusts his ashes to her, the crazy great-uncle who puts a curse on a small child.

It is popular to say that this victim ideology has gone too far—"now everyone's a victim," say the critics who believe themselves to be superior to popular culture. But in some very real sense, the victim ideology is true. Those who rail against what might be called a "victim culture" exclaim that by calling everyone a victim we are not doing justice to "real" victims. They then go on to describe some of the most horrifying cases of abuse imaginable. But they fall into the trap of overpurifying victims. The only examples of victimhood they can conjure up are the extreme cases. Are these the only true victims? How completely tortured, coerced, and incapacitated must a person be to earn the label of "victim"?

It is my belief that, as in the imaginary town of Killick-Claw, we might all be victims, even the perpetrators, and that it is not necessarily self-indulgent to see oneself as a victim of harm or cruelty, pernicious advertising, heartless parents, insensitive lovers, poverty, or verbal abuse. It's what is meant by the word "victim" that counts, and victimization should not mean absolution from all responsibility. But if being a victim means being that ship tossed about, if it is about having no responsibility for who one is and who one has become, then yes, these people are using the word victim unfairly.

2

Victims blame themselves. This fact has not gone un-noticed by clinicians, researchers, hot-line workers, friends of victims, and the popular media. "It's not your fault" is the one response that the newly victim-compassionate public has learned well, and this phrase is used with much hope as an inoculation against post-victimization reactions. Elevated almost to a bat-tle cry, the phrase is a perfect response to the senseless victim-blaming once so common, the kind of blaming that assumed if a girl was sexually abused, she was provocative, and if a woman was beaten or raped, she provoked it.

Yet if we truly listen to victims and honor their perspectives, we see that by advocating a cognitive view of their experience that is so at odds with what they themselves are feeling, by telling them that we know more about their agency in the world than they do, and by informing them that they are sadly mis-taken in their perception of choice and free will we do them an injustice. Of course, psychotherapists often advocate a different way of looking at oneself or one's situation. But doesn't it seem strange to advocate a totally deterministic view to women who themselves do not hold that view and to women we hope to empower?

The argument that victims' self-blame is only an illusion, a side effect of depression, or an unconscious internalization of the aggressor is unsatisfying. Whereas it is important to argue vociferously with the perpetrator who seeks to blame his victim for his own actions, it may be wise to hold back before erasing the sense of agency and responsibility a victim feels for her own victimization. Can we raise as separate issues the question of perpetrator responsibility and victim responsibility? Does blame have to be a mathematical equation in which if one side is diminished the other is enhanced? Can we acknowledge that there is some validity to the victim's self-blaming while still maintaining that the perpetrator is thoroughly accountable for his violence?

Feminists and grassroots workers in the field of abuse and victimization have accomplished a great deal in promoting a social perspective of the victimization of women and children. Decades of research on why women stay in abusive relationships and why sexually abused children and rape victims are afraid to tell have revealed factors that help explain their continued victimization. The unblanketing of social forces, in an attempt to understand why women and children make choices that seem to be against their own best interests, has served to take discussions out of the realm of mental health and away from the area of individual psychology.

It is not my intention to question these social forces—indeed, I will give them their due weight in the discussion that follows—but I do wish to argue that an exclusively external view is problematic, not only because it underestimates the validity of what the victim herself is telling us, but because of an inherent contradiction between the social-forces account (which is almost always presented in its most deterministic way) and the possibilities for change.

In the recent past, the discussion of victim innocence and perpetrator responsibility has been too radical, leading to an overemphasis on victimization.[1] When everyone's purported victimization is overemphasized in this way, those who already doubt victims and support perpetrators use these exaggerations as proof that little victimization actually occurs. One current debate concerns what has been given the sound-byte term of "date-rape hype." In this debate one more woman, Katie Roiphe, has gained notoriety by giving a new (and female) voice to a very old male perspective. Her book, *The Morning After,* has provided a media opportunity to question the validity of accusations of date rape even though multiple, solid research studies support the existence of the phenomenon.[2] Another movement concerned with "false" memories argues against the extreme position once taken that "children never lie about sexual abuse." Gaining some support from academia, this movement is hard to dismiss because there is some fairness to its claim, as there are some grounds for Roiphe's claim that campus movements to fight date rape may have some overzealous, overachieving women warriors. The "False Memory Syndrome" advocates have gained support and are able to sway public opinion because the good fight has been waged too radically, however understandable and useful this radical method has been.

In looking for that aspect of self-blame that may yield to the victim, I seek not to discount the real and horrible abuse that each victim has suffered, the results of which many still suffer from, but instead to make a more consistent argument, the better with which to hold perpetrators more responsible for their acts than current practice allows.

FORMS OF SELF-BLAME

There is a general tendency in people to blame others. There seems to be a powerful need to be rid of guilt,[3] to accept responsibility for successes more than failures, and to disaffiliate with losers.[4] People will tend to blame others for a negative event particularly when another person is present, when that other person is an authority figure, when that authority figure is known to them, and when the outcome is severe.[5] If we were to extend what we know about other-blaming to incest survivors, however, we would expect them to be among the least likely victims to blame themselves. Yet they do, and often with little mercy. Victims of violence, and particularly female victims of male violence, do not fit into this other-blaming mold.

A number of writers have commented on the tendency of individuals to blame themselves for interpersonal misfortunes versus catastrophes of fate. Victimizations perpetrated by humans lead to more negative assumptions about the self than other kinds of victimizations. For example, we do not blame ourselves as severely when we are victims of a flood as when we are victims of an act of human aggression.[6] In the latter case, someone has actually decided to harm us, singled us out. But it is as if we so want to believe in the goodness or righteousness of the other that we would rather sacrifice our belief in ourselves than our belief in them.

Victims of violence, particularly women, are different from other victims. Whereas most of us will respond to failure by asking, why now? the victim of an assault or sexual abuse will ask, why me? She will personalize the attack, wondering what made *her* the object of rape or those sexually abusive advances. It is interesting to note that women who have been abused by their husbands derive comfort from hearing that their husbands had abused other women, and not just them.[7]

There are several explanations that seem plausible when we ask why victims blame themselves. Some of these explanations have enjoyed more popularity than others. They have their foundations in psychoanalytic theory, cognitive schema theory, and social / feminist positions, and though there is some merit in each, they may not tell the whole story.

Internalization of the Aggressor

There is an almost masochistic quality in the self-blaming of victims, although masochism is certainly the wrong word, since it implies the enjoyment of suffering. But the deliberateness and tenaciousness of self-blame make it seem so masochistic. Self-blame can be viewed alongside other post-trauma symptoms, the self-negating, self-demeaning, and self-punitive behaviors that victims maintain as a result of their abuse. Victims see themselves as worthless and soulless. They can be suicidal or self-mutilators, and we are dismayed at the continuation of these self-destructive behaviors. Haven't these victims suffered enough?

There are diverse psychoanalytic views of self-blame. Whereas some theorists view self-blame as problematic, a symptom, a defense against anxiety, others, including Freud at times, emphasize the goal of mastering the traumatic experience that may be enacted by self-blame. Let us begin by examining what Anna Freud calls "identification with the aggressor," a defense against the anxiety or fear the victim experienced while under attack. Building on her father's theory of the oedipal complex, Anna Freud talks about identification with the aggressor as a normal part of maturing, the preliminary step in the development of conscience, the process by which children internalize the qualities of authority of the people bringing them up. In normal development, identification with the aggressor contributes to the mastery of instinct.[8]

Important to this conceptualization is the idea of mastery. For when we apply the theory to victims of abuse, we see their identification with the aggressor as a way of mastering their anxiety. In identification with her abuser the victim joins the powerful other and hides from her own feelings of helplessness. If a victim later becomes abusive, she is like her attackers and no longer needs to fear them. Lenore Terr sheds light on the issue when she describes the play of various children who have been traumatized as repetitive, aggressive, and reenacting. She sees the play as very literal, its meaning not difficult to discern, and occurring even when the child does not actually remember the trauma.[9] I have seen this play in my own practice: a six-year-old boy who had been tortured and sexually abused by his father would play the game of "mad scientist" during which he would "force" the therapist to sit on "the chair of the slippery snakes"; the boy, although agitated, would derive great pleasure from his pretend power.

Identification with the abuser helps explain why some victims in turn victimize others; but why would victims victimize themselves or perpetuate their own victimization through self-blame and other demeaning behavior? There are two answers to this question: one deals with the urge to repeat the trauma and the other deals with the issue of rage.

In *Introductory Lectures in Psychoanalysis* and other works, Freud addresses the issue of why a person might choose unpleasant experiences that seem to violate "the pleasure principle," if we are all of us motivated to maximize pleasure and gratification and avoid anything unpleasant. In thinking about those who suffer from trauma, he wrote, "It is as though these patients had not finished with the traumatic situation, as though they were still faced by it as an immediate task which has not been dealt with."[10] Under the sway of the "repetition compulsion," as Freud called it, victims attempt to find some way for their trauma to be repeated so that they might master and resolve the overwhelming feelings of fear, rage, guilt, and even sexual pleasure that may have been evoked at the time.

One can call the acting out of aggression on one's self a repetition of the abuse, a back-handed mastery phenomenon. In abusing the self the victim says, "I am master of my own defeat." As a child might repeat the trauma in play, so the child or adult repeats the trauma in her abuse of herself, as exemplified in the self-mutilating behavior of sexual abuse survivors or the tendency to find oneself in a second abusive relationship after one is out of the first, or through more subtle thoughts and behaviors: the way victims will say that they are "bad" people or that they have brought their abuse on themselves. This kind of repetition of trauma, while costing them self-esteem, safety, and mental health, can give victims a feeling of control over their lives. And the feeling of mastery, of self-control, wards off the unbearable anxiety that they could be passive again in the face of trauma. Freud describes repetition in place of remembering as a positive effect of trauma, while he calls a phobic response to trauma, avoidance of remembering, and inhibition negative effects.[11]

Another psychoanalytic view holds that the victim's guilt and self-blaming are a defense against her own rage. In Freudian terms this rage can be explained by the death instinct, but one need not turn to this undersupported and problematic area of psychoanalytic theory; it is easier to view repressed rage as a natural reaction to being attacked, and draw on the social / feminist perspective to explain why women might be afraid of their own rage and encouraged in their guilt.

Current psychoanalytic theory suggests more convincingly that the rage may have been in place before the abuse. For example, the child who is attacked or abused by her parents may feel that such treatment is justified as a response to her own aggressive feelings toward them. That is, the guilt stemming from destructive wishes already exists so that parental violence can only be interpreted as a just punishment for such wishes.

The omnipotent feelings of the child and her belief in her own destructive capabilities can lead her to see herself as having forced the two most powerful people in her life to do something terrible to her.[12]

One need not conjecture rage, however; temptations toward instinctual satisfactions may alone give rise to a person's desire for self-punishment. As Freud wrote in *Civilization and Its Discontents,* "As long as things go well with a man, his conscience is lenient and lets the ego do all sorts of things; but when misfortune befalls him, he searches his soul, acknowledges his sinfulness, heightens the demands of his conscience, imposes abstinences on himself, and punishes himself with penances." The "sinner" sees fate as the parental agent.[13]

Finally, not rage, nor instinctual temptation, but loss may drive the self-punishing behavior. Object relations theorists hold that the victim who blames herself may be attempting to ward off the loss of a loved one, a loss that would ensue were she to see the aggressor realistically. It may be better for her to preserve the image of the loved one who is an aggressor and make herself the bad one. As Judith Herman writes, "The child victim takes the evil of the abuser into herself and thereby preserves her primary attachments to her parents. Because the inner sense of badness preserves a relationship, it is not readily given up even after the abuse has stopped; rather, it becomes a stable part of the child's personality structure." In acting like their aggressors, victims also take upon themselves the shame and guilt of their abusers.[14] Why would one put the "other" in so superior a position to the self? If we think about the vulnerability of the child and his or her dependence, it makes sense that the relationship has priority over self-development, for without a trusting relationship, how can the self develop? The eyes of the "other" bestow selfhood on an individual as clearly as the individual defines his- or herself.

This explanation of loss works reasonably well for those victims abused by loved ones; however, one has to invoke some defense mechanism of projection onto the aggressor to explain the self-blame of the victim who is abused by a stranger. (It is not surprising that these victims express less self-blame than those raped by someone they know.) One might say that the guilt over one's own destructive power is ever-present and so is enhanced by any attack, that unconsciously the avenging parent is projected on the attacker, thus redefining the attack as punishment. It is difficult, however, to apply an object relations view of loss without making a much greater leap.

Although there may be an element of mastery in the self-blaming behavior of victims, it can still be problematic, especially when seen as part of a package of self-punitive behaviors. Depression among victims is well documented, and the relationship between self-blame and depression has been established. But another view argues that there exists a certain kind of self-blame that is protective and healing.

Maintaining a Positive View of the World

Cognitive-behavioral theorists see self-blame as either a cause of depression (a result of faulty thinking) or a by-product of depression.[15] But a number of authors from the field of social psychology speak of schemas and cognitions too, and describe victims' self-blaming as a way of maintaining beliefs that the world is a just and meaningful place, and that they have control over their own lives.

From the "just world" perspective of the victim, it would be easier to see oneself as blameworthy than to give up the more important belief that the world is a fair place and that people get what they deserve in life.[16] Victims, like Job, atone for some undiscovered sin, for if there is no sin, then the world (or God) is unjust, unpredictable, and very frightening. "Just world" research has shown that subjects in experiments will devalue victims who suffer misfortunes, presumably in an effort to make their characters match their fate. Along these lines, Baruch Fischoff has written of an effect he calls "creeping determinism." People are so convinced that negative events have a predetermined reason that once they know of an outcome they will overestimate its inevitability.[17]

Like the psychoanalytic version of mastery, some cognitive versions see victims' self-blaming as a way of trying to maintain an illusion of control over their lives. Underlying this view is the understanding that the victim has, in actuality, very little control over her victimization. Ellen Langer has shown that people tend to believe they can control more than they actually do.[18] One of the oldest beliefs shared by those who suffer from chronic or life-threatening diseases is that their sickness is divine retribution.[19] Thus this general principle may apply to victims of rape or sexual abuse. Rape victims consider themselves responsible for the rape in order to establish some control over it,[20] and one way of gaining control is to view the rape as a punishment for some prior behavior.[21]

It has been said that there are three beliefs that are shattered when a person becomes a victim of violence and that are preserved when a victim deals with her trauma by blaming herself: the belief that the self is worthy, that the world is meaningful, and that we live in a benevolent world.[22] According to Ronnie Janoff-Bulman, for those who have experienced trauma

> nothing seems to be as they had thought, their inner world is in turmoil. Suddenly, the self- and worldviews they had taken for granted are unreliable. They can no longer assume that the world is a good place or that other people are kind and trustworthy. They can no longer assume that the world is meaningful or what happens makes sense.

They can no longer assume that they have control over negative outcomes or will reap benefits because they are good people. The very nature of the world and self seems to have changed; neither can be trusted, neither guarantees security.[23]

With much supporting research from the field of social psychology, Janoff-Bulman argues that we have a tendency toward cognitive conservatism—or, simply put, it is difficult to change our beliefs. She also argues that self-blame is adaptive, that it reflects a "need to minimize the threatening, meaningless nature of the event." Even though self-blame is associated with depression, she argues that it may be better for an individual to blame herself than to live in an unsafe, unpredictable, and malevolent world.

Janoff-Bulman draws a distinction between two kinds of self-blame, one that is more adaptive and one that is problematic. The first, behavioral self-blame, attributes the victimization to the victim's behavior ("I should never have gone out that late at night without a friend"). The second, characterological self-blame, attributes the victimization to something internal or unchanging about the victim herself ("I'm provocative," or "I'm always getting victimized").

Although there is a considerable body of research that predominantly supports the idea that behavioral self-blame is adaptive whereas characterological self-blame is not, other research has been less conclusive.[24] Most recently Janoff-Bulman herself has shown that even internal attributions, the characterological ones, can be adaptive if they are about specific aspects of personality and are not applied globally, to one's whole character.[25] But the adaptiveness may be more of a wish than a fact. Another recent study by Patricia Frazier found that rape victims tend to rate external factors as more causal than factors involving the self, and that when asked about the causes of rape, they do not distinguish between behavioral and characterological self-blame; that is, victims of rape engage in both kinds of self-blame when they search for clues as to why it happened and happened to them. An interesting finding of this research is that *any* self-blame was associated with poorer adjustment (there was earlier support for this in several other studies of rape, incest, and sexual harassment), whereas the belief that one could avoid future attacks went along with better adjustment.[26]

THE SOCIAL-FORCES PERSPECTIVE

In a standard test, familiar to every training psychologist, there is a picture of an angry or impatient man attempting to leap into action and a beautiful woman holding him back, restraining him.[27] It is one of a standard battery of pictures dealt out when psychologists administer the Thematic Apperception Test (TAT) to adults. This test is designed to evoke projections of an individual's inner conflicts, but in response to the picture cards there are some "answers" that are more typical than others and not necessarily viewed as unconscious projections of inner conflict. The psychologist holds up the picture and asks the person being evaluated to make up a story with a beginning, middle, and end, to tell about the people in the story and what they might be feeling. A common story told for this card would be one in which the man feels compelled to go off and fight for what he thinks is right and the woman holds him back, trying to restrain his anger. The woman is responsible for keeping the man from acting passionately, impulsively, or violently.

What is the process that socializes women to accept victimization and take responsibility for male anger? In the book *Bound by Love,* Lucy Gilbert and Paula Webster argue that the earliest lesson of daughterhood is that obedience equals survival.

Women are conditioned to believe in men's benevolence toward women, that there is a special role for men as protectors and defenders. If women believe that men have an agenda to protect and defend them, they will think that only provocation could deter men from this mission.[28] Women therefore often greatly underestimate the degree of male hostility toward them.[29]

These authors go on to examine female self-hatred and view self-blame as a fight against oppression. To feel bad inside is painful, but it is also important. They write, "We prefer the grandiose notion of an evil core to the pathetic recognition of our own arbitrary oppression. . . . We prefer being the bad one to being a mere vehicle for men's tantrums, a punching bag men use while they go about their business. Who wouldn't?"[30] Thus, in this conceptualization, self-blame is a kind of feminist statement arising from the humiliation of domination.

The co-dependency movement is the quintessential example of women's assuming responsibility for male behavior. What began as a movement to help alcoholics assume responsibility for their alcoholism (although paradoxically that responsibility is handed over to a higher power) has become even more popular as a movement to examine the wives of alcoholics as enablers. Thus it has become yet "another tool in the oppression of women, fostering denial of male accountability."[31] A woman who sees her relationship as "enmeshed" will assume part of the responsibility for her husband's behavior.

The co-dependency movement has enjoyed great popularity for many reasons, one being that it addresses accurately and sometimes disturbingly the way in which women tend to define themselves in relationship. Although the strengths of this tendency have been amply noted of late, problems also exist if defining oneself in relationship makes one take responsibility for another's acts.[32]

The feminist / social-forces perspective thus points to various aspects of women's experience (historical and socialized) to explain self-blaming: the tendency of women to assume too much responsibility, to leave themselves out of the equation when calculating what other people need and deserve, to respond passively to attack, and to consider themselves the property of men, as well as the object of men's experiences rather than the subject of their own. Whether this tendency to assume too much responsibility is applauded as an expression of compassion and a greater or different moral awareness, or considered a cause for concern, an expression of neglect of self and lack of boundaries, it is a choice supported by social processes.

A different social-forces explanation of self-blame claims less universality and points to the specific experience of abuse as defining and overwhelming the victim's personal thinking and reacting. The victim's self-blaming can be seen as an actual reenactment of the very real blaming of her perpetrator or her own guilt (however irrational) aroused during the abuse. We can thus talk about internalization of the aggressor without referring to the more complex psychoanalytic notions. Perpetrators will tell their victims that they are worthless, or sluts, or seductresses, or manipulating bitches, and because of the perpetrator's relationship to the victim, the consistency and sheer repetition of such remarks, these words can be both deafening and defining. In addition, the perpetrator will sometimes blame the victim outright by pointing out ways in which a wife could have avoided getting hit ("If only you had . . ."), or by pointing out ways in which a child "wanted" or "was interested in" the sexual abuse. In articulating to his victim these justifications for his abuse, the perpetrator reinforces her self-blame.[33]

In the case of child sexual abuse, contributing to the self-blame is any sexual pleasure the child may have experienced during the abuse. The overstimulation of sexual excitation before a child's body is prepared for it can be overwhelming. But even if there were no sexual feelings present, the fact that the abuse was an act of sex (in rape or child sexual abuse) touches the experience with guilt and stigmatizes the child.[34]

Victims of abuse sometimes begin to abuse others, thereby fueling their self-blame, reinforcing their image of themselves as bad and deserving of punishment. Difficulties in modulating anger enhance their conviction of badness.[35] The feeling of living a double life because of the secrets a victim keeps or the lies a victim tells also contributes to the idea of an inner self that is less than one's public self.

WHY AREN'T VICTIMS TO BLAME?

To many in the field of victimization, this question is insulting, the answer obvious. But if it were so obvious why would victim-blaming continue, and why would victims continue to blame themselves? Let us start from a more general and philosophical perspective regarding responsibility in order to tease apart the varieties of ways in which a person is said not to be responsible for an act. Usually philosophy provides these excuses by turning to the legal questions surrounding culpability for a crime, and so it may seem unusual to apply these legal notions to a victim, but we do so anyway, with the understanding that from the victim's perspective she may be partly responsible for the crime.

Of great importance here is the fact that we do not hold people responsible for their behavior if they were coerced, meaning that the necessary cause of the act was something external to the victim. Someone is coerced if he or she could not have acted differently.

Coercion is most clearly seen when there is a physical threat. In rape, for example, the attacker often physically coerces a woman into engaging in sex by means of a weapon or by his greater physical strength. A woman's being raped by a man who has a gun or a knife is similar to her being raped by a man who is physically more powerful than she. She could not have escaped without great bodily harm and so says to herself, "There was nothing I could do." She tends to blame herself less if she sees herself as having avoided penetration.[36] The well-publicized date-rape trial of Mike Tyson ended with a conviction in spite of the difficulty in convicting date rapists, perhaps because of the difference in size between the victim and the perpetrator. He was large, a boxer, and she was petite; it was as if his body itself were a lethal weapon. This sort of physical coercion is not as common in child sexual abuse, although one could argue that the greater physical strength of the adult plays some part in the coercion.

In the case of men beating their wives or girlfriends, physical violence may be used to coerce, or simply for its own sake. Although it may seem unusual to talk about coercion in such situations, it is clear that if a wife "submits to" the violent relationship or marriage, she is coerced by the violence into submitting to the beating. To the extent that she remains in the relationship, we can say that she is coerced by fear of violence and fear of retaliation should she separate from her abuser.

Another way we find people not responsible for their actions is if we see that they had no other choice, or, to use a phrase that has previously been applied to concentration camp victims, they had only choiceless choices.[37] This explanation applies to the wives or girlfriends of batterers who remain with their partners because they do not have the economic resources or support systems that would enable them to make a successful and clean break from their batterers. They are financially dependent on their husbands or boyfriends, and with the problems of day care and lack of job training, they doubt that they would be able successfully to start a life without them. Women also worry about the burden they may place on their friends and families should they choose to leave their abusers.[38]

Children who have been sexually abused by their fathers or stepfathers are confronted with such choiceless choices also; all too often if they have the courage to tell someone of their abuse, the result of their disclosure is their removal from the household, placement in a series of foster homes, or the loss of many other aspects of their lives that they treasure and that make them secure. Although they may see themselves as making a choice to keep the family together, or taking care of a "sick" daddy, this is still a choiceless choice, in that either way these victims lose.

Finally, we do not hold victims responsible for their behavior if they were mentally incapacitated in some way. Legally this could mean innately incapacitated, for example, by impaired intellectual development, or developmentally incapacitated, as a result of childhood or insanity.[39] Psychological coercion often depends on mental incapacitation and, at times, facilitates it.

In the case of a child, we say that she cannot be held morally responsible for her behavior because she has "diminished understanding." She cannot make an informed decision about the matter of sexual relations with an adult. Unaware of the social regulations governing sexual behavior, she is unable to judge the acceptability of a sexual partner. And even if she did not resist, or even consented to the act, she is not likely to fully understand the consequences.[40]

Also by virtue of her dependence on powerful adults around her, the child is not held responsible for her submission to the authority of adults. Diminished capacity is an issue of education and development; dependence is an issue of freedom. Because of her age, the child is under the authority of adults and will be responsive to both incentives and their exercise of authority; thus, we could say, she will be conflicted in her effort to make wise decisions on her own behalf.

We could also apply this thinking to the wife or partner of a batterer if we consider that the authority a man has over his wife or girlfriend is something socially bestowed rather than a legal right, as it once was. In this way of thinking (which is not popular because it demeans the subject), the woman is mentally incapacitated by the authority her partner has over her and the socially constructed authority of men over women in our culture. This argument could be extended to rape victims as well.

One could also maintain that children and women are incapacitated by certain emotions. While this argument may seem degrading, those working in the area of victim support do actually argue for incapacitation via emotions, even though these emotions can be seen as strengths in the context of a better world or in relation to people who are not abusive. For instance, the child is seen as trusting and compliant and thus easily manipulated and taken advantage of; the qualities that may serve her well in most of her relationships incapacitate her when confronted by a perpetrator. Attitudes that have been traditionally associated with women in our culture and have traditionally benefited men (the desire to preserve relationships, trust, compassion, and the ability to take another's perspective) are all qualities that can incapacitate a woman when faced by a perpetrator of abuse. In the post-violence assessment of the situation, for example, the wife may "feel badly about her husband's frustration with her or his situation in life, and thus "understand" her beating. The rape victim may try to see herself from the perpetrator's point of view and think that perhaps she *was* provocative. Lenore Walker and Angela Browne have written that women's socialization for passivity, submissiveness, politeness, and helpfulness make them more vulnerable to victimization.[41] There are also social penalties for women who violate the norm of passivity.[42]

The very act of abuse can mentally incapacitate the victim and contribute to her ongoing psychological coercion. In chronic abuse situations, men establish control over their victims through fear, unpredictability, intermittent rewards, and by destroying the victim's other relationships.[43] The abuse itself is demeaning and degrading and destroys the will of the victim. When a woman or child is used as an object, it is difficult for her not to feel that she is an object, a nonperson. Self-esteem has always been a problem for the survivor of abuse, and low self-esteem will hinder a victim from protecting herself further.

Fear, in particular, incapacitates. During the abuse, victims often become immobilized, and after the abuse the terror continues to keep them from action even though they judge themselves harshly for this inability to respond. In this way the abuse itself further incapacitates a victim.

The strongest argument regarding incapacitation comes from those who describe a total state of captivity, one that completely incapacitates the victim. This argument was made for Hedda Nussbaum, the mother who did little to prevent her daughter's sexual abuse and beatings, and was present, using drugs with her husband, as her daughter lay nearby, on the floor, dying. Those who came to Hedda's defense saw her as a victim of Battered Woman's Syndrome. They argued that she was trapped in a relationship by virtue of a dependency her husband had systematically created through beatings, drugs, and other "brainwashing" techniques, and that her insistence that she was not afraid of her husband was consistent with the numbness experienced by those who live in daily terror.[44] It is worth noting that there also exists a condition known as "The Stockholm Syndrome," which documents how hostages, over time, and even after their release, maintain a strong bond with their captors, understanding their plight, and ignoring their own.[45] Child sexual abuse victims and the wives and partners of batterers can be seen in an extreme sense as hostages in their own homes.

The hard line in the argument for victims' incapacitation is embodied in the description of captivity. And cases like Hedda Nussbaum's are emphasized to paint a picture of almost total sadism on the part of the perpetrator and total incapacitation on the part of the victim. But abuse as well as incapacitation occurs in degrees. Children are more or less incapacitated by their age, and as they get older they are held more culpable for their actions. Women are more or less incapacitated by the authority of their husbands or boyfriends, the economics of their situation, and violence itself. Victims are more or less fearful of their abuse. The hard line has been emphasized to combat victim-blaming.

But victims resist this hard line. As Herman puts it, "Traumatized people struggle to arrive at a fair and reasonable assessment of their conduct, finding a balance between unrealistic guilt and denial of all moral responsibility." They seek "not absolution but fairness, compassion, and the willingness to share the guilty knowledge of what happens to people in extremity."[46]

The role of victim is socially constructed. To be a victim is to have been harmed and to have been powerless, a reactor to an external force. Until recently it has been a deviant label, a shameful category, a name to be avoided. (The current trend in which people are seemingly proud to be victims, where everyone increasingly sees herself as victim can be viewed as a kind of reaction formation, an expression of the opposite in order to defend against the feelings of shame.) One victim states, "It belittles you to admit you're a battered woman. I don't like the name. I'd rather be referred to as temporarily abused."[47] It is not the physical harm that makes victimization feel so demeaning but the powerlessness. The powerlessness is exactly what victims chide themselves for.

"I could have fought harder," claims the rape victim. "Why didn't I leave him?" asks the wife of the battering husband. "I can't believe that after fifty years of living I'm such a bad judge of character." "I was so weak to believe him." "I was stupid to trust him." "I shouldn't have been tricked." What victims rail against is their passivity and, more generally, their character. As noted earlier, all victims show some sort of characterological blaming; they ask, why *me?* not just, why?

Therapists all too often tell victims that there was nothing they could have done, or show them the ways in which they were made passive, incapacitated by their perpetrators. "He had a gun; you did what you did to save your life." "He was your father, you were taught to obey him and comply with his wishes." "If you had fought harder do you think you really could have escaped?" "You were only three; you didn't know how to call the police."

There is another strategy of counseling that attempts to empower. "You *did* do what you could; you fought the best way you could but it wasn't enough to prevent *him*." "Your character was fine, these are wonderful qualities, they were just manipulated by the wrong person." "Anyone would have reacted that way in that situation." These empowering voices are preferable to the ones that reinforce the passivity, but they leave open the possibility that the victim can argue about the degree to which any of these "reasons" are true. The victim answers, "But other people have escaped rapists; others *did* do more than I did." "Other children did say no. Other children did tell." They move beyond the general case and ask, "Why didn't I make myself the exception?" There are enough stories of the pride of victims who overcome their victimization to demoralize those who do not.

Victims drown in the sea of degrees of powerlessness. Aristotle wrote that an act is compelled when "the cause is external circumstances and the agent contributes nothing."[48] This "nothing" is what the victim, in her search for fairness, questions. How powerless was she? Did she react more helplessly than she needed to? Had she done something or said something else, could she have protected herself better? Questions of blame and responsibility are obliterated only by the most extreme cases (abuse involving captivity or very young children); otherwise, victimization cannot help raising issues of character. Perhaps this is why almost all victims claim that their victimization changed their lives. Therapists can help them grapple with these issues of character, but if we choose a road that emphasizes the victimization and does not deal directly with issues of self, character, and responsibility, then we risk turning victims into victims for life.

VICTIMS' RESPONSIBILITY

Issues of character and selfhood are crucial to a victim's struggle with blame for her victimization. The victim examines the degrees of powerlessness during the abuse and after. What power did she have during the abuse, when did it stop, when did it or does it begin again? Some victims of sexual abuse must continually contend with the fact that they may have felt sexually excited during the abuse. Although most therapists will deal with these feelings by insisting that the body has a mind of its own and that these were merely physiological reactions, such a response would seem to encourage the symptoms of dissociation while the victim herself is trying to feel connected (if ashamed) to her body and its reactions.

Another aspect of the self-blame of victims is their anger at themselves for not "getting over it." Friends and family encourage them to get on with their lives and "not think about it anymore," perhaps because it is so difficult for them to hear about the abuse and its ramifications in the victim's life. A victim's inability to "get over" the abuse can be seen as a continuation of the abuse in some respects. The suffering doesn't end. Years later, she is still depressed and may even perpetrate abuse on herself, acting in a way that is not protective and, in the very least, not life-enhancing.

The general view is that victims are in a sense not responsible for the way they respond and are in a continual state of reacting to their abuse. Although a hard-line libertarian view would hold individuals responsible for their reactions to events in their past, few would take this extreme a position with regard to victims.[49] Nor would many say that victims have no responsibility for their post-trauma reactions and behaviors.

This is a difficult issue, as illustrated by the case of a mother I once interviewed for a research project.[50] Her daughter had been sexually abused by her sons' godfather. She had allowed this man to baby-sit her daughter several times in his basement apartment. What was so dramatic about this case was that the mother allowed this to happen after the man had served time in prison for having sexually abused her two sons a few years earlier! When asked why she had allowed him to baby-sit her daughter knowing full well that he had been convicted of child sexual abuse, she first said that she thought he had learned his lesson by being sent to jail, and second, that she thought he did this only to boys. This mother herself had had multiple experiences of abuse while growing up, having been sexually abused as a child and gang-raped as a teenager.

Let us consider what our reactions to this mother would be if she had put *herself* in a dangerous situation and been raped; would we view her more compassionately? We would perhaps find her incapacitated in her judgment because of her low self-esteem and possible counterphobic reactions caused by her earlier experiences. Next, we can go back in time to this mother's gang rape. Would we blame her at all for that act, knowing her history of sexual abuse? Probably not. We might say that she lived in an environment that put her at constant risk for rape, or that she was unlucky to have been chosen for the rape, or that because of her limited resources she had to depend on people or situations that were less protective than people or situations a middle-class woman depends on or finds herself in. If we do see her behavior as putting her at risk for that gang rape, we might go back and blame perpetrator number one, who victimized her and caused certain symptoms and reactions that would make her more vulnerable to the second attack.

If we move in the other direction, to the point in time after her daughter has been abused, we probably would blame this mother more. But how is it that she is not responsible for her *own* behavior, which might have led to her second abuse, yet responsible for behavior that leads to her *daughter's* abuse? Is she less responsible for herself than she is for her daughter? Some may argue that this mother should not be blamed for her daughter's abuse, that, like Hedda Nussbaum, she was "incapacitated" by her own victimization. But many would not find this incapacitation argument so persuasive.

How can we say a person is responsible for her symptoms? her reactions? How can we say that the character that develops as a result of her abuse is her own responsibility? It is a difficult task, especially as these reactions to trauma are given medical labels such as symptoms and syndromes.

The list of symptoms experienced by victims of abuse is in fact enormous. In the early stages of research in this area, study after study showed the deleterious effects of abuse, as if to shout to the public, "See! Take abuse seriously. It is harmful." Victims of child sexual abuse have problems with self-esteem, intimacy, interpersonal relationships, and work. As adults they continue to have symptoms of depression, anxiety, suicidality, and sexual dysfunction. These symptoms are worse with longer durations of abuse, use of force, penetration, when the perpetrator was a father or other close family member, and the earlier the abuse started.[51] Rape victims and women who have been battered do not fare better.

It has been important to show these outcomes of victimization and their seriousness, but if one sets up one side of the issue in its extreme form, the other side can use the weak points in the argument to attack the whole concept of victimization. We must admit that there has been some exaggeration in presenting the most dramatic cases, and not only on the part of the media. The politics of research have caused many studies to have been undertaken in a less than complete way. For example, we know very little about what kinds of circumstances mediate positive and negative outcomes after sexual abuse. There has been little acknowledgment of the fact that although rape, child sexual abuse, and wife battering are terrible experiences to have gone through, many people have "survived" and moved beyond them, feeling as if their victimization is not something that has defined them or continues to affect them.

But let us return to the issue of responsibility for one's reactions to victimization. So comprehensive is the list of symptoms that it virtually defines the victim, suggesting that who she is is not of her own making. So, like the issue of whether a victim can be held responsible for any aspect of her character that may have made her susceptible to her victimization, there is the similar question of whether or not she is responsible for any of her reactions. The fundamental question is, what is the relation of a person to her own psychology?

POST-TRAUMATIC STRESS REACTIONS

Post-Traumatic Stress Disorder (PTSD) is a syndrome that describes a pattern of symptoms sometimes found in a person who has been traumatized, and it is generally considered to be an involuntary response. Who, after all, would *choose* to have symptoms such as overwhelming anxiety, flashbacks, and depression? Although developed originally to describe reactions of veterans who had been in combat, it is generally acknowledged as a useful term in describing the victims of child sexual abuse, rape, and battering, and was accepted as a syndrome into the Diagnostic and Statistical Manual for Mental Disorders (DSM) in 1980. (Whereas Lenore Terr has argued that only acute (one time), not chronic, trauma should qualify as the event that triggered the symptoms, others have argued that although the violence may be chronic, each single event shares aspects of the unpredictability, uncontrollability, and menace of any acute trauma.)[52]

The creation of a syndrome to describe a person's response to the stress of abuse "medicalizes" a victim's reactions. In some sense it has been a long-needed acknowledgment of the suffering of victims, and a pathway by which they can get treatment and support. A great deal of money for mental healthcare is tied into psychiatry (hospitals, research, medication, insurance) rather than, for example, neighborhood women's clinics; the creation of a syndrome for post-trauma victims helps women to get the support they need, but only from more mainstream institutions.

Post-Traumatic Stress Disorder is defined by the following criteria. First, the stressor must be acknowledged as "outside the range of usual human experience" and "markedly distressing to anyone."[53] Second, the victim must display symptoms from three different categories: reexperiencing symptoms (such as flashbacks, nightmares, and distress at events symbolizing or associated with the trauma); avoidance symptoms (such as amnesia, feelings of detachment, and restriction of affect); and symptoms of increased arousal (such as hypervigilance, irritability, and difficulty falling asleep). Although many survivors have some of the symptoms, the rate of PTSD among survivors is not so high as to claim it as an inevitable reaction to abuse.[54] Researchers have found that the greater the stressor, the greater the risk for developing PTSD.[55] With regard to abuse, we can add that as coercion increases, choice diminishes, and as choice diminishes, symptoms increase.

We might ask what evidence there is that the PTSD reactions constitute a syndrome. The medical answer to the question is that there is a cluster of characteristics that seem to occur together, that this cluster has stability over time, and that the constituent characteristics can be defined "without recourse to social phenomena."[56] There are a few sociocultural answers to the question also. The philosopher Lawrie Reznek writes that, by classifying a condition as an illness, "we inform medical scientists that they should try to discover a cure for the condition. We inform benefactors that they should support such research. We direct medical care towards the condition . . . [and we] inform the courts that it is inappropriate to hold people responsible for the manifestations of the condition."[57] Thus there is much to be gained from the classification or invention of a disorder.[58] The more patterns we can determine, the better we can support the mental health "industry" as a whole. And a narrower definition of mental illness would limit the mental health field by encouraging fewer people to seek services, thereby limiting the number of problems for which insurance companies would pay for treatment, and requiring fewer highly trained clinicians.[59]

There is currently a debate within the medical profession about the ethics of treating people who play a large part in bringing on their own illnesses, for example, liver disease in the alcoholic, or lung problems in the heavy smoker. This is not to say that victims bring on their own illnesses, but to say that the more a person is seen as a victim of her illness, a reactor and not an agent, the more she is seen as deserving of or needing treatment. Unlike many disorders that could be said to institutionalize "deviant" behavior, PTSD legitimizes reactions so that victims can garner more support.

But why are these reactions to external stressors considered an illness? There are plenty of reactions to stressors that do not become syndromes.[60] Take, for example, the inner-city youth who does not show an interest in education. He looks listless in school, his eyes glazed over; he may even engage in some delinquent behavior outside of school. A certain pattern of symptoms and easily identified external stressors are present here—poverty, lack of job opportunities for him and his peers, the uncaring attitude of his parents or the school system—and these stressors probably cause disinterest in school and its concomitant symptoms about as often if not more often than violence causes PTSD. We could label his syndrome "school dissociation disorder," but we don't.

There are those who would argue that the PTSD symptoms constitute a "disease" because they are largely involuntary. These supporters also discuss research based on learning theory (according to stimulus / response research), biological mechanisms, or some combination of the two. These kinds of "medical model" descriptions are rampant in the psychiatric literature.

The behavioral model argues that the PTSD symptoms one sees in survivors of abuse (particularly the amnesia, restricted affect, and detachment) are similar to the avoidance and escape behaviors that emerge in rats who experience uncontrollable and unpredictable pain. Avoidance, for example, increases in animals if the shock they receive—or whatever traumatic experience is administered—is also accompanied by something that was previously associated with safety.[61] That is, the avoidance reactions are "conditioned" by virtue of factors external to the subject (unpredictability and uncontrollability) as well as internal factors (memories and associations of safety). Edna Foa and her associates argue that research supports this view,[62] for a victim is more likely to develop PTSD symptoms if her life was endangered or she believes it was in danger (unpredictability, uncontrollability),[63] and the abuse occurred in a situation (during the day, at home) or was perpetrated by someone (a date, one's father) she had previously associated with safety.[64] According to behavioral therapists, PTSD anxiety symptoms in particular are so unyielding to human thought and empathy that they must be treated behaviorally, through "flooding." "Flooding" is a technique in which the person is forced to reexperience her trauma, for example, by actively repeating what happened in order to relive it so often and so continuously that her physiological response to it will be retrained.[65]

Biological views begin by pointing to basic responses to trauma that are "hard-wired." "The first line of defense against trauma is reflexive," writes Elizabeth Waites in her book *Trauma and Its Wake*.[66] Summarizing biological studies of human responses to chronic trauma, she offers that the "wear and tear" on biological systems that regulate arousal results in a depletion of energy for coping with simple stressors, and can fundamentally change a person's neurochemistry, resulting in a new kind of homeostasis. Some symptoms can be seen as a result of a chronic state of depletion of norepinephrine. It has been argued that the heightened arousal during trauma that calls for more of the neurotransmitter creates additional receptors for it. When the trauma ends, the extra receptors remain and the victim will have a chronic depletion of norepinephrine. This depletion has also been associated with problems in memory storage.[67]

It has been hypothesized that "addiction to trauma," or the reexperiencing symptomatology, is caused by a depletion of naturally occurring opioids (chemicals that produce a "high") in the body. Like norepinephrine, these opioids are overworked when responding to the stress, thus creating additional receptors for them in the brain. The victim then seeks out opioid-supplementing experiences to attain the new homeostasis her body needs, through drug use or even compulsive self-abuse.[68]

If these symptoms seem to have some biological connection, then how can a victim be responsible for her reactions to or her character after the abuse? They are reactions, involuntary symptoms, and in this sense not one's own, not *to be* owned by the individual. But most people would agree that symptoms are "overdetermined," and that "the human brain is not a slave to reflex."[69] There are multiple determinants to any reaction and biological readiness, or genetic endowment is not always enough to produce a reaction. Moreover, there have been many studies that show the reverse effect, the effect of thinking or experience on biology. Describing a biological component does not, then, argue against responsibility for one's reactions, if we take reactions to mean something more than the immediate, reflexive response.

Biology has been used before in psychiatry to avoid tricky issues of responsibility. For example, if alcoholism is genetic or part of one's biology, then the alcoholic need not feel ashamed.[70] Psychiatrists tell depressed individuals that there is something wrong with the chemistry in their brains, and that the medication prescribed is like insulin for a diabetic. Newer temperament data lead parents to ignore parenting style and overemphasize the biology of the child, to argue that his temperament makes him a "difficult" or "spirited" child. Biology, in this sense, is like one of the rival agents described by the philosopher Daniel

Dennett in his book *Elbow Room:* the nefarious neurosurgeon who has strapped us down and inserted electrodes in our brains, or the Peremptory Puppeteer who controls our movements as if we were marionettes. *They* are the supreme agents who control us, determine our future, and take away our free will.[71]

If physiology is not like the "mad scientist" controlling his victims, and if symptoms are not merely physiological reactions to stress, there is still one remaining rival agent: the stressor, or perpetrator, himself. For example, can the low self-esteem, the feeling of not having a self, and particularly the automaton-like behavior with accompanying dissociative symptoms seem truly to derive from the experience of abuse that deprived the victim of selfhood for a time (giving Dennett's "pitiful human puppet" and "zombie of Dr. Svengali" new meaning)? If biology is not the nefarious neurosurgeon controlling us from afar, surely the specter of one's actual perpetrator determines the victim's life, self, and future. But when the abuse stops, this perpetrator mainly exists in the victim's own head—indeed, as a specter.

Let us consider, then, what our vision of therapeutic change would be if the victim's reactions to the stress were completely determined by external forces. There could be biological change. The body could perhaps readjust to its pre-trauma physiology after time, much as women recover from the hormonal on-slaught of childbirth. There could be more behavioral ap-proaches, in the manner of Foa, where the victim is helped to unlearn or decondition determined responses—behavioral work that is led, taught, and enforced by a behavior therapist who could create an opposing response to combat the anxiety reac-tions. We could imagine a different therapist who could suggest new ways of thinking that would help the victim to reevaluate herself and her situation. Or we could see the therapist as providing a rehabilitating, nurturing experience to replace some of the bad affect that had developed from the abuse. In any of these circumstances, the change comes from the outside, the victim is determined by her abuse, she is determined by her biology, or she is determined by the kind of therapy or therapist that attempts to change her. As a psychotherapist, I certainly believe in the importance of this kind of change and the ability of therapists to help victims overcome their trauma. But I am sure we are all unhappy with this reliance on external forces in its extreme. Even the most regimented behavioral or biological therapies need one thing to work: patient compliance. We want to see the victim as having some input into her own healing, some self through which she makes choices, some determination. Indeed, victims do a tremendous amount on their own to heal themselves—through disclosure, journal writing, art, and other forms of "processing" the event. In their activities they seem, much more than we, to hold themselves responsible for their outcomes, for their symptoms, and for their characters. Yet if they have free will at this point in their recovery, why hadn't they free will earlier, as they were experiencing post-trauma symptoms?

LIMITED RESPONSIBILITY

If a victim is a product of her victimization and never an agent, then she needs to be reborn, to rebuild her character from scratch. Victim-support agencies and therapists see anger as the source of this agenthood, since anger and resentment are a proper response to abuse. When the victim owns the anger and the resentment, it is as if she is saying that she is a person whose rights have been violated. As the philosopher P. F. Strawson says, if we do not react with resentment when our rights are violated then we do not take our rights very seriously.[72]

In his books the Marquis de Sade rendered his victims passive and faceless because he knew that the face of a victim was a powerful weapon. That is why perpetrators must render their victims passive, stripping them not only of their rights but of their dignity.[73] Crucial to our dignity is being held responsible for things that have happened to us.

Some may be comfortable with the extreme but popular view that victims are *not* responsible for their characters or their disorders, and that their abuse has made them the way they are. And we too might be able to live with this view of heavy determinism, until we turn our attention to the perpetrators. Will we then decide that their prior abuse or current disorders lessens their responsibility for the abuse? Will we argue that they are not responsible for their characters?

Did victims have real power to change their abuse? Some did, many probably did not. For those who did, it would have been very difficult. Still, rape and sexual abuse prevention courses emphasize what children and women can do if they are attacked or approached, which does seem to imply that one has a responsibility for one's character, a responsibility to assume the assertiveness that will protect one's rights.

Consider an adolescent girl who had been sexually abused by her father for more than four years, and who told the members of her therapy group the following story.[74] At work she asked for a free burger. Her manager in turn asked, "What will you give me for it?" She said, "Nothing," to which he responded, "How about a hug?" She consented, and he asked, "How about a hug in the back room?" She followed him to the back room, and when she hugged him he squeezed her buttocks and fondled her breast. She went out and continued working, although she was upset and felt abused and violated.

The members of her group, in as gentle a way as these adolescent girls knew how, told her she was stupid to agree to the hug, stupid to go in the back room, and stupid not to have left work right then and there. Realizing that they may be right, she asked them all, "What is it about me that makes men do this to me?" This was a good question.

3

In the quintessential horror tale *Dr. Jekyll and Mr. Hyde*, Mr. Hyde's first act of villainy is, significantly, the "trampling" of a little girl.[1] As Mr. Hyde rushes through the streets of London, he literally runs into a child and "tramples" her; the use of the verb "to trample" conveys the combined carelessness, brutality, and selfishness of the act. The narrator, Mr. Utterson, along with the girl's family and neighbors who happened to see the incident, is horrified that a man could be so "hell-bent" as not to notice or care about the effects of his self-absorption. The horror is also at his sense of entitlement, reminiscent of the modern phrase "driving"—or in this case running—"as if he owned the road." And so, true evil is defined in an act in which a victim is harmed simply for being in the way, an act in which no concern is shown for the victim nor any thought given to consequences for the onlookers and society at large.

Does Mr. Hyde represent the deep inner nature of all men, or is he a thing created by external circumstances, induced by drugs, or stemming from the civilized, polite culture of the time? Is Dr. Jekyll, who continues to take the drug that transforms him into Mr. Hyde, an addict, in modern parlance? The words of one incest perpetrator evoke the feeling of addiction and of the secret self so relished and feared by Dr. Jekyll: "I knew before

I left the hospital that I was not straight, that despite all that was available there, nobody was sharp enough to pick up my secret. And I didn't want anyone to learn my secret."[2]

The task of this chapter, at the outset, seems simple enough: to support and substantiate a view that holds perpetrators responsible for their evil acts, a view that presents them as agents of their acts who possess the requisite free will to be blamed. The task becomes more complex, however, when we seriously consider the arguments for why an individual perpetrator may *not* be blameworthy; why, according to some, his actions, like those of Dr. Jekyll's alter ego, may not be called his own. Some have argued that the perpetrator's acts are overdetermined or predetermined by the culture of male violence, our biological history, male sexuality, the cycle of abuse, alcohol, drug addiction—all of the reasons that make abusive acts seem to be about someone's impulses rather than his deliberations, and that make his deliberations look like rote learning. Philosophers commonly hold that free will depends on a person's ability to "have done otherwise," that an act is free only if the actor had realistic alternatives. Intuitively we say to ourselves that any individual perpetrator of abuse must have been able to have done otherwise. It seems clear. But just as in Chapter 2 there were reasons beyond the "tie-down, physical coercion" that explained what the victim sometimes called her participation in the act of violence or her response to it, there are "reasons" that the perpetrator puts forth in explaining his acts.

It is well established that perpetrators rarely take responsibility for their acts; they deny their offenses. Even those perpetrators who do admit to them initially have excuses.[3] A primary focus of most therapies for perpetrators is, in fact, getting them to hold themselves accountable for their actions. Psychologists who have studied the ways people excuse themselves for bad behavior or failures differentiate three kinds of excuses. The first kind of excuse is outright denial; "I didn't do it," most perpetrators claim when caught. This kind of "excuse," if used by a perpetrator, is easily dismissed, for most perpetrators are aware that they are lying and merely deny the act to avoid punishment. The second kind of excuse-making minimizes the act's importance or effects: "It wasn't so bad," or "It wasn't rape," or "She asked for it." This kind of excuse could indicate that the perpetrator is either misreading cues or fooling himself, and we shall see in Chapter 4 that minimization of impact has been supported in subtle and more overt ways by cultural practices. The third type of excuse, the focus of this chapter, is the "Yes, but . . . ," which sounds like "I didn't mean to," "I couldn't help it," and "It wasn't really me," or "It wasn't the true me who committed that abominable act." At the heart of this kind of excuse is the question of whether a perpetrator has a direct claim to the act he commits, and whether he can use the excuses of childhood history, impulsivity, biology, and cultural context to make his act appear externally determined or separate from a core sense of his self.[4]

Excuse-making theory states that people are motivated to present a positive image of themselves; that is why perpetrators extend blame outward. This has also been known as "self-esteem maintenance" and "attributional egotism," among other catchy concepts. Sensing that negative evaluations of behavior are influenced by a number of factors (intentionality, foreseeability, harm done, whether the behavior had been exhibited before, whether it was distinctive, and whether the judge would have done the same in the same circumstances), the perpetrators incorporate many of these elements into their excuses.[5] If an act can be made to seem impulsive, then it is not intentional; if the actor lives in a society replete with images of violence toward women, then his act is not so distinctive; and if there was provocation, or alcohol, or a history of abuse, or any combination of these variables, then anyone might have acted the same way in the same circumstances.

At the outset, we can hear a distant cry from philosophers asking that we differentiate between holding someone responsible and claiming that he "caused" his act, between explaining an act (which presumably makes no evaluative comment and merely provides facts of causality), justifying it (which claims that, given the circumstances, the act was permissible), and excusing it (which says that the act was not permissible but that the person had a good reason for committing it). But let us keep those philosophers distant for the present, and look at reasons and responsibility in the way the public hears those words and the way they are most often meant by the perpetrators.

When a perpetrator, or any guilty party, gives a reason for bad behavior, if he does not mean for that reason to serve as a justification for it, he customarily adds, "I know that doesn't excuse what I did." People add this phrase to their reasoning fairly consistently whether or not it is said with sincerity. Why is this linguistic tag added on to explanations? It is needed because there is something inherent in explanations that smacks of "excusing" the act, that makes a bid to the recipient that the act be viewed as not entirely one's own, that looks like one is asking for leniency in judgment.

In offering the supposed reasons for his act (for example, his childhood history, his alcoholism, his life stresses), a perpetrator attempts to explain in what way he was coerced and to invite the listener to imagine a self that is not connected to the evil act, the "good" self that sits back and reflects on the event (as in Corrado's character theory).[6] This is also the effect the psychologist and the defense lawyer often aim for when presenting the context of an act of abuse or events leading up to it, such as the childhood history of the perpetrator; they argue for the "determinedness" of the act.

So, for the purposes of this chapter, though all explanations need not be justifications, and all reasons need not be excuses, let us think of them as being used in this way and look at whether they actually work to show the past or present coercion of the perpetrator of violence. I wish first to examine the excuse of a history of physical or sexual abuse and then the excuse of passion, which also could be seen as impulsivity or impulsive anger. I will examine these grander excuses because they pull at our compassionate sensibilities the strongest, but I will also look at other kinds of excuses, some related and some more distant to the excuses of childhood abuse and impulsivity. For example, the appeal to biological determinism is made through excuses of anger, but also addiction. The claim that it was the other person's fault needs to be examined simply because perpetrators rely on it so often. And the plea that the acts they commit are not truly representative of their inner selves, although not a direct claim of perpetrators, needs to be examined because it underlies so many of the more overt excuses.

EXCUSES: THE CYCLE OF ABUSE

One of the most compelling reasons for a compassionate approach to perpetrators is that many perpetrators of violence against women and children were themselves victims of violence or sexual abuse. In almost any media presentation of an abusive man, his own history of sexual or physical abuse is trotted out in an attempt to soften questions regarding the origins of evil. But though a history of physical or sexual abuse appears to be related to adult men's acting out sexually and violently, a causal relationship is not especially clear. In fact, we currently find that so many adults have suffered from childhood sexual or physical abuse, lived with an alcoholic parent or a dysfunctional family, that it may be the commonality of these experiences that makes it so easy to find them in the history of abusers. After considering the evidence for the claim made of the intergenerational transmission of abusive behavior, I want to explore whether and in what ways such a history can serve to lessen the blameworthiness of perpetrators for their acts.

The Research

One of the primary problems of research that attempts to demonstrate what has been called the "cycle of abuse" is that the research takes the form of retrospective studies. A retrospective study is one in which a group of perpetrators or a collection of prison or hospital records on perpetrators are examined by researchers in order to determine whether the subjects were abused as children. Usually this involves direct questioning of the subjects of the study, but sometimes the information has to be gleaned from official files or public sources of information. Retrospective research results in the presentation of a percentage figure that indicates how many perpetrators have a history of abuse, but it does not answer the question of what percentage of children who are abused grow up to be perpetrators themselves.

Prospective studies, few in number and difficult to conduct, are those that take a sample of children who have been sexually or physically abused and follow them over time, sometimes for years. At some point in the course of the study, it is determined whether the subjects, now adults, are physically or sexually abusive themselves, and a somewhat truer percentage of the cycle of abuse is derived. If the prospective study should reveal that 30 percent of the group under consideration grew up to abuse their children while a retrospective study shows that 60 percent of the perpetrators had a history of being abused, there are several ways to make sense of this variation. The lower percentage could be due to the fact that it is difficult to determine whether an adult is or has been physically or sexually abusive (one could rely on police or child-services reports, but what about those cases that go undetected and unconfessed?). Or the lower percentage could mean that the majority of children who have been abused do not grow up to be abusive.

This retrospective versus prospective data dilemma was addressed in the late 1980s by two researchers who analyzed studies that claimed the existence of a cycle of abuse for parents who maltreat their children. They concluded that for such a widely held belief there was minimal evidence.[7] In one prospective study they cited, 82 percent of the parents who had been abused as children broke the cycle of abuse. In a different, very high risk sample of abused parents, only 34 percent were abusive. In total, they determined that a fairly good estimate of the rate of transmission would be about 30 percent, plus or minus 5 percent.

Few of these prospective studies exist for rapists, batterers, and child molesters, and, as in the studies of the abusive parents, retrospective research always appears to suggest that there is a cycle of abuse. Although researchers claim that they are still inconclusive, retrospective studies show high percentages of childhood abuse for physically and sexually aggressive adults.[8]

When comparing incest offenders with nonoffending men of similar age and background, researchers found that five to ten times as many incest offenders had a history of sexual abuse.[9] Others have found history of sexual abuse to be close to 30 or 40 percent among incest offenders.[10] But in an extensive sample of nearly four hundred men who were obtained for the study through prisons, mental health facilities, a group called Parents United, and therapists in private practice, researchers found that from 49 to 65 percent of perpetrators had a history of sexual abuse, and 41 to 68 percent had a history of physical abuse. Those perpetrators who had been sexually abused themselves were more likely to have started abusing at a younger age and to have had more victims than the other perpetrators.[11] In fact, in a different study, one-third of adolescent offenders who had been admitted to a youth treatment center had a history of sexual abuse.[12] Those juvenile sex offenders who had reported any kind of abuse were similar in history to those who had not except for one factor. Those juveniles who had had more early sexual "experiences" had committed rape more frequently.

One prospective study of thirty-four children who had been sexually abused in a "sex ring" followed these children for six to eight years and compared them to a control group of children who had not been sexually abused. The study found that, over time, those children who had been sexually abused were more likely to become involved with drug abuse and criminal behavior. Of seventeen boys in one study, three had been convicted of rape, and there was more aggressive behavior among them when compared with those in the control group.[13]

A study of incarcerated serial rapists showed that 38 percent had been physically abused and 52 percent sexually abused as children. Of eighty-three men convicted of raping women, 59 percent had been molested by older women (at a mean age of eleven years).[14] In general, rapists are more likely than child molesters to have come from violent homes.[15]

The studies of wife-batterers yield similar information. In one study, three-quarters of the participants reported having witnessed violence between their parents, and almost one-half were abused themselves.[16] Childhood history of abuse was strongly related to battering in another study; however, this study relied on reports from the wives about their husbands' childhoods.[17]

Why Do Victims Become Perpetrators?
Why would someone who has been sexually or physically abused grow up to perpetrate the abuse on another? And why would

this be so much truer for males than for females? Is the answer as simple as the well-worn phrase "Children learn what they live"?

Just as we saw the victims' tendency toward self-blame as an attempt at mastery, some have seen the perpetrator (who initially was a victim) as attempting to master his own trauma by enacting what happened to him, but this time placing himself in the more powerful position. Just as the victim was seen as compelled to relive the traumatic moment, the perpetrator relives his traumatic moment, only he transforms himself into the abuser and reexperiences the moment through his victim as she expresses the feelings of helplessness and vulnerability that he is avoiding.

The above description can be seen through the lens of mastery theories or theories of PTSD which indicate that the perpetrator reenacts his victimization to master it or because he cannot help doing so. Along the lines of this latter theory, others have seen the propensity to rape or sexually abuse as resulting from the pathology of the perpetrator's own abuse.[18] It is suggested that these kinds of behaviors are a result of "massive blocking" at the sensory level (numbness), the perceptual level (lack of response to interpersonal cues), and the cognitive level (the shutting out of social condemnation). The child who has been abused is "turned off" physically and emotionally and later rapes to "stimulate himself" (not unlike the female victim who might drink or self-mutilate to "feel more real"), or because he is unaware of and indifferent to the consequences for other people and society. In a study comparing only fifteen male hospital inpatient records to more than sixty female ones, researchers found that men with a history of sexual or physical abuse were much more likely to be aggressive and to have abused others than were women with a history of abuse.[19] Sex-role theory would help to explain why the pathologies of male and female victims diverge in this way, a topic to which I will return in Chapter 5.

The most persuasive theory of wife-beating is modeling, which arose from Albert Bandura's social-learning theory. According to Bandura, children who commit violent acts are imitating their parents, and children tend to use as their model the same-sex parent. Thus "techniques" of violence and violent ways of coping with stress are passed down through the generations.

Modeling also helps to explain the sex differences in aggression resulting from abuse. Some have suggested that the sex-role behaviors of aggression versus passivity become exaggerated, and that for men aggression becomes a defense against intolerable feelings of helplessness and vulnerability. These kinds of feelings are better tolerated by women because they are more consistent with socially accepted sex roles. The methods by which men and women deal with frustration and feelings of helplessness are already determined by so many additional cultural variables.

Is Prior Victimization an Excuse?
Leaving aside any quibbling over statistics, prospective versus retrospective studies, and which theory best explains why abused children grow up to abuse, we can still ask whether or not a perpetrator deserves in any way to be excused for his act and whether he must be seen as a tragic victim rather than a criminal. We can imagine him as a child, crying out in pain, a heartbreaking situation in which his frustrated crying might have been met with kicks, or disregard, or insults. We can visualize the pouting lips or the resigned droop of the head of a child defeated. We can imagine him being sodomized by his father, scared or passive, wincing or protectively blank-faced. And so the perpetrator becomes the victim to us, and we seek to offer comfort, not condemnation. In our deep belief in the continuity between childhood and adulthood, we connect that

sad little boy to the grown perpetrator. But in what way is he connected? Some would say that sad little boy still exists within the adult abuser. Others would say he has been transformed. Still others would say he is lost forever.

I raise the question, but I do not think we need to disprove the continuity between childhood experience and adulthood in order to address the question of culpability.[20] We may ask first, would anyone, given these same life circumstances, have done the same? And second, does childhood abuse cause such a degree of duress that we cannot hope for a person to overcome whatever urges might result from it?

Childhood abuse, though not as strong a mitigating circumstance as insanity or physical coercion, might still meet one of the criteria that have been established by philosophers and legal scholars that excuse an individual from responsibility for his actions. The philosopher Strawson, for example, states that we give special consideration to people for their bad acts if they were "under great strain": "We shall not feel resentment against the man he is for the action done by the man he is not."[21] This excuse seems to work better if we use it to refer only to a specific moment in time. Can we rightly say that a perpetrator's whole life is one of great strain, and, given this condition of great strain, he is not the man he could have been, and thus cannot be responsible for most of his actions?

If we do, we then must make sense of the fact that not all people who were abused grow up to abuse, probably not even the majority. There are, of course, additional circumstances that differentiate those who do from those who do not. Some psychological studies show which factors differentiate the two, in part, but psychological studies cannot capture the moment of choice. There are moments of choice, of opportunity, that potential perpetrators live through, the result of which divides them. When perpetrators draw attention to their histories, they draw attention away from their moments of choice, as well as from the gruesome details of the abusive act. Were we to focus on the abusive act, the face wincing in pain would be transformed from that of the perpetrator in youth into that of his later victim.

Another dilemma regarding the free will of perpetrators is that we know that people can reflect on who they are, what happened to them, and how they behave, and that this reflection can be a powerful restraint or a motivator toward good. So, to what extent can we count on this capacity for reflection to support responsibility? When the perpetrator asks us to see his self divided (an evil actor with a good, reflective inner self), it becomes possible to hold that reflective, inner self responsible for its actions. In one large study, less than 10 percent of perpetrators of sexual abuse had discussed their feelings or tried to get help before committing an abusive act.[22] The compassionate psychologist might say, "Well, but they were helpless; prior experience had yielded men with little belief in their ability to control their impulses." But when these men were also asked, "Did you think that anything could have been done prior to the incest to prevent it?" 77 percent answered yes.[23] Where did they see this prevention coming from? Most likely from outside of themselves.

PASSION, IMPULSE, AND THE EXERCISE
OF SELF-CONTROL

Somehow, if a person commits an evil act spontaneously, with little forethought, he is considered less culpable than someone acting premeditatively, as if his act were almost accidental. We excuse the impulsive act because we tend to think that it does not reflect an evil soul, and because we sometimes identify with the perpetrator in that we have all felt regret over bad behavior borne of a moment's passion. When we consider the issue of self-control, there are two important arguments that vie with the argument for the free choice of perpetrators; one has to do with impulsivity, the other, biology, which I will refer to as "sphexishness" to draw attention to an example used by the philosopher Daniel Dennett. This example is interesting because it does not evoke a simple version of biological determinism but incorporates the concept of interaction with the environment.

Dennett, in his book *Elbow Room,* discusses the digger wasp, *Sphex ichneumoneus,* who seems to be acting as a "free" agent but is actually being driven by features of her environment that are outside her control. The wasp digs a nest, stings a cricket to paralyze it, drags it to the threshold of her nest, inspects the nest, then drags the cricket inside, lays her eggs next to the bundled up, paralyzed insect, and flies away. When the eggs hatch, the baby wasps have the cricket nearby as a kind of "freeze-dried" breakfast (it had not been killed and so can serve as food). But Wooldridge, the scientist who discovered this phenomenon, reports that if while the wasp is inspecting her nest the cricket is moved an inch or two away by the scientist-cum-prankster, the wasp upon her return will move the cricket back to the threshold of the nest and go in for another inspection. The cruel scientist can move the cricket bundle two inches away again and again, and the wasp will repeatedly drag the bundle to the threshold and move to the next stage of inspecting the nest, never reaching the point of bringing the cricket inside.[24]

The wasp, then, who might appear to be a free agent performing a rational act, is not free, and ultimately irrational. Dennett compares this view of the wasp with a philosophical view of the "disappearing self": "All that bustling activity but *there's nobody home!*" In many biological explanations of criminal behavior we encounter this phenomenon of sphexishness. Responding to features in the environment, the biology, or the "program," if you will, is said to control the actor.[25]

The excuse of impulsivity is different from sphexishness, and with it the perpetrator seems to say, "I couldn't help it, it was an impulse, not representative of my character or even my intention but something that overcame me—yes, got the better of me." The excuse of sphexishness goes further, seeming to say, "Not only is this behavior not rational or controlled by me, but it's controlled by something bigger than me, biology, or evolution." With both kinds of excuses the perpetrator focuses on the moment as opposed to the past, and yet he as agent is mysteriously absent from the moment.

Anger

The excuse of anger makes an appeal to both impulse and biological inevitability. For example, the perpetrator who wanted to portray his anger as impulsive might argue, "It wasn't really me; it was the anger talking." A prominent theory of emotions that differentiates them from moods claims that emotions actually last for only a few seconds. (They are physiological events over which we have little control, as opposed to moods, which last longer and are more amenable to external influence.) Emotions flare up so quickly that the person may not even be aware of them until moments later.[26] But one important point is rarely remembered about anger, even after Carol Tavris's excellent book on the subject, and that is that anger and aggression are different. The former does not have to produce the latter. The former does not even have to be expressed.[27]

Here we are talking not about deep-seated, long-lasting anger (which theorists might instead call the mood of anger) but about the anger that gets acted on impulsively. The "impulsively angry" excuse is more common among batterers than among child molesters or incest perpetrators because the latter two kinds of abusers often need to plan their offenses in order to avoid getting caught. Even so, perpetrators in general tend to describe their acts as impulsive.[28] Criminology theory concurs, claiming that most crimes are committed because there is an impulse and there is an opportunity.

There is an aspect of impulsive anger that might excuse the perpetrator if we view him in much the same way psychotherapists tend to see trauma victims. You may recall that the victim, feeling powerless and unable to escape her perpetrator, dissociates. She "blanks out" and contributes to her own powerlessness in a sort of semibiological reaction to the overwhelming stress. This dissociation is akin to one of the primary symptoms of PTSD and underlies serious reactions to the abuse such as Multiple Personality Disorder.

The perpetrator's angry acting out can be seen as a kind of dissociation. I balk at the suggestion, but a case can be made for, and is consistent with, a view of anger that has been described as "blind rage." Similar to "temporary insanity," anger is a cognitively mediated, semibiological reaction, unjustified as it can be, to some perceived slight or insult. That is, the perceived insult motivates some momentary physiological reactions we call anger. Particularly for perpetrators who have been abused, dissociative anger may be a way of regulating uncomfortable affect. As the victim dissociates into an extreme form of passivity (according to gender-role socialization lines), the perpetrator may dissociate into an extreme form of aggression: rage. To be consistent, if we hold the perpetrator responsible for moments of blind, dissociative rage, then mustn't we take a similar view to the dissociation of the victim? And if we try to distinguish between "justified" temporary insanity (as in the case of Lorena Bobbitt, who cut off her abusive husband's penis) and "unjustified" temporary insanity (as could be argued for her husband, who allegedly beat her and raped her, though he was not convicted of this in court) then we render the term "insanity" meaningless.

The impulsively angry excuse does not hold strong once examined in greater detail. For example, one director of a treatment center for perpetrators claims, "These persons spend hours and hours planning sexual offenses. They work on these incredible scenarios in their minds and have a whole variety of game plans that they can use."[29] Nicholas Groth concurs, describing rapists as "rehearsing" their offenses at home.[30] It has also been pointed out that the batterer usually beats his wife or girlfriend at home. Why does he lose control at home but not when out? Why, when he is angry, might he express his anger in one context and not in another?

Anger may make it difficult to control oneself, but wouldn't it be going too far to say that anger made it impossible not to hit someone? Another important question is whether or not perpetrators have options *before* they get angry. Emotions do not arise out of nowhere but are shaped by the ideas we hold, the perceptions we interpret. Some may argue that emotions are "irrational," but those same "romantics" would argue that ideas and thoughts are not. Hence we may ask, can't we hold a perpetrator responsible for the ideas he has that would shape his response to be an angry one? If the perpetrator had avoided getting into a state of rage, through, for example, the examination of his ideas and perceptions, he would have avoided the limitations that were placed on him by being in this "less rational" state.[31] The philosopher Robert Adams writes that although we cannot blame the inner state of a person (which can be seen as involuntary), we can blame the "voluntary behavior in which that state is apt to be manifested."[32] It is possible that one can even cultivate rage as a personality trait.[33]

Although the perpetrator might be viewed as "dissociating" when confronted with helpless or vulnerable behavior, he can also be viewed as choosing to exercise self-control only in situations where his self-image is most likely to be damaged by disapproval or legal consequences. Therapists who use paradox have found a sense of control inherent in the loss of control. They have learned that if you assign a man the task of losing his temper every day, he finds the task difficult, and sooner or later, he finds it hard to lose his temper at all.[34] Anger-control training has been one response to the view that perpetrators of wife abuse lose control, but has had mixed results. Some have argued that anger-control training misses the point, since many perpetrators, before the angry outburst, use a variety of nonviolent but controlling strategies to demean and humiliate their future victims.

If we change our tack and think about a different kind of anger that may lead to acting out, long-standing anger rather than momentary rage (mood rather than emotion), we will encounter the still-common theory of perpetrators' anger toward their mothers. In this theory, violence toward women is viewed as the workings of a defense mechanism called "displacement." The perpetrator is seen as displacing his anger toward his mother onto another woman and thereby leaving his mother unharmed, preserving the relationship that he desperately needs in spite of all his mother's shortcomings. Others have spoken of the perpetrators' anger at their fathers for their absence,[35] but more recently for their fathers' earlier violence toward them.[36] We can even extend this kind of displacement theory to the perpetrator's anger at all the social injustices that have befallen him, anger displaced onto wives, girlfriends, and children. And if we then ask, why displace onto women, since there is also a tremendous amount of male-to-male violence? we could answer that women and children have traditionally afforded special opportunities in terms of their accessibility, their nonviolent responsiveness to their own harm, and their tendencies to want to protect their perpetrators.

Biological Anger?

There are also the "biology is destiny" arguments regarding anger that are related to the excuses of both impulsive anger and long-standing anger. "Biological anger" and "genetically determined aggression" have periodically been fashionable topics of discussion in the literature for decades. Studies of twins and adoptees have attempted to support the view that aggressive tendencies or criminality are inherited and will be expressed given adequate or, shall we say, inadequate (as with *Sphex ichneumoneus*), circumstances.[37] We are also in the decade of Prozac, when more and more people believe that they have a certain brain chemistry that influences their feelings and behaviors and that is more easily overcome by medication than psychotherapy. Finally, we have a renewed interest in individual differences in temperament, which have been put to use already as a sort of excuse for "bad behavior" in children.[38] The philosopher Judith Shklar remarks that people have always attempted to justify cruelty with arguments on the biological determinism of aggression.[39]

In what way is anger biological? To what extent is aggression controllable? One analysis of emotion words supports the idea that anger is one of five basic emotions.[40] Researchers have also suggested that an action plan may be associated with each of the basic emotions; however, researchers seem to agree that there are forms of anger associated with approaching the source as well as forms of anger associated with avoiding the source.[41] The discovery that when a person is angry blood goes to the hands and other extremities has been seen as evidence that the physiology of anger has some evolutionary connection to preparing one to fight.[42] But couldn't blood rush to the hands to prepare them to soothe? We must also keep in mind that preparation is not the same as motivation.

Addressing biological-determinism arguments from a different direction, we can look cross-culturally and find that some cultures do not even associate anger with fighting. In Micronesia the Ifaluk use the word *song* to refer to something like "justified anger," but rarely does *song* lead to physical violence; it is much more likely to cause a person to pout or refuse to eat. Most often *song* is expressed by an elder disapproving of a younger person who has broken a rule.[43] Violence and physical aggression among the Ifaluk are rarer than among those in the United States. The Ilongot of the Philippines, who do not have a word specifically for anger, have the word *liget,* which refers to something like a desire to prove oneself and show that one is not inferior to others.[44] Speakers of Polish distinguish between a kind of anger that is a childish rage, almost like animal aggression, and a more dignified, adult anger that seems to refer to something like "that person did something bad."[45] While in most languages the emotion anger has an essential component of "that person did something bad," and so is other-directed, how one acts in response to this realization seems ultimately socially constructed.[46] Thus though there may be a biological component to anger and perhaps even some evolutionary connection of anger to aggression, social beliefs and practices have great influence over its expression.

In this light, the implications of straight biological explanations are curious. The idea that something is inherited or has a biological component does not, after all, have to indicate that it is unchangeable or even harder to change than other traits or habits. As an extreme example, let us consider a biological urge that everyone can relate to: bowel movements. Moving one's bowels has a biological function and a sense of urgency about it. If we were to attempt to prevent this natural and biological moment for more than a couple of days, we would be in deep physiological trouble. After about the age of three, however, almost the entire world controls this biological urge and "expresses" it in the culturally appropriate place and suitable manner. What does it tell us about our culture and social training that some men seem to have a problem with where and how they express anger but have controlled their bowels exceptionally well? This harks back once again to Carol Tavris's point in her book on anger: anger may be overwhelming and involuntary, but aggression is a choice. Dennett put it wisely:

> Although we arrive on this planet with a built-in biologically endorsed set of biases, although we innately prefer certain states of affairs to others, we can nevertheless build lives from this base that overthrow those innate preferences. We can tame and rescind and (if need be) repress those preferences in favor of "higher" preferences, which are no less real for not being directly biologically (that is, genetically) endorsed.[47]

Sex
The need for sex has been used as an impulse excuse, particularly in the case of date rape, where men have argued that they were led on to a point of no return and thus needed to continue. Historically, feminists have tried to remove the discussion of sexual urges from the discussion of rape or child molestation, because from the victim's point of view these acts are acts of

violence, assertions of power by means of sex, rather than assertions of sexual needs or urges by means of power.

Men's lack of control over their sex drive is a concept that has been discounted somewhat since the 1950s but has still been described by some as the dominant discourse of sexuality widely believed and accepted in our culture.[48] As Rachel Hare-Mustin writes, "The woman is seen as the object that arouses and precipitates men's sexual urges. Men's sexual urges are assumed to be natural and compelling." This vision of male sexuality makes it appear as if choice is overwhelmed by urge. We hear this in the words of one rapist: "When I had this urge, nothing else mattered; I would do anything."[49] One wonders whether current "men's movements" like Robert Bly's that encourage men to return to more "animal," primeval images see choice as a burden and instinct as a relief, and whether they support the dominant discourse of uncontrollable male sexuality.

The idea of the sex addict has gained some support and serves to take sex, once again, out of the realm of choice and responsibility. We tend to show more compassion to those whose conditions we regard as being beyond their control. Is being compelled to do something similar to being sick or insane? Is it a disease? And why are some compulsions mental disorders and others not?

The addiction argument surfaces in literature about certain kinds of child molesters who have been labeled "fixated offenders." Some of the descriptions of these men seem to imply a biological fixation to young children.

Like perpetrators of abuse, sex addicts are presented as adults with abusive histories. One sex addict is described as "numbing" his pain, loneliness, and shame through a sexual fix. Again we see a description of a sort of dissociation, a dissociation from which victims also suffer. According to Patrick Carnes, sexual addiction begins with a faulty belief system, and so the therapy must ultimately change a person's beliefs.[50] But are beliefs to be seen like behaviors, "things" one has acquired but which do not actually belong to the self? According to this kind of cognitive view of sexual addiction, beliefs along with behaviors are merely appendages of the self, beliefs such as "I am a worthless human being" and "my needs can only be fulfilled by sex," which can be removed or transformed through therapy. If beliefs *and* behaviors are to be viewed as appendages of the self, what is left to compose the inner self?

Alcohol

Another excuse used by perpetrators that relies on the notion of self-control and biology is that of being drunk at the time of the abuse or having an addiction to alcohol. The "regressed offender" often uses alcohol to enhance the loss of self-control. Although less than a third of child sexual abuse acts occur when a perpetrator is under the influence of alcohol, alcohol seems to work as an excuse.[51] Undergraduates are less likely to judge perpetrators as harshly when they commit their acts under the influence of alcohol, for example.[52] Our own culture supports the belief that alcohol causes people to do outrageous things, impulsive and violent; however, there are many societies in which alcohol is connected with peaceful behavior.[53] In our culture alcohol is used to provide a kind of "time out" from responsible behavior.[54] In one experiment this "time out" perception was proven: A group of adults were given a drink. Some were told that what they drank was alcohol and some were told that it was something else. Half of each group did drink alcohol and everyone in the experiment met with the same (experimentally configured) anger-evoking experience. Interestingly enough, those who believed they had consumed alcohol but actually had not acted more aggressively than those who had consumed alcohol but believed they had not.[55] Thus, the knowledge, whether accurate or not, that they had drunk alcohol seemed to give them permission to act aggressively.

Self-Control

In an argument that discredits traditional individual versus situation arguments, Jack Katz, in *Seductions of Crime,* writes that the criminal seems to need to arrange the context so that he may see himself as being ruled by external forces. The seduction of crime is the possibility of experiencing oneself as no longer a subject or an agent but as an object of transcendent forces that carry one into another world.[56] Katz reminds us that the criminal alone is in charge of his transition from being a subject of his own experience to being an object, and refers to this transition as "pacifying one's subjectivity."[57] This helps us to understand how perpetrators can be seen as arranging the loss of self-control, even participating in the addictive process, yet still see themselves as the ones who are put upon, as reactors to, rather than the prime motivators of, their acts. This idea also serves to explain their lack of empathy for the victim, their tendency to blame others, and even the perpetrators' leap into conceptualizations of themselves as victims.[58] We as onlookers collude in this transformation to passivity when we begin to see the perpetrator as object rather than subject of his acts.

BLAMING THE OTHER

At the root of all victim-blaming are the perpetrator's own attempts to present the victim as the cause of his violence or abuse. Some of this other-blaming can be caused by the misreading of cues, another aspect of it comes from a sense of entitlement, and finally, some of it derives from self-deception, or image-preserving lying. Perpetrators of sexual abuse may say to their potential victims (as Dora's seducer said to her in Freud's *Dora: An Analysis of a Case of Hysteria*), "I get nothing from my wife." The truth is, sexual satisfaction in marriage is no greater or no worse for incest perpetrators than it is for others.[59]

Perpetrators may also blame the cultural expectations imposed on men: "Women expect too much from men." Groth cites a perpetrator who says, "I wish there were more aggressive girls around," as if to imply that if there were more, he would not have to rape. Or perpetrators may blame women for not living up to cultural expectations, for being too aggressive rather than not aggressive enough. A woman who fights back in a rape, for example, is more likely to anger her perpetrator (even though she is also more likely to escape).[60] In the case of the wife-beater, it is what the perpetrator perceives as disrespect or insubordination that is as likely as anything to set him off. Underlying this is the perpetrator's view that wives should serve (in reference to a host of "wifely duties") and that women should be compliant (since some do take on the responsibility for their men's egos).

Perpetrators will also claim that their victims are almost directly responsible for their fates, that the little girl wanted to be fondled, that the raped woman was asking for it by her behavior and dress, and that the abused wife provoked her beating with her comments or behavior. This kind of excuse has been labeled "dissonance reduction," and serves the perpetrator because it is easier for him to believe that he has harmed a bad or provocative person than an innocent one.[61]

Some of this other-blaming may actually derive from exceptionally poor social skills that lead the perpetrator to misread the situation. Aggressive boys, for example, have been shown to perceive ambiguous behaviors to be aggressive ones, and they therefore respond in kind, in a sort of projection of their own motivation onto others.[62] This is reminiscent of the explanation of a murderer on the *Oprah Winfrey Show* who stated about his victim and himself, "We exchanged blows, only he didn't get a chance to exchange any."[63] It may be more likely that the perpetrator does not think about the other person's motivations or behaviors at all, but is, rather, self-absorbed.

While a good amount of other-blaming has to do with provocation, and projecting one's own disavowed anger onto another, a different kind of other-blaming has to do with the perpetrator's belief that the victim is responsible for stopping him from committing his act. "If she wanted me to stop, she could have fought me," says one adolescent child molester. "My wife knows how to push my buttons. She knew, when she made that last comment, that she was asking for a beating," says the wife-beater. Each of these perpetrators holds the other, the child or woman, responsible for his self-regulation, a role that women have taken on for many years, beginning with mothering. Mothers teach children to wield unwieldy emotions, to soothe themselves or seek appropriate methods of self-soothing. And it has recently been argued that the wife is the one who "controls" the escalation of arguments through her reactions to her husband.[64] But it may be that boys are not expected to soothe or calm themselves, that they are allowed somewhat freer reign with their anger, particularly in a culture that subscribes to the view that anger and aggression are biologically more connected to men than to women. From the perpetrator's perspective, the woman should have soothed him, or stopped him, but instead she incited him and provoked him.

Many have asked why the wife-beater beats his wife as opposed to somebody else (although it has been shown that wife-beaters certainly are also more aggressive outside of the home than non-wife-beating husbands). The answer to the question is related to the idea that the perpetrator may think that the woman in question is responsible for soothing him; and so any provocation (and we all must admit that spouses do say provocative things to each other, though these provocative remarks never deserve to be met with violence) angers him.

When men project blame outward they do so with a sense of entitlement. We hear in their excuses the conviction that, no matter how victimized they themselves were, they live in a culture that seems to have promised them some entitlements that they deserve but are not getting. One hears a range of entitlements, some reasonable, some not: they deserve a good childhood, respect, parents who treat them toughly when they get out of control and whip them into shape with a firm but loving hand, and a culture that does not make it hard for them to find sex when they want it. Whereas victims talk about how they deserved their abuse, perpetrators talk about how slighted they feel and thus how entitled they are to the sexual pleasure they can seek out of situations. We should wonder then at the usefulness of showing perpetrators their own victimization. Many of them feel victimized already. Isn't their reaction to their own victimization (the entitlement) that which leads to more harm? If so, we may not want to encourage a sense of entitlement; it may be that perpetrators feel entitled enough.

DISTINGUISHING THE PERPETRATOR FROM THE ACT

"It was their behavior that was not acceptable, not them," state Sandra Ingersoll and Susan Patton, two therapists, warriors, if you will, battling the perpetration of incest through their work with perpetrators, good-hearted people who view the perpetrator with a compassionate eye, yet are smart enough to be harsh when needed and to emphasize the perpetrator's responsibility for every last aspect of the abuse. They battle not only incest but shame in general, believing that perpetrators have a long-standing history of shame buried within—a shamefulness that in fact contributes to their perpetration of abuse.[65]

But in their presentation of perpetrators as "acting" badly but not "being" bad, a new-age kind of "character excuse," they slip up. They say they believe that perpetrators who successfully complete their program will still need maintenance counseling for the rest of their lives. How can it be that their behavior is not representative of their true selves and yet the recurrence of their behavior is a definite possibility, as if it eternally lurks inside? Once again we run into two classic ideas that constitute perpetrators' thinking about themselves, as well as our thinking about them: that there is a separate inner self that deserves comfort and support rather than blame (and that this self is the real them); and that their behavior is externally caused, representative of their culture, their parents, their biology, anything but them.

If their behavior is viewed as arising from a "bad habit," one they need fight against, it is still as if this bad habit is not a part of them but something conditioned into them through other external influences. If their acts are viewed as coming from a moment's impulse, blind rage, does this mean that this rage is imposed on them from without? Now, even if this were to be true, it would seem that when, as the philosopher Robert Adams suggests, data are rich enough to permit an adequate set of expectations of the consequences or intentions of one's inner state, that is, if there is enough information available to the agent relating to such an internal state, wouldn't this make the agent responsible for that state of mind or, in the very least, the actions that result from it?[66] The deterministic view that everyone's beliefs are externally caused fails to account for what has been called our "information-gathering apparatus . . . our most impressive causal interface with our surroundings."[67]

If we rely on intentionality as our guide for moral culpability we will be in deep water. First, a man can be cruel without this being his primary aim. As Philip Hallie writes, "He does not need to want to hurt his victim—he needs only to want something that requires him to hurt the victim . . ."[68] Indeed, Hallie notes, a process that ends in violence can often begin gently, and this gentleness will help the perpetrator claim his victim.[69] We see this over and over again with child victims of sexual abuse. Second, the perpetrator can dissociate his character from the act in many ways. And many perpetrators have blameless characters in other areas of their lives; consider, for example, the "pillar of the community" who rapes or molests. Perhaps this is why an act necessarily refers back to character, to redefine it. If the perpetrator will not identify himself with the act or the deliberation it took to commit that act, we may need to provide him with a definition of himself.

The Hidden Shame of the Perpetrator?

There is a school of thought that holds that all of the excuses a perpetrator uses are defense mechanisms, ways that he guards against confronting the deep sense of shame buried within. According to one treatment director, "There is probably no more ashamed a group, if you can ever get to it—and if you do not get to it you can forget about treatment."[70] Those believers in the deep shame of perpetrators say that perpetrators feel so badly about themselves that this feeling of incorrigibility keeps them on the self-destructive and other-destructive path of abuse. There may be something to this explanation. After all, the majority of perpetrators believe that what they did was wrong.[71] Still, these same perpetrators are the ones who avoid responsibility in all of the ways already mentioned.

How do we know that perpetrators actually do feel ashamed before they are caught? We have only their word for it. I am reminded of that hoary Zen question, if a tree falls in a forest and nobody hears it, was there a sound? Likewise, if a man is ashamed of his acts, but is not aware of his shame until after he is caught, was he truly ashamed? Perhaps we should ask, in what important and practical ways did his earlier shame (not remorse) mean something? The psychoanalyst might say that this buried shame was indeed the motivation for abusive behavior, as if the man were saying, "Look at me, how bad a person I truly am," just as the child gets what has been called "negative attention" by misbehaving.

Shame that is exposed after the fact, as well as regret and remorse, is a convenient emotion. A recent book on the subject of regret argues that in this simple emotion humanity can be saved.[72] But this seems so paltry an expectation. Regret is easy after the act is done; what gives regret its power? We have examined the grandiose self, the entitled self that perpetrates the acts. After the act, though, we are confronted with the small self, a self that has been made so puny that all the external circumstances loom large. Are we to believe in either of these views of the self?

If a perpetrator truly were ashamed, how might he act? He would hide—behind defenses, from the law, even from psychotherapy and help. The shame might be so unbearable that he needed to hide it from himself, propping himself up with grandiose but ultimately false conceptions of himself and his entitlements. This is consistent with perpetrators' behavior (although this behavior could also be explained more simply as fear of punishment). So, if we grant that perpetrators truly are ashamed, why can't this shame be motivational?

The Evil Perpetrator?

If we do not see the perpetrator as shameful, then is the alternative to this dilemma a simplistic view that perpetrators of violence are just plain evil?—that they have evil motives, evil inner selves, evil souls? In part yes, for if we continue to mystify perpetrators' responsibility, and to mollify their bad senses of self, then it will be impossible to enter into an honest discussion of victim responsibility and the varying degrees of coercion. We may get stuck on judgmental words such as "bad" and "evil," not only because they seem so absolute, but because we think that they convey that a person is irredeemable. We seem to believe that if something is a trait, a part of one's personhood, it is permanent. Instead, we might think of these traits as long-standing. The difference lies in the possibility for change.

The cover of January 1994's *American Psychological Association Monitor* addresses Jeffrey Dahmer, the man who murdered many men and adolescent boys, having sex with them sometimes before and after he tortured, murdered, and dismembered them, and performed bizarre scientific experiments. Judith Becker, the renowned psychologist who has researched and worked with adolescent sex offenders for years, interviewed Dahmer and said of him, "Jeffrey Dahmer is a tragic figure. He in a sense was an incredibly lonely person who believed that nobody would elect to stay with him. . . . He felt so powerless that he found [the violent acts] to be the only way to have power."[73] The title of the article in the *Monitor* was "Sexual Deviancy a Disorder, Not an Evil." Those who work intimately with perpetrators may have to believe in their essential goodness, must need to remind themselves of the once-young victim of circumstances who at one time was this perpetrator. The philosopher John Kekes notes that the more we know someone, the more we understand his motivations, circumstances, constraints, the less likely we are to say that his evil act reflects his character.[74]

The religious question, if God is good, then why does evil exist? has been transformed into a secular one; we ask, if man is good, then why does he do bad? I have argued earlier that despite the perpetrator's past or present circumstances, there remained an element of choice, that excuses such as impulsivity and addiction are not as "choiceless" as they appear, and that there is a cruel or insensitive kind of entitlement that motivates perpetrators.

But what if I exaggerate, what if circumstances are such that these perpetrators actually do not have the choices I presume they have? Whereas they might have once had a choice regarding the development or prevention of their impulsivity or wrong-doing, what if it is now "beyond their control"? The philosopher John Kekes addresses this issue in his book *Facing Evil.*

In this book Kekes draws our attention to the cliché of the "banality of evil," which is harm "caused by casual, unthinking, low-grade human meanness," and describes the "hard reaction to evil" as a point of view that much of the evil that exists is caused by "characteristic but unchosen actions." He argues against "choice morality" and claims that "habitual evildoers" have no choices. They have such deficiencies of character that they cannot meet the conditions of choice: the ability to under-stand the situation at hand, the ability to prevent themselves from being overwhelmed by emotion, and the capacity to exer-cise self-control. Human vices such as insensitivity, dogmatism, and entitlement have become so habitual to perpetrators, so intrinsic to the character of these individuals, that they no longer have choices. Kekes writes of both the "soft" view one can take toward "habitual evildoers" and the "hard" view.

The soft view of perpetrators is eloquently described:

> If the agents really did not choose to be in these deplorable ways, then the feeling is, they are not acting on their own behalf. They are merely carriers of the evil that the world has instilled in them, not originators of it. It is readily agreed that the world would be a better place if people were not made to cause evil by it, but we still should not

make scapegoats of those who are affected in these unfortunate ways. What has happened to agents of unchosen evil is that the essential conditions of life—contingency, indifference, and destructiveness—have come to inform their characters. So, the appropriate objects of censure are those formative conditions, not the agents formed by them.[75]

But the hard view, Kekes's own view, holds that choicelessness doesn't mean that we can't hold habitual evildoers culpable for their evil. The fact that they have caused undeserved harm should be enough to censure them, even when they did not have the self-control to prevent the harm.[76] The problem with the soft view is that it focuses on the helplessness of evil agents rather than on the undeserved harm of the victims. It diverts our attention from the evil done, and, claims Kekes, if we want to succeed in minimizing evil, we need to focus on the harm done and censure those who cause it, regardless of their choice or lack of it.

In the following chapter, I will examine our attention and where it falls in the larger debate about the responsibility of victims and perpetrators. Onlookers have a responsibility too, and in their efforts to minimize the evil in the world they are sometimes misguided. I examine as onlookers the psychotherapists who treat victims and perpetrators, the academics who research and write about them, and the media-consuming public.

ONLOOKERS

4

We live in a period in which victims are idealized. The various audiences for accounts of abuse seek out the innocent victim to such an extent that even perpetrators have come to be seen as victims in their own right. The philosopher Judith Shklar writes of victims: "They are being used untruthfully, as a means to nourish our self-esteem and to control our own fears. They are forced to serve the onlookers. Who indeed knows how best to think about victims? . . . We are often not even sure who the victims are. Are the tormenters who may once have suffered some injustice or deprivation also victims? . . . Are we all victims of our circumstances? Can we all be divided into victim and victimizers at any moment?"[1]

When perpetrators are not seen as victims they are presented as monsters. The perpetrators whom we face and give coverage to on TV and in print are the least banal and most violent. They are the ones who have abused and murdered and tortured and dismembered and sometimes even cannibalized their victims. As counterparts to the innocent victims, these are the perpetrators to whom we turn our deepest attention and our longest gaze in our search for understanding. How could these acts have occurred? How could such evil exist in one man?

The problem with wanting to see victims as absolutely pure

and perpetrators as absolutely evil is that few in either group actually live up (or down) to these expectations. In order for our prescribed story line to work, they would need to transform themselves into our view of them. And if they cannot change themselves to fit into our molds of purity and monstrosity then we tend to blame the victims more, the perpetrators less, and sometimes even reverse blame by holding the victim (who may be more privileged, intelligent, and sane) ultimately responsible and seeing the perpetrator (who may come from a disadvantaged background, be less intelligent, and less sane) as ultimately a victim.

Our expectations of victims force them to paint a public picture of themselves as more innocent and less self-blaming than they actually are. Analyses of images associated with sexual abuse on TV and in newspapers reveal the typical portrayal of a young victim to be a child sitting limp, gazing wistfully out from behind a window, or a broken doll, accompanied by the tinkling of a music box or a prop of strewn hair ribbons. But, warns Jenny Kitzinger, the critic who called attention to these images, it is counterproductive to rely on innocence as an emotive symbol to provoke public revulsion. First, it will stigmatize a child who does not meet the criterion, and second, the innocence itself is a titillation for abusers who respond to our society's use of innocence as a kind of sexual commodity.[2]

Those in the therapeutic community may categorize victims in absolute terms in order to protect them from the suspicious public who will condemn them if they confess to anything but the most extreme position of passivity or innocence. It may be true that if a victim were to reveal her self-doubt and uncertainty about her own contribution to her victimization, the public would leap to define her as responsible for the abuse perpetrated on her. But the public who urges a victim not to blame herself creates a category of victimhood that requires blamelessness, leaving real victims with a private sense of guilt that they dare not talk about and that may prevent them from carrying on the task of living.

The view of the victim as innocent is inextricable from the view of the victim as long-suffering. If the victim accepts and makes use of the claim of total innocence, she is strongly tempted to maintain that she has been scarred for life. Although it has taken considerable effort on the part of feminists and abuse researchers to convince the public that there *are* significant and long-term effects of abuse, and that for some victims the horror of the abuse never ends, those who are not affected so lastingly cannot say so without being accused of denial.

The media promote a certain story line that exploits victims. They begin by showing that the victim is just like you and me, then allow the audience to feel a bit of what the victim felt, and then claim that her life has been changed forever and that she will never be the woman she was before her victimization.[3] The public and the media seem to want to diagnose all victims as suffering from a syndrome, whether they fit into the pattern or not. The resulting problem, then, with research that investigates the effects of abuse on survivors is that these researchers may ask questions about the effects of a survivor's abuse under conditions in which the victim feels compelled to report lifelong consequences.[4]

This creation of a purified, generalized victim figure also has consequences for the way we hold or do not hold perpetrators responsible for their acts. On the one hand, the media focus primarily on those perpetrators who have committed extreme acts of violence and ignore the everyday, more common cases of abuse, in which perpetrators seem more ordinary. On the other hand, the recent "discovery" of victimization in the lives of perpetrators confuses the public, and a portion of that sanctified-victim persona can be borrowed to help diffuse some of the perpetrator's responsibility for his behavior.[5] This diffusion is evident in the speech a judge made when sentencing a man who had sexually abused his two stepchildren: "On your behalf, there are many things that you are not. You are not a violent rapist who drags women and girls off the street and into the bushes or into your car from a parking lot; you are not a child chaser, one whose obsession with sex causes him to seek neighborhood children or children in parks or in playgrounds . . . you are a man who has warm personal feelings for your stepchildren, but you let them get out of hand."[6] By summoning up these other, more horrifying images, the judge excuses this stepfather to some extent, forgetting that what may have prevented this man from seeking out neighborhood children was that it was so easy to take advantage of the accessibility and warm feelings of his stepchildren.

Another consequence of our overemphasis on the horrors of victimization is that the more we see abuse as inevitably causing a devastating outcome, the more we can excuse perpetrators who have been abused for their present and future abusive behavior.

WHOM DO WE BLAME AND WHY?

The main problem with the onlookers of abuse and victimization is not that they don't blame anymore, because sometimes they do and do so vociferously. Indeed, in any general account of rape, child sexual abuse, or domestic violence there is horror and outrage at the perpetrator. When attention turns to the specifics of an individual case, however, this outrage often gets diluted, strong moral sensibility gets dissipated, and all that is left is timid questioning in the face of cruelty.

For decades now, an entire field of social psychology has been dedicated to understanding how and why people make certain attributions, precisely why and under what circumstances they blame one person rather than another. More often than not researchers focus on the biases and foolishness of people in making the attributions they make. For example, one of the most significant findings is what has been called "actor-observer divergence," which refers to the tendency of people to attribute their own behavior to situational circumstances but the behavior of another to a deep-seated personality characteristic.[7] For any given person committing a cruel act, the tendency will be for him to refer to the situational circumstances that influenced him (as we have seen with perpetrators). For any given person explaining the act of another (for example, my writing a chapter about perpetrators), the tendency will be to attribute the person's behavior to a personality characteristic. Victim self-blaming does not, however, fit into this theory very neatly. As noted in Chapter 2, victims tend to explain what happened to them in terms of both situational circumstances and character, and they tend to assess the perpetrator's behavior according to both character and situation as well. Early research on attributions also suggests that people tend to attribute less blame to, and use circumstantial explanations more often for, people whom they see as similar to themselves.[8] In this way, the sex, race, and socioeconomic status of any victim or perpetrator will influence us in our attempts to apportion blame. Not surprisingly, people are prejudiced in favor of themselves.

A considerable amount of this kind of research has been conducted on attributions about rape. The research usually involves giving college students different vignettes to read or sometimes having them watch videotapes with different rape scenarios varied systematically. For example, a portion of the people participating in the study are given a vignette to read about a rape victim from a low-income neighborhood who is flirting in a bar and is then raped by an upper-middle-class advertising executive; another group is given a vignette about the same rape victim raped by a member of her own social class. All other aspects of the vignette remain the same so that if the students who read the first scenario end up rating the victim as more responsible, it is probably because these students are biased favorably toward the middle-class advertising executive.

These kinds of studies have shown that in making attributions about a rape, people blame the victim more if there was less force involved, if she protested rather late in the act, and if she had been raped before. People generally believe that if a woman could have anticipated the rape, she should be held more responsible than a victim who could not have anticipated it. A victim is also blamed more if she is attractive, or if her assailant was well-dressed, or if she did not resist his attack. If the rape was completed, the victim is held more responsible for it. If the victim dated cross-racially or was provocative or was divorced rather than married she is blamed more. All of these findings, of course, are relative to other hypothetical victims who were not attractive, provocative, and so on. This kind of research finds overwhelmingly that if the person assessing blame is male, and particularly if he has more traditional and stereotypical ideas about women and women's roles, he is more likely to blame the victim.[9]

The research regarding date rape reveals similar findings. If a victim has had sex previously with the person who rapes her, or even if she has engaged in foreplay prior to the rape, she will be blamed more. If she knew the rapist, initiated the date, allowed the man to pay for the date, or went to his apartment, she will be blamed more for her rape than a woman who did not.[10]

An assessment of responsibility for incest and sexual abuse is trickier and, as expected, depends very much on the age of the victim.[11] But interestingly enough, the public seems ready to blame the victim more if she was passive rather than defensive, or if the perpetrator committing the act was threatening or coercive.[12] In the rape and date-rape attribution research, men also seem to blame sexual abuse victims more than women do.[13]

Finally, with regard to marital abuse, research shows that more than three-quarters of men justify their actions by blaming the victim or by discounting their behavior because it was "uncontrollable," but there is less research on how the public views their acts.[14] Men with more traditional attitudes toward women blamed and derogated wives more when reading vignettes about wife abuse; women who held beliefs that the world is a just place blamed but did not tend to derogate abused wives.[15] In different research, wives were seen as more responsible for solving the problem of "wife abuse" than men were, whereas husbands were seen as more responsible for the origin of the problem.[16] Short-term members of Alcoholics Anonymous were more likely to hold a wife-beater responsible for his actions when he was drunk than were long-term members, who tended to emphasize the role of external factors.[17]

It is interesting to note that in one research study concerned with attributions that blame the person rather than the situation, participants who were told to try to empathize with the victim attributed more responsibility to the personality of the perpetrator than to the situation, whereas those asked to sympathize with the perpetrator blamed the situation more.[18] The more intimate the relationship between the victim and the perpetrator (married as opposed to acquainted or living together), the more the character of the woman was blamed. And knowledge of a husband's loss of a job seemed to make participants in one study blame the situation rather than the man's character. In this same study, only the most flagrant case of violence, in which a male struck an acquaintance, led to character attributions.[19]

In reviewing the voluminous literature on attributions of responsibility following a rape, sexual abuse, or battering, one is left with many questions: Why is it that certain characteristics of the woman or the woman's behavior make a man less responsible? Why does most research focus on the characteristics of victims rather than the characteristics of perpetrators? And why isn't there general acknowledgment that rape, for example, is always wrong, the perpetrator, always ultimately and weightily responsible for harm done? The only answer can be that a man's self-control and actions resulting from a lack thereof are viewed as dependent in some way on what a woman does, that she is, in a sense, responsible for his actions, or that his actions are contingent on her behavior. The underlying principle also seems to be one of zero sum; that is, if some responsibility is given to one side, the responsibility of the other side is reduced.

One research study seems to point to another attributional error. Investigators found that when you compare people's reactions to male victims with their reactions to female victims, more blame is generally attributed to the character of the female victim, and more blame attributed to the behavior of the man.[20] This tendency supports and predicts women's self-blaming and men's other-blaming and can be extended to perpetrators who tend to see their behavior as something apart from themselves, something a-characterological. They release themselves from some of the blame and the responsibility for their characters that seems necessary for change. If the idea of blame rests on an assumption that the self is a unitary, unfragmented entity, then the separation of behavior from character can only lead to a diffusion of responsibility.[21]

In sum, several blaming biases stand out that help explain the "overresponsibility" of victims and the "underresponsibility" of male perpetrators. First, given the victim-focused orientation of this research (supported by the public and the victims themselves), the discussion of perpetrator responsibility remains unspoken and relatively unassessed. And if victims are apportioned more blame, or any bit of blame, there is an automatic assumption that the perpetrator is apportioned less. This is what I mean by a zero-sum equation. The implication is that if the victim takes or can be apportioned some responsibility, the perpetrator is off the hook. But it doesn't have to be that way.

A second bias that emerges involves the problem of sex-role stereotypes. It is overwhelmingly clear that women who veer away from traditional roles are considered more blameworthy. This fits into the formulation that behavior that is "unusual" tends to get attributed to character rather than situation. But this does not explain why it should reflect poorly on behavior. If a woman can be seen as deviant, even in the purest notion of that word, the deviant experiences of abuse, rape, and beating will seem in accordance with her natural deserts. Women may be seen not only as deviant but also as deserving of punishment for not conforming to the requirements of innocence that are a part of victimization.

The third bias concerns character. Why would we focus so much more directly on the character of the female victim and not the character of the perpetrator? Why must we support the perpetrator's view that his behavior is separate from his self? This attributional tendency may show why backlash movements can gain in acceptance, competing with our now declining interest in victims' rights.

THE BACKLASH MOVEMENTS

There are some individuals who question the existence of the social problems we call child sexual abuse, rape, date rape, and domestic abuse. These groups and individuals attempt to persuade the public that reports of extensive victimization are exaggerated or made up. The attacks and unsubtle arguments against the existence of these social evils often come from people who have been wronged by the system or by false abuse allegations. They are reacting to what they see as an overemphasis on victimization, but they in turn distort the facts to present an oversimplified backlash view. Like the audience who strives to find the innocent victim and the monstrous perpetrator, these individuals dichotomize the issue in another unhelpful way by saying that there is no abuse, that the extent of the abuse is greatly exaggerated, or that the real evil is the system.

Sexual Abuse

The backlash regarding sexual abuse takes several forms. Some groups or individuals vehemently argue that the fervor created over sexual abuse is out of proportion to actual cases and that many innocent men are being sent to jail because of these "witch hunts." There is also an academic component to the backlash movement in which qualified researchers ask the empirical questions of whether children can have memories induced, what the effects are of repeated questioning, whether children ever lie, and whether memories can be implanted. Some of these academics have even joined forces with backlash grassroots movements such as the False Memory Syndrome Foundation, an organization combining popular rhetoric and academic research.

Richard Gardner, a clinician long recognized for his controversial views, has written a book provocatively entitled *Sex Abuse Hysteria: Salem Witch Trials Revisited*, which I would like to examine as an example of the kind of accusations "backlash" authors make regarding the sexual abuse of children. Gardner has spent about twenty-five years in the field of child custody litigation and therefore may be qualified to speak about the seamier side of human nature. He has also spent a considerable portion of his practice testifying and analyzing reports of sexual abuse allegations in the context of custody disputes. In his opening chapter he argues that the likelihood of an allegation of sexual abuse being false or true depends primarily on the situation in which it arises. For example, he claims that incest allegations generally have a high likelihood of being true, whereas allegations made in the context of a bitter custody dispute do not. He adds at the end of his first chapter that he appreciates that "genuine sex abuse of children is widespread" and that "perhaps 95 percent or more" of child sexual abuse allegations are probably justified. But Gardner's book is about the other 5 percent, and therein lies the problem.

Because he believes that only about 5 percent of these allegations are false, one must seriously regret Gardner's choice of the title *Sex Abuse Hysteria,* and wonder too about the subtitle *Salem Witch Trials Revisited.*[22] Our present-day outrage and horror at the injustice and torture perpetrated at the witch trials in Salem come from a well-grounded belief that *there are no witches!* It is simply not the case that back in the 1600s in Salem, Massachusetts, a few innocents among the many guilty were burnt unjustly. One hundred percent of the women burned or drowned or stoned were innocent, and, as Anne Llewellyn Barstow suggests, they were possibly persecuted because they were women who broke the mold of male-defined femininity.[23] (One is reminded of the attribution biases reviewed earlier that punished women through blame if they did not fit into stereotypical roles for females.)

To compare the current-day preoccupation with sexual abuse to the Salem witch trials is akin to comparing anti-Semitism in America today to the Holocaust. Gardner's initial figure of 5 percent for false accusations, followed through time to see which actually result in a trial, makes the word "hysteria" seem even more overblown.[24] Research indicates that sexual abuse is a grossly underreported crime. Figures show that at best maybe half of sexual abuse incidents get reported. This is consistent with common knowledge that it is difficult for children to disclose sexual abuse because of threats from the perpetrator, their desire to sometimes protect the perpetrator, feelings of shame and guilt, and fears that they will be punished. Of those cases reported only about 10 percent go to trial.[25] If 10 percent of Gardner's purported 5 percent of false allegations were to go to trial, then we would end up with one-half of 1 percent of all *reported* sexual abuse cases going to trial. And if all of these men were unjustly found guilty we would have a problem of one-half of 1 percent of all *reported* sexual abuse cases being wrongly judged—one-half of 1 percent of men accused of sexual abuse wrongly suffering. One wonders whether the law could boast so low a wrongful conviction rate for other crimes.

Gardner's statement that there is a high likelihood of false allegations in divorce-custody disputes is exaggerated. There may be a high rate compared with false allegations *not* in custody disputes, but research shows that the likelihood is still relatively small. There is no difference in physical evidence of sexual abuse in cases that involve custody disputes and those that do not.[26] Studies that used large samples of children involved in divorce-custody battles showed the rate of false allegations to be around 14 percent,[27] and an even larger study involving nine thousand custody disputes found that only 2 percent included sexual abuse accusations, with only about half of these accusations unlikely to be substantiated.[28]

These figures address the question of "hysteria" and the comparison with the witch trials somewhat, but we still need to address that one-half of 1 percent of false allegations for sexual abuse in general and that 1 percent of false allegations in divorce-custody disputes. To some, the low incidence of false allegations seems like a small price to pay; to the wrongly accused it is an enormous price to pay. More important, to men who believe that there is a remote possibility that they might someday be wrongly accused, 1 percent or one-half of 1 percent looms large.

Why, though, is there such a fuss created about the possibility of wrongly accusing a few men? Those who bring up the issue of wrongful accusations attempt to equalize the issue. They put it like this: on the one hand we want to protect young children, and on the other hand we want to protect innocent men. But this artificially balanced scale does not weigh true. The equalizing tendency in our rhetoric about sexual abuse just isn't right. In terms of the power accorded to each side weighing in, we can see why the issue of innocent men gets set up as equally weighted against the prevention of sexual abuse; to preserve one innocent man from being punished we would probably sacrifice two hundred children.

Gardner, along with the members of VOCAL (Victims of Child Abuse Laws) and the False Memory Syndrome Foundation, would like to focus more on the harm done by the legal system, therapists, and investigators than that inflicted by the perpetrator. Members of the False Memory Syndrome Foundation believe that sexual abuse memories are suggested by therapists to vulnerable clients searching for something in their past to explain their current unhappiness. Their concerns are so well publicized that people seem to believe such a "syndrome" exists, although no such syndrome or diagnosis has been proposed formally in writing by the American Psychological or Psychiatric Associations.

There is also widespread belief that even when allegations are accurate they should not be acted upon because the judicial, therapeutic, and criminal systems cause more harm to the victim than the perpetrator. In an article in the *Philadelphia Inquirer* entitled "Twisted Love," Frank Bruni writes: "Child molesters leave scars on their victims. Sometimes society, in its frantic response, can leave gaping wounds [on victims]."[29] To be fair, there are cases in which the system has brutalized a youngster so that she wishes she had never disclosed her abuse. But is there research that suggests that these investigations are traumatic?[30] It isn't the effect of repeated questioning that the youngster complains most about; it is the process by which the accuser rather than the accused has to leave the family and live somewhere else in order to be protected, and the process through which, after all the effort a child goes through, the perpetrator is not punished. A recent large-scale report on children who go to court for sexual abuse found that there was little harm done by the repeated questioning or any other aspect of the legal process *if* the child had a supportive mother, a mother who believed her and stood by her.[31]

There are admittedly some cases in which a therapist has suggested that sexual abuse occurred when it had not. And it is not difficult to encounter people nowadays who wonder aloud whether they have ever been sexually abused in view of their current symptoms. (The sexual abuse victim is a tempting category for several reasons.) When people are troubled, believing that the cause of their suffering is external can release them from all sorts of mental anguish and guilt. To be able to relate one's troubles to an event in one's past, to cast blame specifically, can be a relief, particularly from the incessant and difficult looking-inward that most psychotherapy requires. Also, the effects of abuse are so wide-ranging and nonspecific that many current maladies can fit into a syndrome developed from a history of abuse: depression, anxiety, suicidality, phobias, low self-esteem, and so on.

False Memory Syndrome advocates have argued that there is no such thing as repression and that all recovered memories are false. And yet there are documentable cases of recovered memory. For example, Michael Yapko, in his book *Suggestions of*

Abuse (which was, incidentally, advertised as a book supporting those who think there is hysteria about abuse), discusses a case reported in the *New York Times* in July of 1992. A man who had been sexually abused by a priest repressed the memory until adulthood. When he recovered the memory, he asked the priest about it and the priest admitted to committing the abuse. Through the publicity and this victim's active searching out of other victims, fifty people came forward to say that they also had been abused by this priest. Three of the fifty-one victims claimed to have repressed the abuse, the others had always remembered the abuse but had not discussed it with anyone.

What can we deduce from this story? One side can point to the evidence of repression; the other can point to the fact that most of the abused remembered (although presumably there may still exist some repressors with unrecovered memories out there). A more recent study, conducted by Linda Meyer Williams, shows that 38 percent of the women interviewed did not recall their sexual abuse. In this study interviewers carefully questioned one hundred women approximately seventeen years after they had come to an emergency room to be treated for sexual abuse. Of the women who *did* recall their abuse, 16 percent said that there had been a time when they had forgotten it.[32]

The False Memory Syndrome Foundation attacks not only the notion of repression but also therapists who they believe are implanting memories in the minds of their patients. The problem with their argument is lack of real evidence that this implanting of memory by therapists or suggestion of past abuse occurs often (despite the lengthy reference list from which they draw unsubstantiated conclusions). They have found people whose therapists have vigorously and stupidly promoted the notion that they had been sexually abused, but the foundation has not been able to prove that this is widespread. And there are decent clinicians who, despite the lack of evidence, are "at risk of being ambushed by established opposition" if they help a client uncover a lost memory.[33]

The recovered memory debate is actually a side issue, not a central one, in the protection of children. Admittedly, the idea of recovered memories is controversial, but it is probable that very few cases presented to a prosecutor are based on recovered memories. Indeed, most child sexual abuse reports, and especially those made when the victim is still a child, do not document events that the victim had once forgotten and then remembered.

The idea of false allegations by children is a more interesting topic. Groups like VOCAL have argued that the high rates of unsubstantiated reports indicate that false allegations are abundant.[34] But false allegations are different from unsubstantiated cases. As any social service worker will agree, it is extremely difficult to substantiate a case of child sexual abuse, and, more often than not, cases are dropped because the child will not repeat her or his claims or because there is no physical evidence.

The research on false allegations is mixed. Researchers have used different laboratory scenarios as well as naturally occurring situations such as doctors' visits to test whether a child might make a false allegation, and what would lead her to do so. For example, a month after a doctor's visit a child might be asked whether the doctor examined her throat (true) or even kissed her (false). The results have not been overwhelmingly against the child. They have indicated the possibility that a child or a small percentage of children, given the right circumstances, might lie or even be made to believe that something that didn't happen did. These results have caused a stir, but only because they contradict the overstated original position that children never lie, a position consonant with the overpurification of victimhood.

Research on the suggestibility of children or false allegations made by children, even in the context of a divorce-custody dispute, shows that the public need not be so skeptical. Most false reports are made by adults, and many of the allegations that arise in the context of a divorce-custody battle are actually true.[35] Of greater concern is the possibility that adults can implant false memories in children merely through repeated or suggestive questioning. Elizabeth Loftus claims that it is very easy to suggest information to people in a way that changes their memory of an event. She states, "We have gotten people to tell us that they saw broken glass (when there was none), if we ask a question about cars smashing into each other (rather than 'hitting' each other). We've gotten people to tell us red lights were green lights, if we ask a leading question that suggested that the light was green. We've gotten people to tell us that an individual has curly hair when in fact he had straight hair."[36] Although adults have succumbed to these particular suggestions about details of the events they witnessed, it is important to remember that they probably would not have succumbed so easily to the suggestion that (1) they did not witness a car accident at all; (2) there was no traffic light; and (3) the individual was bald or even that there was no individual, all of which are suggestions that more closely parallel the disclosure or recanting of sexual abuse. Another problem with such research is that it often applies more readily to witnesses of, rather than participants in, an event.

Loftus admits that children are most susceptible to suggestion between the ages of three and five. (Only a percentage of the sexual abuse cases of children aged two to sixteen that are brought to social services offices and police stations in this nation involve children who are of this age group, of course.) Gail Goodman and her associates found children generally very resistant to suggestions that they had been abused.[37] Experts on children's memory seem to think that the primary problem with children is not how much they remember, their suggestibility, or errors of commission (stating that things happened when they did not), but rather errors of omission, the underreporting of what they remember.[38] In my research with Bhavna Shyamalan, I have found that pre-schoolers are much more likely to deny a true event after repeated questioning than to report a false event. Stress and intimidation can decrease a child's willingness to report as well as her ability to retrieve information,[39] though stress, when severe, can enhance memory.[40] For example, children who experienced pain during a doctor's visit more accurately described people present in the room at the time.[41]

The discussion of children's memories divides academics as well as those in the judicial system into two highly researched and somewhat cautious camps. Absent, however, from this discussion of children's lying or substituting memories is a discussion of the perpetrator's lying or fooling himself or encoding into his own memory a different version of the events that occurred. One wonders if the lies of the perpetrator are taken for granted—if they are considered not so interesting because they are assumed to be common.

Perpetrators lie all the time about their abuse, but perhaps it is unfair to compare perpetrators to children. Perhaps the comparison should be made between children (potential victims) and men (potential perpetrators). No one has yet done research to discover whether, by setting up a study in a certain way, one that encouraged a man to lose control, or act out in an angry or quasi-sexual way, men can be made to lie and to say that something that did happen did not. This is because the fear is much greater that an innocent man will be accused by a child than that a guilty man will go free to abuse again.

Date-Rape Hype?

Few questioned crime statistics on rape until Katie Roiphe's book *The Morning After,* in which she takes on date rape, specifically date rape on college campuses, but also more generally questions the validity of women's fears of being raped. After reading plenty of impassioned reviews, letters to the editor, and magazine analyses of Roiphe's book, I took a look. It is an essay that cites the wisdom of the author's grandmother and mother as often as it does academic journal articles. It is admittedly a book that states a strong opinion, and so one seems justified in examining the source of the opinion, Roiphe herself.

Roiphe begins by telling us that before entering Harvard she was educated in all-girls schools, protected by her feminist mother from sexist TV shows, and "sequestered from the normal libidinous jostle of coeducation." (Only someone sequestered as she had been could call the modern-day high school experience a "libidinous jostle," particularly in view of the current recognition of unwanted sexual advances that female students typically ward off from their unrestrained and unpunished male peers.) Her description of who she is and where she comes from sketches Roiphe's innocent upbringing. Although she may have learned a great deal from her feminist mother about the early feminist movement, Ms. Roiphe was protected from the kinds of insults and assaults that those older women had experienced and were fighting against. This innocence is celebrated as she comments about the Take Back the Night marches at Harvard: "I wondered whom they wanted the night back from and what they wanted it back for." [42]

The narrative she constructs is on one level the story of a girl who has been protected from sexism, a girl brought up in such a way as to be "more afraid of wild geese than rapists." [43] On another level it is a typical female adolescence narrative in which a girl defines herself over and against her mother. By painting her mother and what her mother stands for in an extreme light, the girl can emerge a woman different from and independent of what society has condemned as the suffocating arms of motherhood. Her "brave" (see Wendy Kaminer's review) step away from other feminists is an adolescent girl's step away from her mother, who, she reminds us over and over again, was a founding feminist in the 1970s.[44] My own response to her youthful exhortations is to worry about her, as a mother would worry about a daughter staying out late at night. Roiphe's analysis, at every point, seems to try to reassure me, "Don't worry Mom, we'll be all right with this sex thing. It's not as dangerous as you think it is." But youth is reckless.

If we set aside the underlying personal story that can be read between the lines, Roiphe's argument is right in one sense. There is little territory that is open to dispute among feminists talking about violence against women. Even in my own work on this book I have encountered both rejection from mainstream abuse researchers and cooptation from people who believe there is mass hysteria over abuse.

Roiphe claims that feminism makes women out to be fragile victims, suppressing any notion of agency and sexual desire—notions, she informs us, that she is quite familiar with herself. To set herself in a superior position to her college peers, she describes them as delicate intellectuals who have no intellectual agency; they cannot think for themselves and are being pushed around by first-wave feminists, older women who are attempting to hold younger women back from their freedom and separation.

Roiphe insults her peers further when she describes their shaky voices at a Take Back the Night march. These voices of female students recounting their date rapes all seem to sound the same to Roiphe; they sound "rehearsed." Some probably are rehearsed, and some probably borrow narrative structure from other sexual abuse stories. But we need not discount what they say simply because they follow a story structure or what can be called "rape genre" just as heroes of old retold their stories along certain narrative genre lines (for example, utilizing "voyage stories" or "battle stories"). It may be helpful to look at why these women's tales come out in story form, why they sound rehearsed.

First, a story line provides someone with a supporting framework to speak about something she has trouble speaking about. Second, victims are so terrified of others blaming them, and so automatically self-blaming, that when they hear a version of a story that "works," that helps them to lessen some of their self-blame and make them the "hero of their own lives," as Linda Gordon once put it, they might latch onto it.[45] Yes, many stories are probably distorted to underestimate the amount of victim "participation," but you can be certain that internally the victims overestimate their participation and fault. Most rape victims take more than their share of the blame, but Roiphe doesn't seem to know this.

What she is hearing from students on campus is a celebration of one side of their ambivalence, the side that says, "It was all his fault." Like Katie Roiphe as she wrote *The Morning After,* these students take one side of an issue and define themselves over and against the other side.

But the complexities of date rape and victims' responses to it are beyond the black and white thinking of adolescence. For example, Roiphe is irritated by the constant and formulaic refrain of victims that they have been silenced. But women *have* been silenced, even if they have been complicit in their own silencing. The fact that women may collude in their own silencing and powerlessness does not take away the fact that their silence is supported and encouraged by other external forces, and that certain people have something to gain from women's silence about abuse. Roiphe cites Neil Gilbert on the fact that 42 percent of women who had been date-raped later had sex with the man who had raped them.[46] But if a wife were to be beaten by her husband, and stayed with him after that beating, would that mean that he really didn't beat her?

Roiphe thinks that victims are trying to throw off responsibility, but that is because, as she admits, women don't talk to her very personally about their rapes or sexual abuse. She has gathered her information from public speeches, which represent one side of the victims' reactions. I have spoken to students who participate energetically in such marches, spoken about the shame and guilt they feel for having gotten drunk prior to being raped, for possibly misleading moves they may have made, for not protesting strongly enough. One tearful former student of mine described a scene in which her boyfriend raped her, forcefully holding her down. This was in the context of an ongoing relationship. She had many talks with him afterwards trying to convince him that what he had done was rape, and they finally broke up, not because of the rape, but because he could not acknowledge that his actions constituted rape. Like wife-beating or wife-raping this assault occurred within a complex relationship, but that doesn't mean that the act wasn't cruel, violent, unwanted, and harmful.

Roiphe's book was as celebrated as it was because it simplistically took one side of the issue. For media producers and editors it had a "hook." One imagines that the kind of guest that TV talk-show producers avoid are the ones who preface their statements with "This is a very complicated subject." It may be true that college-age feminists yearn to uncomplicate a difficult issue in order to help them define themselves and what they believe in, but when the press and media do the same, there is a real disservice to society. If we are victims, we are usually not all victim, and when we are perpetrators (as in the recent

Menendez trial), we are usually not all perpetrator. But we can still call violence, violence, rape, rape, and cruelty, cruelty. Or can we?

Wives Who Beat Their Husbands

The backlash regarding wife abuse is rooted in one study that is forever branded into the minds of social psychologists. It is the study conducted by Straus, Gelles, and Steinmetz of more than two thousand U.S. households that shows that women are violent within the household just about as often as men.[47] The study's findings were replicated by the authors six years later.[48] Daniel Saunders, commenting on this research, reminds us that the authors originally qualified their reports by adding that husbands had higher rates of dangerous behavior, were likely to do more damage, and that many women were defending themselves.[49] Still, despite these qualifications, there was controversy over whether there existed a "battered husband's" or "battered data" syndrome.[50]

Mutually violent male-female relationships are rare, or, at least, much rarer than articles about women's violence toward men and the continuing controversy over it suggest.[51] Writing about the conceptualization of "mutual combat," the researcher Richard Berk and his associates have shown that when injury is of primary concern, the terminology is misleading. Their study of more than two hundred couples showed that so-called mutual disputes overwhelmingly involved female injury and rarely involved male injury. These authors write that it is "downright pernicious to equate (men's) experiences with those of the enormous number of women who are routinely and severely victimized."[52]

We must also consider once again the context in which this research is pursued. Empirical researchers often need to be reminded that the questions they ask, the way they ask them, and the questions they leave out influence the answers they get. Feminist researchers have at times argued against quantitative methodology, fearing that such methods, in the hands of the typical supporters of empirical social science, would lead to findings that support the status quo.[53] For example, Saunders points out that, in interviewing women, the concepts of self-defense and fighting back are merged, and while women might label their legally defined self-defense aggression as fighting back, this aggression is still a response to fights initiated by men.[54] It is interesting to note that the use of the term "fighting back" indicates a kind of active view of the self, an unvictim-like stance, as if, once again, the victim takes more responsibility for the act than her perpetrator does. This unvictim-like stance is both an accomplishment and a burden, and it may reflect women's overresponsibility for male violence and encourage male lack of responsibility. Susan Schechter has noted that in her interviews with battered women, many of the victims refused to call themselves "battered women" because they saw themselves as actively preventing their abuse (even though sometimes they were unsuccessful at it).[55]

Backlash Realities
The backlash movement aims to counteract the extremeness, or what has been referred to as a "moral panic," inherent in the victims' rights movement, but backlash supporters do so by going to the other extreme. Still, these backlash writers bring to light some realities that should not be dismissed.

Such writers are sensitive to the overpurification of victims. They clearly see the current discourse on women's and children's victimization as undermining the expression of female assertiveness. And they clearly are right that the prominence of the issue has directed efforts away from other important concerns that compete for funding and services from the government. For example, child welfare agencies may be so busy following up alleged reports of abuse that the more prevalent problem of child neglect, which can often be helped by intervention and education, is ignored.[56] My own research with Lisa Hessenauer Sheehan suggests that children who experience neglect suffer just as much from PTSD and depression as children who have been physically or sexually abused.

With regard to sexual abuse in particular, these writers may be right to tie the movement to right-wing elements that fear childhood sexuality. Historians have shown us that childhood sexual abuse is not a new phenomenon, and that there have been various crusades against it in the past, some led by feminists and child "savers," and some co-opted by the criminal justice system. That child sexual abuse has existed for hundreds of years is wholly substantiated through legal and historical accounts.[57]

Of significant interest to our modern crusade is the period in the early twentieth century when male violence toward women was a major issue, taken up by churchmen and sex reformers as well as by feminists. In the 1940s and 1950s, however, this issue was taken over by new "professionals" and, of all people, J. Edgar Hoover, who redefined the problem of male sexual privilege as one of male psychopathology.[58] During the 1940s and 1950s the category of "sex fiend" was developed, "locating most sexual abuse outside the respectable family, criminalizing its young victims, and pathologizing child abuse crusaders by labelling them as sexually abnormal."[59] A sex offender was seen as a hyper- or hypo-masculine predator, with an "utter lack of power to control his impulses"; a mentally ill individual who should be institutionalized rather than jailed.[60] In this way, what began as female and moral (or religious) monitoring of male behavior was taken over by male institutions. There was little female interest in this concern and no feminist leadership on this issue at the time. The central concern was men and the defining and categorizing of a specific sub-group of men as deviant.[61]

The feminism that spawned the battered wives' movement was also subsumed under more male-oriented institutions. To gain funding and more federal support for shelters and research, wife abuse was redefined as a "family" issue rather than a woman's issue, and feminists gladly portrayed the problem as widespread, cutting across class and race lines, to ensure more funding and a more institutionalized treatment of a problem that had before depended on grassroots support. But when the Reagan era began, this redefinition backfired and was seen by the New Right as an attack on the family; they even interpreted antiviolence campaigns as attempts to prohibit parents from spanking their children.[62]

But let us return to the issue of the "correctness" of backlash authors. It is wrong to think that they are the underdogs in this fight. Their work aids and abets perpetrators in the excuses they make for their behavior. And authors such as Gardner and Roiphe have only become so popular because they reflect deep fears of the public, fears grounded in the protection of men and male dominance. When we look beyond what seems to be an incessant march of information about victimization, we can see forces still at work to protect perpetrators and hold victims accountable for more than their share of the blame.

ABSENTING PERPETRATORS AND DIFFUSING BLAME

As victimization becomes the focus, and perpetration the background, it is difficult to find perpetrators in the recounting of an event and in the daily narratives of evil. We recount the perpetration of evil, but we write and speak in such a way as to describe acts without agents, harm without guilt. The evil described is made linguistically palatable, and this whitewashes victims' pain, humiliation, and horror.

Linguistic Avoidance

If language categorizes and clarifies the world, then the way we use language is inherently a moral consideration. Through language, for example, we assign agency to acts and imply causality. Social norms then get expressed through these linguistic devices of agency and causality, holding certain groups or individuals responsible for certain acts. These norms and morals of our society, expressed linguistically, can become self-perpetuating and self-validating, regardless of the reality to which they refer.

For more than two decades feminist thinkers have shown us the numerous ways that our everyday language is devoid of the female voice[63] and contains subtle underlying messages that support the status quo of male domination.[64] Julia Penelope argues, "White men benefit directly when we believe their words are harmless," and explains that "language obstructs our ability to conceive of ourselves as agents in the world or as capable of rebelling against male tyranny."[65]

The ubiquitous use of the passive voice in media and academic reports of male violence against women contributes to the description of violence with no perpetrators. It is not uncommon to see a statistical report of violence against women that reads something like this: "This year, over one million women were beaten or otherwise abused in their homes." Excluded is the end phrase "by men," which, if included, would draw extra attention to the perpetrators but, when excluded, influences readers to focus primarily on the victim. When agency is suppressed in this way the reader becomes more distant from the acts the author describes, but also begins to assume an understanding that no one is actually responsible for them.[66] Some research even suggests that use of the passive voice leads readers to attribute blame and responsibility differently than they would had they read an account of violence written in the active voice. By absenting the perpetrator, Nancy Henley and her associates found, readers are more likely to blame victims.[67]

Sonia Johnson speaks passionately about the problem of the passive voice. When she was running for president on a radical feminist platform, she used the phrase "Today over 2,000 women in this country will be raped" in a campaign speech. She later argued, "By using the passive voice, I made rape sound as innocuous as 'today it will rain,' as if rape just falls out of the sky on women, just 'happens' to us. As though there were no rapists."[68] Researchers have even shown that in newspaper writing the word "raped" is found in a passive-voice construction more often than many other verbs.[69]

There are several reasons why the passive voice appeals to authors in academia and the media even though most writing manuals warn against its use. The passive voice, minus the agent, protects the author from libel, as it protects the guilty party. There is also a pseudo-objective sound to that kind of writing, what has been referred to as "intellectual pretense."[70] When authors use the truncated passive voice they "try to imply grander forces at work . . . appealing to an unspecified, perhaps illusory, universality or evading the issue of who will be or is responsible for some action."[71]

Two other linguistic devices authors use are nominalization and gender obfuscation. Words such as "the battery" and "the violence," when overused, once again prevent the agent of the act from being named. Gender is obfuscated in words such as "victim," "assailant" and "perpetrator" (without assigning proper pronouns such as "he" or "she" to each), so that men beating women becomes a broad social problem rather than a problem of *male* violence in particular.

Another, more insidious way that perpetrators are made absent from media and academic reports is through terminology that focuses on the couple, both victim and perpetrator together, and writes them in as joint agents of actions. Language including the terms "domestic violence" and "family violence," which originally was developed to include battered women's problems in public funding discussions, when used in newspaper reports leads readers to hold perpetrators less individually responsible and to assess blame more evenhandedly, even when it is made clear that the only violent acts that occurred were male to female violence.[72] Even the phrase "battered women" is problematic because, in emphasizing the physical damage, the term "battered" masks the deliberate intimidation and controlling behaviors that lead up to and follow the physical abuse.[73]

Obscuring language can be found in the literature and presentation of child sexual abuse also. Unlike the 1940s and 1950s, when the "sex fiend" was the focus of sexual abuse prevention efforts, today the formulation of child sexual abuse as a problem is consistently one in which the perpetrator simply does not feature. When it is time to turn to the "normal" male, the fathers we know and care about, and the "average" husband, the press and academia are less interested. Authors write about "parents" and present them ungendered, as couples and not as individual men and women. This presentation was perhaps consciously acquired in order to make child sexual abuse a more fundable project under the domain of "family issues," but the backlash has turned the issue into one of family against state rather than of abused against abuser.[74]

While the absenting of perpetrators from reports (and I like to use this made-up verb "absenting" because it implies a choice made by the writer, whereas "absence" makes it sound as if it simply occurs) contributes to victim focus and thus victim-blaming, the diffusion of blame between victim and perpetrator is more subtle and thus more damaging. Such diffusion of blame is supported not only in writing styles and changes in terminology, but also within a broad area of thinking and therapeutic practice called the Systems Approach, which deserves examination given its wide influence.

The Systemic View of Things
The tendency to equalize victim and perpetrator, to see each member of the duo as a victim or to see the duo in a circle of causality, can be traced to the spread of systems thinking. To understand the presuppositions of systems theory as it is applied to human behavior, one must see it as a response to the geneticism of the 1920s and to the deterministic slant of psychoanalytic thought with its historical nature and its emphasis on the individual as a passive recipient of instincts, complexes, and neuroses.

Early applications of systems theory to psychology in Gregory Bateson's work on the "double bind" theory suggested that an identified patient (the most disturbed member of a family) was not "sick" but carrying around a burden for the entire family system. The illness was redefined as the only possible response to communication problems in the system. This kind of thinking is present today in our view of the sexual abuse victim's dissociation as an adaptive response to a hopeless situation. And there are other systems conceptualizations of incest as the only possible response to a sick family. The key point is that the symptoms of anyone in the family serve to preserve the stability of the family's patterns of interaction.

If we borrow terms from systems applications in the sciences, we can see families as "open" or "closed" systems, as maintaining or disrupting homeostasis. The unit under examination is the interaction, and any response from an element of the system, be it a cell (in biological theories) or an individual, can only be understood in terms of the broader context. The observer is urged to focus on the interaction, the situation, and the relationship, rather than the individual. Through complex feedback processes and checks and balances, systems perpetuate and reinforce their own behaviors.

Donald Jackson, working in the 1950s, clarified what was to become an important tool of analysis for systems therapists in his article entitled "Family Rules: Marital Quid Pro Quos."[75] He claimed that marital rules are worked out in a mutual exchange. The rules are practical, but men and women are not necessarily conscious of them. The emphasis on practicality highlights an aspect of systems theory that describes all elements of a system as cooperating to maintain the status quo. When a family comes into therapy with, for example, a symptomatic child, a systems therapist will wonder first how the family cooperates in maintaining the system in such a way that the symptom perpetuates, and second, in what way the family *needs* this person to be sick (what each member has to gain by cooperating in such a way). The symptomatic child is not to blame for his symptom, but neither is either parent. The family is thought to be trapped in their interactions. To use a term introduced earlier to describe perpetrators, we can say that the family's interaction is a "habit."

Another focus of systems theory is the metamessage, sometimes viewed as paradoxical. A direct message from a violent man to his wife might be, "I want to hurt you," whereas a possible metamessage might be, "Control me," or, "I'm really very weak—you need to stop me and take care of me." In listening to a systems therapist one hears these kinds of interpretations of metamessages. For example, at a presentation in a clinic, a structural systems therapist showed a videotape of a family in which the daughter had run away from home many times. During the entire session the stepfather sat sullen and unspeaking, perhaps sending a message (not a metamessage) that he didn't care or that he was angry and withholding. The daughter even accused the stepfather of not really caring about her. The stepfather did not answer, but the therapist replied for him with a positive reframing: "He cares so much that he is paralyzed by it and doesn't know what to say or do." There actually was little evidence that this stepfather *did* care, but the positive reframing by systems therapists arises from a vision of the inner good of people. A typical positive reframing for an abusive husband might be, "If I can't control you, I will lose you and that would be unbearable." The "inner voice" that is "read" by, or introduced by, the therapist is one of a suffering man, an "inner child," to use a more popular term. An atypical metamessage (which can be referred to as a clarifying reframing) that a therapist might read could be, "I control you because I hate you and blame you for all my suffering," or, "I control you because I am entitled to have everything my way because I am superior to you."

There have been major attacks on systems theory in general and in particular as it has been applied to families. One argument points out that all systems are really open systems, and that the drawing of boundaries is arbitrary. The elements of a system that theorists select to examine are also arbitrary; and systems theorists anthropomorphize systems such as the family or the school system or even a biological system in a way that doesn't hold up. Finally, and most important to our own discussion of victims and perpetrators, the term "cooperation" is misleading because some of these systems operate through coercion or misunderstanding.[76]

Indeed, as Michael Nichols and Richard Schwartz summarize, feminist family therapists have trouble with the idea of trusting the family to find its own solutions, "steeped as it is in patriarchal values."[77] These therapists have pointed out how an idea of equal responsibility looks like a way of "rationalizing the status quo," and they insist that gender differences and oppression should be of primary concern to all family therapists.[78] There has been intense debate about such issues within systems theory; however, the fact that feminist family therapists still identify themselves as such goes to show how little impact their work has had on the field at large.[79]

The danger with the systems view of violence or sexual abuse is that if the abuse serves a function in the family, then first, the perpetrator cannot be blamed; second, the violent act is seen as somehow provoked; and third, the violence is reinterpreted as an adaptive response to a sick system.

Systems theory just does not do enough. It isn't broad enough or personal enough. Many have commented on the way that systems theory does not reach far enough beyond the family to look at the historical roots and the economic and social structures that impinge on the internal behaviors of the family members. Most particularly it ignores power inequity within the family. Systems theory also does not spend sufficient time looking at the individual. Some characteristics or habits of individuals are more influential in a family than others, reinforce given power structures, and can even create the power dynamics themselves. Take, for example, the feeling of entitlement. This entitlement, of course, is supported and maintained by numerous economic, political, and social structures at large.

Systems theory sometimes helps the perpetrator who seeks to blame his victim by supporting his excuses.[80] Lola Buckley and associates describe a husband's beating of his wife as "a cyclical interaction in which one or both partners have often experienced violence in their families of origin."[81] Those theorists who speak of family dysfunction with regard to incest claim that it occurs in families in which normal hierarchies have broken down.[82] Within the family, male sexuality is seen as "driven and uncontrollable," especially around a female adolescent, and the father's behavior is a counterpart or a response to the mother's withdrawal. Even when a mother is not blamed directly, she is blamed for the "opportunity" opened for abuse—either she is absent, sick, powerless, or chose an abusive stepfather.[83] Although some mothers must accept partial blame if their children are abused, it is possible to see the mother's weaknesses in light of the father's prior abuse, and in terms of what the historian Linda Gordon calls "the systematic way in which male supremacy gives rise to incest."[84]

Systems thinking about couples violence has also met many challenges from within, as feminist family therapists have objected to its overall implications.[85] Michele Bograd writes, "While systemic formulations help explain the chronicity and redundancy of battering sequences, they also contain subtle but pernicious biases that inadvertently sanction violence against women or that deflect attention away from the social conditions that may engender battering."[86] She and others describe systems formulations that point to the transactional variables that either blame the victim or portray women as "unwitting collaborators."

The ideology of systems theory renders the perpetrator only part of the problem and, in its focus on the present interactions, ignores any history of misogyny or the association of masculinity with domination.[87] When the perpetrator is thus made invisible, it is inevitable that the cruelty and the harm done will remain unmentioned, or in the very least faceless.

MAKING EVIL FACELESS

Wendy Lesser writes in *Pictures at an Execution* that when we look at murder through art, we distance ourselves from it.[88] I am not sure whether the same might be said about the artistic treatment of victims and perpetrators; it certainly seems to be true of the media and academia's portrayal of victims and perpetrators. The widespread dissemination of information on abuse and victimization and the absenting of perpetrators from the description of violent acts within this dissemination support this distancing in different ways.

Intellectual pretense as well as pseudo-objectivity abounds in writing about abuse by academics, backlash supporters, and the media, and it protects the audience from hearing details of the horror in such a way that would evoke empathy with the victim and disgust at the cruelty of the perpetrator. Each academic or reporter who writes about abuse chooses words carefully for publication. He or she considers how to refer to genitals or penetration. One might think penetration is too unemotional a word; someone else might consider "ripped" or "shredded" but dismiss these as overly evocative words.

The careful choice of words in press reports may serve not only to avoid describing cruelty but also to titillate the reader. In her analysis of press reports of rape, Helen Benedict documents the press's preference for descriptions that titillate over "objective" descriptions. She notes that newspaper reporters will write "she was stripped" instead of "her jeans were pulled off"; children were "fondled" rather than "touched"; and she was "naked from the waist down" rather than "wearing only a jacket and a sock."[89] The alternatives that Benedict suggests have a pseudo-objective, journalistic air to them. But distancing the reader may be preferable to titillating him or her.

Within academia not one major researcher brings subjectivity into his or her work. Not one has included anything but an intellectual position in discussion. Not one has revealed whether she or he speaks from a "knowing" position, having been abused her- or himself, although it is likely that at least one in four had a childhood experience of sexual abuse. Probably fearful that a confession of a history of abuse might discredit them as they fight for their victims' rights to be taken seriously, they absent themselves from the discussion and, in so doing, absent their emotional reaction to cruelty. They pretend that what they write about is only a scientific issue, one of facts and not morals. In assuming the writing style of academia, (unemotional, and perhaps, in society's view because of this, less female) they leave the realm of the personal and the emotional to talk shows.

Can a book about how the public reacts to abuse and victimization successfully avoid dealing with talk shows on which abuse is at least a weekly topic? I think not. In the words of Foucault, we have two methods of truth production: the confession and science.[90] Talk-show producers choose the former, academia the latter.

Talk shows combine modern adversariness and romantic self-assertion.[91] They follow from a long line of experts giving advice to women, which started in the late nineteenth century with the *Ladies' Home Journal,* and in which the focus was truly on "enlightened self-improvement" rather than on externalizing blame.[92] But TV has an agenda-setting, ideological effect.[93] It socializes viewers, or gives advice that almost always calls for looking inward. And, given the predominantly female audience for these shows, it reinforces the internalizing stance of victims.

Television talk shows, TV documentaries, and made-for-TV movies bank on the emotionalism of the issues surrounding abuse and victimization, but trivialize it, and, in the end, fare no better than academics in naming cruelty. Neil Postman reminds us of this telling precommercial tag from the now defunct *Vidal Sassoon Show:* "Don't go away. We'll be back with a marvelous new diet and then a quick look at incest."[94]

These shows also cheapen the issues they deal with by focusing so narrowly on the reactions of victims, their shame and rage. A study of these shows and movies would reveal that very little time is spent on the actual events that took place. Events are reviewed quickly at the beginning of the show as important background material for the audience. But the remainder of the show focuses on the victim, usually the long-term consequences of her abuse, and how she has coped with the trauma. The shows reinforce the view that empowerment comes from being a victim and coping with it rather than preventing oneself from being a victim.[95]

Because these talk shows see themselves as self-help venues rather than avenues for societal change, it makes sense that they focus on the victim. And through the victim's confession and narrative of coping, the audience comes to identify with the victim, to borrow some of her courage and purity. On TV, identification has taken the place of empathy. When an audience hears about and sees a victim suffering (apart from and distanced from perpetrator cruelty), they identify but are spared the more gut-wrenching empathy that an encounter with cruelty might evoke. This identification with the victim in such a way helps the perpetrator in his efforts to hide and deny the harm done.

Julia Penelope analyzed a TV documentary called "Kids Don't Tell," and she points out that even in the title the act of incest or sexual abuse is not mentioned, in effect supporting the inclination of children not to tell. She also describes how neither the interviewer nor the interviewees actually name the crime. Perhaps the family was too ashamed to speak the words, but even the reporter adopts the language of the family. Reinforcing the perpetrator's denial, the reporter refers to what he did as "it" or "what happened to your daughter." What happened to his daughter is what "he did" to his daughter. Penelope writes that the reporter, instead of asking, "Why does it keep happening?" could have asked, "Why do you persist in forcing your daughter to have sex with you over and over again?"

This kind of show can be seen as a new form of public entertainment carved out of the experience of abuse in order to distance us from it. Pretending to be factual, it removes us more from the cruelty than art does. Any "play therapist" knows that art helps one deepen the emotional experience of an event rather than distance oneself from it. It may be that only through fiction and other art (as opposed to television shows, the press, and academia) are the aspects of cruelty and harm preserved. The supreme irony is that "fact" and science may be obscuring the realities that art and fiction now preserve.

The onlookers, analyzers, and audience for abuse stories, wrapped up in discussions of victims' rights and tragedies, ignore the perpetrator, and thus do not assess blame accurately. If we look past all the rhetoric, lecturing, and speech-writing, we cannot find a bottom-line moral point of view condemning these acts, a point of view that finds them simply inexcusable.

I want to give an example of how transgressions in my own household would be inexcusable. To use an extreme example, my children are simply not allowed to set fire to the couch. I cannot imagine a single extenuating circumstance, except a state of delirium caused by some illness, in which they would be held less responsible for setting fire to the couch. Were they to set fire to the couch I would be furious. Were I to find out afterward that they were "acting out" because for the past year a Boy Scout leader had been sexually abusing them, I would offer them support and love and care around those issues. But I would be furious that they had put their lives and mine at risk by setting fire to the couch. The point is that there might even be a relationship between my boys' sexual abuse and their setting fire to the couch, but under no circumstance should they have or should they ever in the future set fire to the couch. And, if that couch happened to belong to just about anybody else (save the Boy Scout leader), then I would insist on their making reparations to the family who lost a couch and who may have been frightened or distressed by the fire. There are some things you just do not do. One of them is harm other people or put their lives at risk.

Why doesn't the public feel this way about violence against women, or the sexual abuse of children? Why can it sometimes be partially justified? We must refer back to two interpretations discussed earlier—that of seeing the victim as somewhat deserving, and that of seeing the perpetrator as not fully in control. And now we are faced with the opposite of the dichotomy we started out with: instead of the innocent victim and the monstrous perpetrator, we are left with the guilty victim and the helpless perpetrator. Blame is diffused.

We focus so exclusively on issues of rights violated and blame-worthiness because we may not really think of violence toward women or children as cruelty.[96] For if we were to focus on the cruelty or the harm done in the act itself (not in the long-term consequences), rather than the rights, or "right to," or "justification" of the people involved, then we would be face to face with the perpetrator and his lack of empathy, his heartless self-centeredness.

Successful jail programs that do rehabilitate focus on the cruelty and lack of empathy of perpetrators. For one show, *20/20* filmed a group meeting in a state hospital in Seattle in which rapists participated in an empathy-enhancing program. At this group meeting of convicted rapists, a tape of a woman who had called 911 after a man had broken into her house was played. It brought some of the men to shameful tears. The woman's voice contained so much fear, and was so disquieting, that the hosts of the show warned the audience that what they were about to hear was disturbing and they should turn off their TV sets if they thought it would be too much for them to handle. Oddly enough, rapes and other violent acts in TV movies rarely receive such warnings; yet the mere sound of a voice accurately rendering the terror of an impending rape was seen as warranting additional warning. And it very well did. When audience members face (or in this case, simply hear) the immediate harm and the cruelty of acts done, it is terrifying.

THE MAKING OF PERPETRATORS
AND VICTIMS

5

To talk about the life or childhood of a perpetrator or, for that matter, the life or childhood of a victim is a difficult matter. The fact that we discuss someone's childhood at all seems to suggest that we are searching for an excuse, not only for the abusive act, but also for the other-blaming of perpetrators and the self-blaming of victims. As we grapple with issues of nature versus nurture, the inner versus the outer, and the social versus the individual, the dualism of Western psychology seems inescapable. If we accept the argument that people can *be* responsible and also be *held* responsible for their behavior, then we must also determine at what age that responsibility begins, for surely we do not hold an infant responsible for the neglect it suffers, nor a toddler so thoroughly responsible for the extra cookie he grabs. We must also ask what environmental supports an individual needs to help him or her assume that responsibility, and to what extent the lack of such supports is used as an explanation for a perpetrator's cruelty or a victim's self-derogation.

From the outset we need to address the question of whether victims are indeed *made* victims by anything but their victimization, and what is meant when we talk about being made a victim. To be a victim is different from being a victim of *something*. The violent act as well as the sexual offense has the capacity to transform the person affected into a certain kind of victim, a victim who self-derogates, blames herself too much, and cannot move beyond defining herself in terms of her victimization. There are certain predisposing factors that make it more likely for some to react to their abuse in victim-defining ways. These factors are both external and internal, having to do with the nature of the offense as well as the personality and socialization of the victim before the abusive act.

Those who refer to themselves as victimologists would have us look closely at the particular act of abuse, the way it intrudes upon the victim's life, body, and thoughts, the way it shakes up her old, steadfast beliefs about the nature of the world and her place in it. These victimologists would say that there is something in the experience of victimization that marks the victim, that actually makes her a different person. But the process is not entirely unidirectional, not simply a matter of cause and effect: the way the person reacts and responds to her victimization also transforms, creates, and marks her.

What follows are some examples of reactions to relatively mild sexual offenses that I introduce to illustrate how certain responses reinforce cultural stereotypes and mark the victim. The first example involves a teen-age girl who is riding down an escalator in a major department store; a teen-age boy is riding down behind her with his friends, about to gallop past. As he overtakes her, to the great amusement of his friends, he reaches over and grabs her breast. Now, imagine two reactions. In the first reaction, the girl grabs his hand tightly and yells furiously, "How dare you, you fucking asshole!" In the second reaction she pulls away. There is a pained and embarrassed look on her face, and she thinks, "Why me? Was it the shirt I was wearing? Who saw this happen to me?" The boy's response to the first reaction is shock. He had not anticipated her anger and her action. His friends laugh at him because they assess that the girl has "won" the battle and that their friend has been caught and humiliated. Their laughter minimizes the harm of the act, teases their friend, and captures their own discomfort with the girl's expressed outrage. In a weak attempt to gain their approval once more, the offending boy calls her a "bitch," but his friends are still laughing at him. How does the boy respond to the second reaction? Actually, he does not notice the pained and embarrassed expression on the girl's face, or, if he does, it doesn't register for very long. Instead, he basks in the jovial backslapping of his friends; he has "won" something. The girl's first reaction marks her as superior to the boy: "How dare you touch me—yes *me*," it says. The girl's second reaction brands her inferior in some questioning and vague way: I don't think I deserve this; I've been good. What could I have done wrong? How will people judge me?

In the second example, a different teen-age boy, lonely and feeling down, thinks about "copping a feel" down his stepsister's underpants as they hang around the kitchen. He is fourteen and she is ten. He thinks about all the girls he knows in school and how none of them is ever going to be his girlfriend. Or maybe he doesn't think too much at all, but just feels kind of bad. He does it quickly, impulsively, holding her wrists tightly as he puts his hand down her pants. Thought becomes action as quickly as one brushes off an offending mosquito. But his stepsister doesn't react with the same spontaneity, by swatting him or saying, "How dare you?" or even, "What the fuck!" Confusion more than anger overwhelms her, and then silence, and then shame, until at a slumber party she tells a friend, who tells her mother, who tells the stepsister's mother, who reports the incident to a government agency to prove that her daughter should be living with her and not with her father and stepmother.

The boy is evaluated by a psychologist. A Rorschach test, in which a patient responds spontaneously to the psychologist's presentation of inkblots, organizing random spills into clues about the stresses that impinge on a person and his or her organization of the world, indicates that he has few internal resources to deal with emotion. When emotion flares up he may act impulsively because he cannot cope with the moment. Interviews with the boy's father show him to be a likeable man who doesn't understand why his daughter was the target, why this particular boundary was crossed. He asks why his son didn't just do this to some girls at school. When asked about his own high school years he readily admits to being suspended several times for harassing the girls in the hall; he would grab their breasts as they walked by. To this day he considers suspension from school to have been an extreme reaction to what he did: "They didn't mind. They were sluts."

These are true stories. And although they portray mild offenses in the grand scheme of violence against women (surely not punishable by imprisonment), they provide a midway point—in statistical terms, a median—between the violent and terrifying sexual abuse and rape stories that gain the most publicity and the lives of those who never perpetrate and never have been victimized. These are incidents that are likely to go unreported, even though the second example did involve a government agency. But acts like these are probably more widespread than we might think, given that they are unlikely to be reported or even discussed within the family. These stories also contain the kernels of victim and perpetrator behavior.

The girl in reaction two of the first story and the girl in the story of the stepbrother respond with disbelief, immobility, and self-doubt. The lack of immediate anger in the second response of the girl accosted on the escalator is a glaring fact when compared with the first reaction. Her responses betray the kernel of all victim behavior: (1) questioning the actions of the boy, as if he had some right to do what he did; (2) shock and surprise that such a thing was happening; and (3) embarrassment, as if the behavior labeled her in some way.

The boys show many signs of perpetrator behavior. There is the sense of entitlement in considering the girl's body to be theirs for the having, or in their conveyance that they have some right to it to fulfill their own needs. There is also, especially in the first tale, a distinct battle of the sexes, the losing of which brings humiliation and shame to a person in the eyes of his peers. There are impulsivity and a little aggression and some anger and depression. There is also the complete inattention to the girl's reaction.

Why don't girls say, "How dare you?" Why don't they get mad? And why do boys feel entitled to the sexual parts of girls' bodies? Why do they not pay attention to their victims' typical reactions? Why don't they manage bad feelings, depression or anger, in constructive or even *self*-destructive ways?

These questions lead us to examine the cultural assumptions embedded in our socialization practices, practices that make gender such a strong marker for sexually aggressive behavior. Cultural transmission is the process by which the values and beliefs of a culture come to form human beings, their practices, their relationships, and their personalities. The messages implicit in social discourse tell us what to presuppose, value, feel, and how to classify; what is to be taken as self-evident and what it is to be a person.[1] But before we embark on a complex and entangled journey through gender-role socialization and development, it seems important to address the issue of how it is possible to speak of the cultural transmission of values and still hold people responsible for their actions. Does the tyranny of cultural transmission mean that we will have to lay aside the lofty requirements of individual responsibility?

Philosophers have long dealt with this question in more

complex ways. Those who have been called "Incompatibilists" argue that free will and determinism are two incompatible ideas; if everything in nature is caused according to invariant laws— most of which we are far from knowing in anywhere near a complete and predictable way—then people and their actions must also be caused.[2] "Compatibilists" argue that there is no reason to believe that just because everything is caused we have no free will. Indeed, these scholars say causal theory has little to do with morality and responsibility, and that our subjectivity, cognitions, and reactions make us able to attain the kind of free will that is worth wanting—a free will that means our actions are not, in the moment of our acting, "controlled." Rollo May writes that the "world includes the past events which condition my existence and all the vast variety of deterministic influences which operate upon me. But it is these as I relate to them, am aware of them, carry them with me, molding, inevitably form- ing, building them in every minute of relating. For to be aware of one's world means at the same time to be designing it."[3]

Of course, such responsibility for one's actions is always developing and always present. It is evident in the way the mother of a two-year-old will hold her son responsible for the minor household "crimes" he commits, such as spilling his juice on purpose, or throwing his toys across the room. And it is evident in the guilty expressions of three-year-olds when they know that they have transgressed. Internalization of responsibil- ity and conditioning for such occur very early.

And so, if conscience and a sense of one's own responsibility and efficacy in the world develop so naturally in the early environment, what can we look to in order to understand the overresponsibility of victims and what seem to be the lapses or lack of conscience of perpetrators? What childhood acts are we looking at specifically? Do we look at aggression in childhood and blame the absence of the father or the intrusion of the mother, as so many of us have done before? Do we look at moral development, the development of a conscience, of guilt, and its counterpart, the development of empathy? And are there underlying mechanisms associated with the development of a conscience, of guilt, of empathy? Emotional development may be one such mechanism. If we start with how children come to recognize what constitutes a transgression in this culture, we will almost always end up in a study of emotion. What makes a child shameful at transgressing? What makes a child notice the emotion of another? And from whence comes that righteous anger when one has been transgressed upon? In the remainder of this chapter I will work my way "up," from the earliest of moral behaviors, through emotional development, development of anger, guilt, shame, and a sense of entitlement, to, finally, the development of a worldview of the relationship of boys to girls. Within these various areas precursors to both victim and perpetrator behaviors are clear.

DO ALL CHILDREN START OFF MORAL?

Around the second year of life a child begins to show that he or she has a sense of what is right or wrong. This is observed in very small behaviors indicating that the child suddenly cares about these issues.[4] For example, a two-year-old will toddle over to a previously prohibited object and shake his head "no" at it while looking at his mother (we refer to this as "social referencing"). The toddler will also show delight in the violation of a parental standard, for example, teasing the parent by pretending to put her hand in the dirt of a flower pot. The child will begin to negotiate about actions that might be prohibited, to converse about what can be touched or not touched, and to investigate by watching a parent to see what actions he or she can get away with. These small acts can be seen in the behavior of children aged one to two living with adolescent mothers in the most deprived urban conditions, as well as in the middle-class households of the United States.[5] Although the content of values may differ, the toddlers' recognition of the standards remains remarkably similar and comes about at the same age.

The standards that the child can begin to recognize only at around fifteen months have been directly taught by caregivers: "Don't touch," "Don't you dare run away," "No throwing." Children also learn standards and values through modeling, that is, through watching their parents and siblings and noting vicariously which behaviors are acceptable, which are punished, and which are tolerated. Toddlers also begin to understand and cognitively construct various standards of right and wrong through subtle environmental cues and natural consequences of their acts. For example, when you hit someone and hurt him, there usually is some response, some feedback in terms of victim emotion—anger or fear or hurt feelings or retaliation, depending on the age of the victim—and this kind of disturbing feedback occurs quite regularly. Children also understand something of the context in which particular acts occur so that they can distinguish between hitting that is acceptable, as in patty-cake or other games, and hitting that will surely result in negative consequences, hitting that is more a matter of social convention as opposed to hitting that would be wrong just about anywhere and under any circumstances.[6] If toddlers do not choose the good, we can safely assume that they are capable of knowing the good, be it a universal good or merely what their caregiver has requested of them.

The second through third year of life is not only a time of burgeoning moral development but also a time of tantrums and battles of will, in which the word "no" becomes a means of self-assertion, a triumph of separateness and individuality, as well as a plea for recognition by a small person whose wants and needs *ought* to be taken seriously, and taken seriously now! It is probably not coincidental that the beginning of a moral sense coincides with the beginning of a sense of self if one conceptualizes a moral sense as a recognition of standards imposed from the outside.[7] It is at this moment in development when awareness makes a person (or toddler) capable of commenting on, observing, and verbally disagreeing with what is externally imposed.

But then there comes a time after the beginning of morality when children start to learn how to lie, to deceive, and to make excuses. Once they have a "self" they can disengage this self from their acts and the standards they violate in a number of ways. Excuse-making is a part of life, and probably necessary in maintenance of our self-esteem, providing a way in which we can see ourselves as better than we are.[8]

The first way the self can be protectively disengaged from the standard of morality it has transgressed against is through denial: "It wasn't me." The second, most primitive excuse-making comes from a sort of merging with mother, a feeling that she is the one to blame for the mistake. I recall a time when my oldest son, then three, was climbing the stairs ahead of me and stumbled and fell. He was an unusually moralistic three-year-old who took criticism to heart and tried especially hard to be good; he turned around and exclaimed that I had pushed him, that it was my fault that he had fallen. Implicit in this distortion were the more subtle cries "You should have helped me" and "Why didn't you prevent this from happening to me?" My response, and most likely the response of most mothers to such blaming, was one that enforced the responsibility: "I didn't push you, you tripped on the rug." To take the blame, as an extremely lenient mother might be prone to do, would be to endorse a view of reality that simply was not correct, and to allow my son to paint a picture of me as a mother who would push her son. But it might have helped him remove some of the harsh criticism he probably was internally heaping onto himself. A third way the child can disengage his self from the act he has committed is by blaming the object of his transgression. The chair was in the way. The jar was too close to the edge of the table. "Bad chair," says the child. "Not my fault."

A behaviorist might say that, in the development of excuse-making, a violent perpetrator's excuses have been rewarded from very early on. On the local news in Philadelphia, a mother made a plea for her son who was accused of kidnapping to turn himself into the police: "Come home dear. I know you didn't mean it."[9] He didn't mean it? But all parents tend naturally to reward children's excuses, not just the excuses of future perpe- trators. Excusing and holding responsible are part of the moral education of every child.[10] Chiefly it is the law that is one-sided; the law does not consider children responsible for their actions. Parents, by contrast, hold their children responsible for quite a bit from about the age of two.

Both the excusing and the holding responsible give children a chance to see themselves as better than they are, and out of such socialization practices grow a child's ideals. It is evident that parents respond with judgments and high expectations for their children as soon as they begin to transgress and show some awareness of transgression. Some parents do this even before the child shows an awareness. Psychoanalytic literature has talked about these expectations in terms of "ego ideals," which are said to derive both from our parents' expectations of us and from our idealized fantasies of our parents. Instead of seeing the good as already residing within us, we long for the good we may someday attain.

The development of a conscience has been seen by some

researchers more than others as closely related to different patterns of parental responses to transgression. Harsh parental responding (power assertion) has been associated with less moral behavior in children, and parental affection has been associated with more moral behavior in children. Behaviorism has shown us again and again that you get more from the carrot than the stick, and that fear of punishment only goes so far. The child who restrains himself for fear of punishment does so without attachment, so that when the threat of punishment is not present, the restraint flees also. Moreover, when pleasing the parent yields no rewards, love and affection being one of the most important rewards to a child's life and vitality, there is little impetus for the development of ideals or motivation to do good. We see children, some as young as sixteen months, trying to please their parents by "being good"—earning love, so to speak, through moral behavior. The child needs to feel connected to the force out of which morals arise in order to internalize these morals. This is not a new idea.

Indeed, many theories have spoken of loss of love as a motivator for moral behavior, although research on this factor suggests that the withdrawal of love has only an immediate effect on compliance, and no long-term effects on the adoption of new moral standards.[11] Of particular interest to the self-blaming of victims is Justin Aronfreed's concept of internalization.[12] When a child does wrong, Aronfreed conjectures, she becomes anxious about the withdrawal of love that might result from her behavior. The child will then either criticize herself in order to preempt the other's punishment and reduce the anxiety inherent in anticipating the other's reaction, or she will make reparations, confess, or seek out punishment. These are all behaviors that victims tend to engage in—as if they had done something wrong—and all behaviors that perpetrators seem to avoid. Each of these behaviors reflects a connection to a socializing force, a parent; and each also reinforces the connection between the wrongdoer and the rulemaker.

High-risk children who have had those early connections challenged through poverty, abuse, and neglect can overcome the odds in various ways, for example—and this is particularly true for boys—by attaching to some adult outside of the family. One can assume that using this person as the moral base to return to, to please, and to impress can be lifesaving for a child.[13]

Overly harsh parents are not likely to be moved by attempts at reparation. Regret, for example, would probably have little sway with a harsh parent and would not be supported by a return of lost love or affection. If regret or reparation is unlikely, then the child has little recourse but to try to hide his "sins" from his parents. When sins are unseen and hidden a child gets little feedback for his wrongdoing. His crimes go uncommented on and he has only to rely on his individual developing conscience to guide him. If his parents have been overly harsh to begin with and love has not been a motivating force for moral restraint, then the internalized parent also may have little sway and, when the child is older, all society can count on is his fear of punishment. Unfortunately, the kind of punishment that society can provide is inconsistent and variable.

Children seek out knowledge of the good and, through their attachment to loving figures, learn to practice the good in their own behavior. Overly harsh and punitive judgments and reactions, as well as a lack of connection to a caring adult, will impede moral development as it impedes development in so many other ways. In the end, these impediments may disturb the child's development of conscience by disturbing his or her emotional development, for emotion is at the root of early conscience.

THE IMPORTANCE OF EMOTION

Empathy, shame and guilt, the bad feelings that lead some adolescents to offend, anger and its relation to aggression, and even the sense of entitlement are all emotions related to moral sentiment and action.

Empathy

Lack of empathy, for example, has been implicated as one of several factors that lead a perpetrator to commit the offenses he commits. But empathy is not a one-dimensional emotional experience. To empathize with another, one first needs the cognitive ability to identify emotions correctly. We might even assume that if perpetrators really could assess the pain they were causing their victims they might stop. Another assumption we make when we speak of empathy in everyday terms is that the person who may "feel with" the other also cares about the other. Nancy Eisenberg has shown, however, that feeling with someone is not necessarily an empathic response.

Eisenberg and her colleagues at the University of Arizona distinguish between two kinds of responses to distress. Both kinds of responses involve the accurate detection of the other person's emotion, but one response to the distress of another involves personal distress, and the other response is more caring. The research shows that those who respond to the distress of another by becoming distressed themselves (the distress response is measured physiologically and through facial expressions) are less likely to offer help to the person in distress than those who respond with empathy.[14] What we normally consider the empathic response must be differentiated from personal distress. We might even conjecture that for some perpetrators, though they might accurately note the pain and humiliation of their victims, the distress may be a noxious stimulus. In fact, abused toddlers do seem to find the distress of their peers noxious, and they will respond to it by attacking them rather than showing concern, which might suggest to us why perpetrators may remain unmoved by the cries of their victims.[15]

But perpetrators may actually be able to show sympathy or empathy in other situations. For example, one of the techniques Judith Becker uses in working with groups of adolescent sexual offenders is to have them imagine that it is their sisters who are being abused. Feelings of helplessness and fear and empathy emerge, and the adolescents become outraged at the imagined offenders. So, for some perpetrators, selectivity of empathy or sympathy rather than lack of empathy may be the problem. The "ability" to turn off a sympathetic response, to disregard the victim, or to reinterpret her signs of distress may be the mechanisms by which many perpetrators can carry out their abuse. If this is the case, empathy training may not be the answer for many of them.

Shame and Guilt

Shame and guilt both mediate self-control.[16] But it is unclear if the problem with shame and guilt as they apply to perpetrators and victims is one of degree (for example, that the former do not feel enough guilt and shame, and the latter feel too much), or one of management of emotion (that perpetrators and victims feel shame equally but they have been taught different ways to handle it).

The experience of shame is one of intense vulnerability. The shamed person feels "naked, defeated, alienated, lacking in dignity and worth."[17] Since the feeling of exposure is so central to the experience of shame, one can understand Helen Block Lewis's assertion that an individual can only experience shame in the context of an emotional relationship with another person, and only when he or she values that other person's opinions.

One may internalize the other person, and thus feel shame even when not in the presence of the other. This internalization also shows the importance of a child's connection to a moral base in the early years.

Avoidance of shame, rather than shame itself, theoretically should be adaptive, a motive for responsibility—"I will do what's right to avoid that awful feeling of shame." Avoidance of shame should promote self-criticism and social cohesion. But hiding after the act, rather than avoidance before the act, is the most common defense against shame, hiding in the form of secrecy about the acts one has committed, or hiding in its most primitive form, through denial. Some argue that shame does not motivate change but acts to paralyze all efforts at self-improvement.[18]

Shame and aggression may go hand in hand. Lewis noted how easily hostility was directed outward when a person felt ashamed.[19] Some have seen a connection between shame and the desire to punish others.[20] June Tangney and her colleagues found that in the fifth grade there was a direct link between boys' proneness to experience shame and teachers' reports of aggression, and that, in general, adults' proneness to feelings of shame was related to malevolent intentions.[21]

Tangney's research also shows that females consistently experience greater shame and guilt than males, which might suggest that perpetrators simply are less moral, victims more.[22] It is more likely, however, that some perpetrators have no sense of shame, whereas others are deeply ashamed and project this feeling outward, making their victims enact the humiliation and degradation that threatens to surface within their own beings. It is in just this way that the perpetrator admittedly wishes to make the victim experience what he will not allow himself to feel.[23]

The late Erik Erikson, who saw human development as a

series of struggles and opportunities, the outcome of which had lasting effects, wrote of shame. He broadened the Freudian psychosexual stages in several ways, including by extending the concept of development to one of a lifetime process, and by trying to conceptualize each stage as the meeting place of biology, individual personality, and culture. He believed that during the second stage of life, which Freud narrowly labeled the anal stage, the child struggled with feelings of shame and doubt; if a happy outcome could emerge from this stage, these bad feelings could be minimized in favor of autonomy, or the assertion of a self with its own wishes and desires, apart from the wishes and desires of parents.

In this sense, the feeling of shame exists in opposition to a sense of self, and one might even understand the violent projection of shame onto another as a way of asserting a self that is in control, a prideful, autonomous, but ultimately false self set out to compete with the shameful, weak, and degraded self. Is this to say that the perpetrator's toilet training was not handled well? Hardly. This second stage of life, although coinciding with a toddler's first attempts to control his bowels, is more about developing a will, the sense of assertive self that marks the beginnings of moral development. The toddler grasps the self as something separate from the morals and the moral forces (his caregivers) that surround him, a self to control, a self he is expected to control. But it is also a self that is connected to those moral forces who form him and whom he hopes to please. Erikson wrote that when moral forces are overly harsh and punitive, and give little support to the burgeoning self, there "comes a lasting propensity for doubt and shame."

Shame may capture the essence of the "power rapist," in Nicholas Groth's terminology. Shame also captures the essence of the victim who doesn't tell. But the discussion of shame thus far has not explained the different reactions to feeling ashamed: the perpetrator's tendency to project it outward or the victim's tendency to hide from it.

Shame is a healthy reaction of a child who does wrong. As noted earlier, it indicates the presence of a relationship and the urge to hide from any person who has the power to make one's self feel insignificant. In some sense it is an adaptive way to preserve the relationship. But shame becomes unbearable and overpowering if the child is allowed to hide. The neglectful parent, the parent who does not seek out the moral life of the child, risks allowing the child to suffer with shameful feelings. Exposure and the chance to make reparation are crucial for the moral development of a child, not only in teaching the child about the transgression, but also in teaching a way to manage shameful feelings. Exposure that results in harsh punishment only teaches the child to learn to hide his wrongdoings in the future. Psychologists talk about perpetrators' "wanting" to be caught, committing their offenses in careless ways so that someone will expose them. Therapists also speak of sexual abuse victims who try to disclose in so many indirect ways, for example, through their bedwetting or their tantrums. Shame causes one not only to hide from exposure but also to seek drastic means of exposure in order to return to the community and reconnect with loved ones.

The Management of Bad Feelings

Shame is just one of the ways an adolescent boy who begins to perpetrate sexual offenses or to act out through violence toward his girlfriend can feel bad. Research on the relapse of "cured" perpetrators shows that 75 percent of them identify "negative emotional states" as a precursor to a relapse.[24] And it is well known that the perpetrator who might not even be aware of the shame or the bad feelings will fight the expression and recognition of such feelings through projective identification.[25] Projective identification is a term used to describe the way a person, in this case a perpetrator, can unconsciously set out to make another person, a victim, take over his feelings, act in a manner suggestive of the perpetrator's inner feelings and even feel them for him. The victim then represents for the perpetrator all that he is ashamed of and disavows within himself. There are some recipients who make better hosts for these feelings than others—those who are less able to shrug off or avoid internalizing these projected feelings.

Some perpetrators and victims may have a propensity for shame and few tools to manage it. Possibly both have a propensity for depression, but each has different capacities and tendencies with regard to the management of difficult feelings. Internalizing and externalizing symptoms have long differentiated psychopathology between boys and girls.

One can conceptualize internalizing and externalizing symptoms as ways of managing emotion, or as forms of emotion regulation. Sometimes externalizing symptoms are discussed as reactions to internalizing symptoms by those who cannot "sit with" feelings well. For example, conduct disorder and substance abuse have been said to mask depression or anxiety. Thus, one might argue that feeling "down" or feeling "jumpy" may have some basic physiological effect, but the role requirements of men and boys push for a more active expression of the feeling (a pushing away of it or a masking through action), the role requirements of girls, a style more ruminative.[26] Indeed, one could argue that because men have an easier time expressing anger, bad feelings such as depression or anxiety may end up diffused and expressed as anger.[27]

The idea that emotional states may be more fluid than we generally conceive gains support from a cross-cultural view.[28] For example, it is difficult to translate depression cross-culturally to

Eastern societies. In China, because of the stigma of mental illness and other cultural factors, what we Westerners call depression may be experienced by the Chinese as stomachaches or other somatic complaints.[29] It has also been argued that this difference has more to do with the language of emotion than with a lack of psychological-mindedness on the part of Easterners.[30] We may then ask whether there are any true universal emotional responses to experiences. Do the Chinese mask true depression and call it a stomachache? Do Western boys deny and mask true depression and call it anger? Or do Western females construct depression as a response to neglect or stress or loss? Arlie Hochschild has said that we manage feelings through "surface" and "deep" acting; in this way, the culture provides males and females with different roles they can assume in the management of emotion, roles that in the end may transform the emotion itself.[31]

Any discussion about the experiencing or management of emotion is also a discussion about the construction of emotion. Catherine Lutz argues that it may not be accurate to say that "emotion," save anger, in men is suppressed, as popular myth would have it, but more accurate to say that emotion is *created* in women—created as a chaotic, irrational force that needs to be controlled by authority. In this way, the construction of emotion supports the dominance of men over women, and the rhetoric of emotional control suggests a set of roles that gets hierarchized and then linked with gender roles.[32] Some anthropological work shows that hierarchical societies manifest greater concern with how society controls the inner emotional life of people than do egalitarian societies.[33]

If emotions in women are seen as irrational and chaotic forces in need of control, this culturally constructed impression works nicely with the general social rule that anger should be spontaneous and not deliberate.[34] The spontaneous anger rule serves several purposes. If anger is spontaneous, it dissipates after it is expressed and is not something one can pinpoint as a personality trait. It also makes it difficult for the oppressed to organize. If there exist few cultural ways to be angry in a prolonged and planned way and to express anger in a structured, cohesive manner, the recipients of that anger can forget about it as soon as the flare-up is over. As a spontaneous impulse, anger becomes excusable. But it also becomes invisible.

As "women's work," anger is invisible. Arlie Hochschild writes that women do all the emotional labor in a household except for expressing anger.[35] (By emotional labor she means that women induce or suppress feeling to create an outward display of emotion in order to produce a preferred state of mind in others in the family.) Popular myth concurs, holding that women are better at expressing emotion and express it more regularly. Whereas women may have grown up with the idea that emotion is something one needs to control (and Lutz's interviews support this notion), men, who may believe that they are better at controlling emotions, or have fewer emotions to control, may not have grown up with the expectation that controlling emotion is important and essential for human relationships. Women's beliefs in the uncontrollability of their emotional impulses may actually give them more practice in emotional regulation. According to self-reports, women get angry as often as do men.[36] This would suggest that they refrain from acting on their anger more than men.

But we must consider that the control and expression of emotion say something about relationships involving power, dominance, and hierarchy. For men, anger in the household is more visible, more easily expressed. In interpersonal situations, research shows, men report lower levels of fear and sadness and higher levels of anger,[37] and boys who watch angry feelings being expressed on videotapes are more likely than girls to respond with anger.[38] These expressions of anger and entitlement can mark the individual expressing them higher in status than the one to whom such feelings are expressed.[39] It is interesting to note that ten-month-old boys are less likely to accept withdrawal of their mothers' attention than ten-month-old girls.[40] Emotional numbing, by contrast, marks one as inferior and contributes to a person's staying in a dangerous situation.[41]

Peggy Thoits argues that the experience of victimization may require a victim to feel and express a negative reaction, whether or not there is one, in order to confirm the badness of the act.[42] The less able the culture is to acknowledge the badness of the act, the more suffering the victim may feel and express in order to seek out moral confirmation that the victimization should not have happened. Conversely, if the culture were to confirm the idea that this should not be happening to a woman, that her body is her own and no one else has the right to make claims on it, she would then not need to prove how hurt she has been by the act. It is as if she is forced to show suffering and to believe in her own long suffering in order to convince society that this should not be happening.

This is ridiculous, as the Supreme Court recently confirmed with regard to sexual harassment in the workplace. The Court concluded that a woman need not prove she was harmed by the sexual harassment for the law to say that her rights in the workplace have been violated. A woman should not have to suffer deeply from her rape for rape to have been wrong in the first place. She has certain entitlements regardless of pain and suffering. But our culture has for some reason focused on women's expressions of entitlement more in terms of pain and suffering than in terms of their individual rights.

Entitlement

The expression of entitlement as a quasi-emotional state marks one as superior and is the overlaying emotional state of the perpetrator as he intrudes upon the person of the victim. But a sense of entitlement on the part of the perpetrator is also something that victims bestow or support through their reactions and the processing of the experience.

In all this discussion of emotion, we have not addressed the issue of entitlement, primarily because it seems to be not an emotion per se but something akin to an emotion. Healthy entitlement is seen from infancy in the rage of a child who does not get what she wants or needs at a given moment. It is also seen in the development of the self, in the second year, in the toddler's cries of "mine," cries that accompany countless disputes over property that will continue over the next year or more.

Psychoanalytic literature dealt with entitlement as early as Sigmund Freud's 1916 papers on the "exceptions" in psychoanalysis, those patients who seemed to Freud to be unwilling to move from the dominance of the pleasure principle ("I want what I want right now") to the reality principle ("I will wait and work, through whatever practical means I can, to get what I want, taking into consideration a number of other factors"). These patients, he claims, feel entitled to get what they want immediately because of their childhood suffering.[43] As in Heinz Kohut's 1976 description of narcissistic rage, entitlement can sometimes lead to a preemptive attack that would avoid an expected blow to one's narcissism.[44]

But women who suffered deprivations in childhood similar to those experienced by men do not seem to feel they have a right to take what they deserve; they do not seem to have turned their deprivation into a sense of exaggerated entitlement. This must be because the social supports for a man's entitlement are so much greater. When the social and economic world of a woman communicates that she is not entitled to equal pay, equal opportunity, the right to safety, the right to express an opinion, or especially to express her anger, then it is difficult to sustain whatever feelings of entitlement might arise from being mistreated—difficult but not impossible.

We can also see social support for male entitlement in the freer expression of anger allowed boys. Theorists have commented on how entitlement and anger appear to be linked so that anger serves in the expression of entitlement. Some research shows mothers of toddlers supporting sons more than daughters in conflicts over possessions. That is, when two two-year-olds are fighting over a toy, mothers tend to resolve the dispute by passing the toy from their own child to the other child; however, if they are mothers of sons, they tend to do this a little less.[45]

Entitlement within the household may be taught vicariously as children watch their fathers and mothers interact. Women still do more housework than men, regardless of whether or not the wife works or how many kids there are in the household.[46] Fathers issue commands more than mothers, and those commands seems to say much about a person's relative status.[47] Men also control topics of conversation more than women do.[48]

The psychoanalyst Mark Blechner suggests altruism as the opposite of entitlement; the opposite of "I am deserving," he writes, is "You are deserving."[49] Scales of entitlement seem to predict that the more entitled a person feels, the less empathic and socially responsible he will be.[50] And so one wonders about the many victims who have become crusaders for others, who have joined the helping professions, sometimes ignoring their own needs, to work for the entitlements of others. Although this kind of work may be healthier than supporting the needs and entitlements of their perpetrators, in supporting the needs of women and victims they often neglect their own.[51]

The division between healthy and exaggerated entitlement is not so clear when we listen to the voice of one man who is not a perpetrator but who was raised in a culture that encouraged a strong sense of male entitlement. He writes as part of a men's group reexamining masculinity and tells about his prior feelings of entitlement to women and their bodies: "What was so precious about their cunts, I [asked], that I couldn't get access to them?"[52] His words clearly reflect the belief that he should have access to another person's body. It is as if he needed a kidney and because of this legitimate need he should therefore have the right to demand the kidney of another person for his own use. He also reminds us of the father in the second example at the start of the chapter, the father who teaches his son that yes, he had a right to the breasts of the girls in his high school who happened to pass him, but no, not to his sister's body. This "men's group" writer, writing about his *former* views, reflects an upbringing that taught him that women possess some goods, goods that are highly valued, unequally distributed (in that he does not have rightful access to them), and unfairly safeguarded—that women are wrongly preventing him from having what he deserves.

Conversely, women may come to experience their bodies as not their own, and grant entitlement to others. One psychoanalyst writes about a woman who had been sexually abused as a child, and who did not feel that she owned her own genitals. In this case, a sense of entitlement was a developmental step forward.[53]

Turning Anger into Aggression

It seems appropriate in a review of the emotional underpinnings of moral development, emotions that must play some part in the blaming behaviors of perpetrators and victims, to leave anger for last. Anger, the experience of it, its expression, and its meaning, is perhaps the most gendered emotion in our culture. There is something about our culture that trains, transmits, and allows the expression of anger and aggression in boys but not in girls. Women who are notoriously "good" at detecting emotional cues from others are not so good at detecting anger in men. Men who have more trouble recognizing the facial expressions associated with other emotions detect anger better than women.[54] From early on, the socialization practices regarding anger are very different for men and women.

Mothers often ignore the angry expressions of girl babies and respond to the angry expressions of boy babies, thus reinforcing for boy babies the potential of anger to help them get what they want.[55] Thinking back to perpetrators of sexual violence for a moment, we assume that they get what they want through the threat of violence, even if they are not violent. We assume that, because they are bigger and more powerful than their victims, the threat of violence is present. But this is not the case with infants. For male babies the expression of anger is already working to get them what they need without the threat of violence.

Indeed, the frequency of angry outbursts in childhood is the same for girl toddlers and boy toddlers up until eighteen months, at which point it increases for boys and decreases for girls.[56] It is also interesting to keep in mind that this bifurcation occurs in the second year of life, notably, the time when a child's will emerges, and when self-control begins to become a developmental issue. As socialization and gender marking progress, girls report more facial masking of anger.[57] This masking is taught at a very young age, for mothers of two-year-old girls tend to imitate anger suppression expressions and reflect them back to the child, but mothers of two-year-old boys do not.[58] The masking of anger is of great interest if we consider the construction of emotion and agree that the management of emotion can also change the physiological experience of it.[59]

When toddlers' anger results in aggression, mothers and fathers are more likely to discourage the aggression in girls than in boys.[60] Girls aged four to six may find that their mothers are increasingly negative about their aggression and less negative about the aggression of boys of the same age.[61] Oddly enough, boys who tend to be aggressive may feel bad about themselves, but teachers may still perceive them as having a positive self-image.[62] Does responsibility get socialized right out of the child? One can almost imagine a responsible little boy, feeling bad about his aggressive impulses and acts, slowly being socialized to believe that this is an "OK" part of him, as he sees that adults view aggression as a sign of assertiveness and self-esteem. Some research shows that girls are more likely than boys to experience guilty feelings and to confess their transgressions.[63]

As with anger, gender differences in aggression emerge early.[64] Behavior intended to injure another person is more characteristic of males than females, and this conclusion is drawn from several data sources: popular lore, anecdote, crime and delinquency statistics, psychology laboratories, and naturalistic studies.[65] It has also been found that early childhood aggression correlates with adult antisocial and criminal behavior.[66]

The myths we have concocted with regard to the aggressiveness of boys and men have had biological as well as social roots. Most currently, an impressive body of research on the distorted thinking of aggressive boys has emerged. Aggressive preadolescent boys, for example, misattribute hostile intentions to others and attend to fewer interpersonal cues. We do not know, however, if these cognitive deficits are caused by the aggression or precursors to it.[67]

It seems safe to assume that for boys aggression is reinforced or rewarded. Indeed, the most aggressive boys tell researchers that they expect their aggression to be rewarded.[68] They minimize the effects their aggression has on their victims and exaggerate the benefits it will have for them.[69] For example, boys seem to expect that aggression will reduce adverse behavior in others.[70] Boys, more than girls, expect to feel less guilty and expect less disapproval from parents for aggression.[71] And boys are more likely than girls to believe that aggression is acceptable across a wide range of circumstances.[72]

One of the ironic benefits of aggression is that youths can use this social labeling of them as tough, wild, or aggressive as a means of creating a self.[73] Aggressive adolescents believe that aggression enhances their self-esteem.[74] It is not difficult to see why we sometimes associate aggression, anger, and entitlement and see a sense of entitlement as a way of upholding standards in a community.[75]

Entitlement, power, and status are thus linked to anger in our culture in such a way as to create a sense of angry moral indignation; but anger need not be associated with moral indignation. It is not necessarily "natural" to feel angry when one's rights have been violated. Fear might be an appropriate response, or depression. And within the subculture of women, anger often is linked to depression. But anger is the appropriate response to a violation of rights when one feels entitled to those rights—deserving of them—as if one ought to be treated better. In this way, as boys are taught the reaction of anger to violations of the self, they are also taught about their place in the gender hierarchy. Ronald De Sousa writes that, to the extent we are motivated to conform to gender roles in our emotions, men will experience anger as moral indignation, identifying with the social system to which they are more indebted than women, even if this social system is a gang or the more abstract institution of "masculinity."[76] Women will experience anger more as guilt-laden frustration with less self-righteousness; and their responses may not even be recognizable as anger at all.[77]

THE BATTLE OF THE SEXES

When boys and girls are asked to rate their approval of different kinds of aggression, girl to girl, girl to boy, boy to girl, and boy to boy, boys approve most highly of boys' aggression against girls, whereas girls approve least of this kind of aggression.[78] This reveals an implied acceptance among boys that girls are appropriate targets for aggression. The differential socialization of boys and girls in the expression of anger and aggression is disturbing, but even more disturbing is the thought that boys learn so early that girls make appropriate targets.

Barrie Thorne and Zella Luria, in studying the playground games and discussions of grade-school children aged nine to eleven, found that the play conveys three implicit rules of gender roles. First, girls and boys see each other as members of opposing groups; second, cross-gender contact is potentially sexual and contaminating; and third, girls are defined more sexually than boys. The authors noticed that girls are most likely to be named as the ones to give "cooties" or "germs," or to threaten boys with kissing. Girls' kisses and touch are considered especially contaminating.

The authors also noted the heterosexually charged rituals in which sexual scripts are played out and reinforced. For example, cross-gender chasing games get names, such as "boys chase girls" or "cooties," whereas same-gender chasing goes unnamed. This lends a certain importance to and recognition of cross-gender chasing. Thorne and Luria suggest that this is part of the process in which girls and boys are socialized to see each other as members of opposing groups.

Thorne and Luria also describe the interaction among boys as different from the interaction among girls. Boys' play reveals a pattern of building to an intense, aroused state in which rule transgression is particularly exciting. And if, in this state, they end up harming another, they are most likely to excuse their actions by saying, "When you get excited you do things you don't mean," thus using lack of emotional regulation as an excuse at a very early age. One imagines that some teachers accept and reinforce this excuse.[79]

Ruth Goodenough also noted such behavior in one of the two kindergarten classes she studied. In this particular class boys discriminated against girls regularly through the use of minor harassment and verbal put-downs. They exploited the belongings and territory of girls and spoke to them in tones of superiority. The girls, and even the teachers, were unable to stop the boys' behavior even though it was disturbing. One girl, Elena, who "gave it back" to the boys through defiance, was exempt from the harassment, but she seemed also to scare the other girls and be left out of their activities in the classroom. In general, the boys controlled one another by laughing at or deriding any behavior that seemed dependent or any friendly approaches to the girls.[80]

In a day-care center, similar peer-to-peer socializing behaviors were observed among toddlers. Beverly Fagot found that when boys engaged in a behavior or a game that was considered "girlish" and got a negative response from another boy, they would stop that behavior or game; but when boys engaged in typical male behavior, a negative response from a girl, peer, or teacher was not likely to stop them. Overall, the teachers' negative responses were much more effective with girl toddlers, and the negative responding of the other boys' was much more effective with boy toddlers.[81]

This in-depth look at both the external and the internal influences on the perpetrator and the victim can cause us to question how much responsibility each can truly be assigned. For the perpetrator, there may be several precursors to perpetration: in his early years, the lack of a moral base to turn to, the experience of isolation after shaming experiences, the harsh and abusive punishment for minor crimes, the neglect of any punishment for more serious crimes, or the demoralization of the self that leads him to search for aggrandizement. These kinds of experiences all seem to encourage the development of a character who may perpetrate, a character who will use his impulsivity to victimize. Our culture (parents and institutions such as school or church) may give permission for perpetration through several indirect means: the encouragement of aggressive behavior and approval of anger in boys, the construction of the sexes as "opposite" in battle, and hierarchical, and the excusing of such behavior as well as the tolerance of milder versions of it.

But despite overwhelming odds that a potential perpetrator will grow up to perpetrate and not see his victim as equal or as having rights, or even not see his victim at all, he still had the opportunity not to commit the act he committed. To envision a perpetrator as encumbered by the stresses of his upbringing and the failings of our culture does not mean that we have to take away his personhood. Each act still weaves and unweaves his character. A will emerges, and emerges early on, but character is shaped. It is shaped, undone, and "done in" by experiences like the monumental abuse that some parents and institutions in our society heap upon some children, but that kernel of will is also present. This is the kernel that we observe in the two-year-old's assertion "I am not you, I have different feelings, different states, different ideas"; and we observe it in the vigilant glances a child gives the important caregiver before transgressing. This is the will that proclaims, "I want to join, I want to be a part of this larger moral universe." It is personified choice.

To believe so totally in the overwhelming forces of evil as defining and making a person is to give up hope. And when we seek to treat perpetrators, when we invest them with our hope, we appeal to their wills, their observing egos, the part of them that can choose the good. If we give up on the idea of that separate self that is linked to the two-year-old's assertive "no," and woven through the demoralized self that seeks to assert itself destructively, and embedded in the terrible man who blames others for his character, then we can only lock up perpetrators, or burn down their houses, or stone them, or execute them. But if they have the will to change, if they see themselves as having the ability to make a choice, and if we can see them as having a choice, then we can provide the supports that step by step undo an old character and build a new one. Such supports include people who provide a moral base, education about sexism, and the opportunity to speak about shame and shameful experiences. After there is an acknowledgment of responsibility, and after we provide those all-important supports, then we can see real change.

Victims are made victims not only by horrendous abuse but also by social forces, the oppression and abuse and sexism that give the message that their bodies are not whole but composed of parts, parts that are primarily valued as commodities over which they have little presiding rights. And when society supports sexual offenses against them and suppresses victims' speech about their humiliation and anger, they are truly marked from the outside, stigmatized, and seen as victim from without as well as from within. Victims who attach so strongly to society's moral forces are betrayed by them, and their tendency to forgive so that they and their perpetrators will be able to return to the community is premature, growing out of an unwillingness to assert their selves and their rights.

When a perpetrator says, "Oh, my God, what have I done!" and when a victim grabs hold of a perpetrator's arm and screams into his face, "How dare you!" then everything is overturned. How do we achieve this remarkable switch? As we will see in Chapter 6, changing the victim depends on changing the perpetrator.

FORGIVENESS AND PUNISHMENT

6

Should victims forgive their perpetrators? Or, for that matter, should we as a society forgive perpetrators? and if so, when? Forgiveness evokes the same extreme responses as blaming. When faced with the horrible crime of a sex offender, a man who sexually abused many of the children in the parish over which he was in charge, or a violent sex offender who left his rape victim for dead in the forest, people cry for vengeance, often believing that no punishment is harsh enough. When faced with the perpetrator himself, as a human being, possibly a father, possibly remorseful and even tearful, society may see the victim as harsh and unyielding if she doesn't forgive.

Irrespective of whether we *should* forgive perpetrators, is it healing for a victim to forgive her perpetrator? And for that matter, is forgiveness rehabilitative for perpetrators? In the Judeo-Christian tradition the capacity to forgive has been considered a virtue; priests, ministers, and rabbis alike preach that compassion should temper one's anger and desire for vengeance.[1] Christians have generally believed that we need to forgive for two reasons, in order to reform the wrongdoer, and because we ourselves need to be forgiven.[2] This latter reason is based on the conviction that we are all sinners, and is reflected in biblical quotations such as "He that is without sin among you, let him first cast a stone." Indeed, if a Christian forgives a wrongdoer who is not remorseful, who offers no apology nor any reparation, other Christians tend to regard this person as particularly praiseworthy.[3]

Some authors have argued for the therapeutic effects of forgiveness on the forgiver, their arguments sounding almost religious as they speak of the transformation or transfiguration that such forgiveness can provide. Therapy, which utilizes such phrases as "letting go," "working through," and "accepting," seems readily suited to the idea that forgiving is healing.[4] For instance, forgiving purportedly can provide a release from one's anger. And letting go of anger supposedly benefits one's health[5] and one's relationships.[6] Forgiveness can even be elevated to a form of therapy, as with one clinician who devised a cognitive-behavioral technique in which the patient practices forgiving those who have wronged him or her regardless of their offenses.[7]

But not all writers and philosophers have seen forgiveness in so positive a light. For example, Marx believed that Christianity encouraged the development of a meek and forgiving disposition to such an extent that Christians would tolerate oppression and call it a virtue.[8] And Nietzsche referred to forgiveness as sublimated resentment, insisting, unlike Freud, that sublimation was not so great an achievement and resentment even worse.[9]

Victims tend to show premature forgiveness just as readily as they blame themselves. Philosophers have pointed out that to forgive too easily shows a lack of self-respect.[10] Strawson argues that if we do not resent the violation of our rights, then we do not take our rights very seriously.[11]

But victims seldom see this point. When they find themselves unable to forgive, they sometimes feel even worse. The expectation to forgive, which may come from family members, society, or from within, is felt as an additional burden for victims, sometimes even a test, the failing of which leaves them feeling less adequate than before. "Why can't I be a good enough person to forgive this man?" one victim may ask. "I am so surly, and angry, and full of rage that I may deserve to be beaten," thinks another.

When victims do forgive, it can be self-defeating or self-negating. For example, if a victim forgives by telling herself that what the offender did was not so bad, she risks being blind to her own injuries or, in the very least, denying herself the respect and rights she deserves. Sometimes a victim might forgive simply because she feels that the power and responsibility to hold another accountable are just too burdensome; she is already encumbered by her own guilt, and so the responsibility of not forgiving and possibly "hurting" the perpetrator by denying him forgiveness can feel very wrong to her. A victim may forgive in an effort to feel superior to the perpetrator, to be "too good" as a kind of reaction against or an undoing of the feeling that she is too bad and very guilty. A victim also wants very much not to be at all *like* the perpetrator, and so she "dis-identifies" with the man who was angry and vengeful when he attacked her.

A victim may have more pure or altruistic reasons for forgiving. She may forgive in order to take care of her offender, a father or a brother perhaps, as she has taken care of him for years before. She also may empathize with the perpetrator whom she knows, and decide that she cannot bear to see him in jail or even frightened of going to jail. She might also feel for him in his shame and exposure. Having been the vehicle through which he expressed his own shamefulness, she deeply understands this sense of shame and his embarrassment. So the victim who loves her perpetrator may overempathize and neglect herself.

The therapist and author Bonnie Burstow writes of sexually abusive fathers who ask their daughters to forgive them, to show empathy and compassion, and to help them in dealing with their guilt and remorse. She argues that their pleas for forgiveness are in effect similar to the incest itself, an example of "covert incest." By asking for forgiveness, these fathers once again treat their daughters as someone special, the only one who can help them with this special problem, a savior. In so doing, they are asking their daughters to take care of them again. A victim, Burstow warns, is not the proper source of help for her perpetrator.[12] Instead of begging for forgiveness, a perpetrator might plead with a victim, "How can I take care of you? Can I pay for your therapy? Is there anything you need to know from me about the abuse? What can I do to help?" To a victim, this other-centered plea feels very different from the self-centered appeal for forgiveness.

Several family therapists have taken to working with entire families including the incestuous fathers in an effort to keep families together. Cloe Madanes, for example, describes a sixteen-step therapy process during which the father or other incest perpetrator gets down on his knees and begs forgiveness from his victim until the victim and the other family members believe he is sincere. On the one hand, it may be very important to a daughter to hear this from her father (an admission of guilt, his remorse, his worry); on the other hand, the expectation of forgiveness or even the subtle pressure that a "good" daughter would forgive her father seems too great to place on a child, and especially on a child who has been victimized. It creates a dynamic where the father appears to be the warm, loving one, the daughter the cold withholder, even though Madanes warns, "There should be no pressure on the victim to forgive." Burstow writes, "By treating forgiveness as necessary, we effectively pathologize anger, close down the survivor's own process, and reinforce societal messages."[13]

In the case of battered women, forgiveness is one part of the whole "abusive cycle."[14] After the violent episode, after he has beaten her, bruised her, or bloodied her face, the batterer is extremely remorseful and begs forgiveness, trying to make reparations any way he can but, in the end, not changing his behavior to prevent the abuse from happening again. Women who purportedly suffer from Battered Woman's Syndrome forgive their partners repeatedly. This forgiveness contains elements of both loving empathy and lack of self-respect. Any good couples therapist knows that remorse from a habitually battering man means very little if it comes after the violence. The woman's belief, but not the wise therapist's, is that her forgiveness will transform him.

With regard to whether or not society should forgive perpetrators, we must first ask if society has that right. Does anyone have a right to forgive except the person who has been harmed?[15] Dryden wrote: "Forgiveness to the injured doth belong," but if it does, what do we do as a society if the injured forgive too readily?[16]

A distinction can be drawn between forgiveness and absolution. Forgiveness conveys that the victim no longer holds a grudge for the harm done her. It says something about the state of mind of the victim. It is not a retraction of moral judgment nor an escape from punishment—it does not mean that the perpetrator is no longer to blame for his actions.[17] And so, if forgiveness is not directed at blame, what is it directed at? Obviously, the victim's own resentment.[18]

As forgiveness tells us something about the state of mind of the victim, absolution may communicate something about the perpetrator, perhaps that he is no longer to be held responsible for his act, or that he has done enough penance, or that he no longer need face his "just deserts."[19] Forgiveness is a way of cleansing one's own soul or a way of restoring the relationship between wrongdoer and wronged. Absolution addresses the relationship between the wrongdoer and moral forces—the church, the state, the "authorities."

But while philosophers may distinguish between forgiveness and absolution, *we* might not really differentiate. What difference does it make cognitively, emotionally, and culturally whether we forgive or absolve? In practice, forgiveness and absolution are often confused; forgiveness is often felt and talked about as a kind of absolution. Why else do perpetrators seem to be able to demand forgiveness from another person? Why would they want it? If forgiveness were only about the victim's state of mind, why would a perpetrator make a claim, demand, or request for it? Because it pains him so to see his victim in the sorry state of resentment? Probably not. Forgiveness must have some meaning to the perpetrator, and not just to the victim, or perpetrators would not demand it. And if forgiveness did not mean something to or affect a perpetrator, why would we judge someone harshly if she did not forgive when we think she ought to have? If forgiving affected only the state of mind of the victim we would see her as unfortunate and not harsh enough. It must also have some meaning to society whether a victim forgives or not. Thus forgiveness is not the same as absolution, not to perpetrators and not to society, whether or not victims perceive it to be so.

Forgiveness may be used by victims, perpetrators, and society as a way to avoid blaming. As discussed in Chapter 1, we have great difficulty maintaining a blaming stance, and this may interfere with perpetrators' accountability. How can we reconcile the problem that to be blamed may be good for perpetrators, but to be blaming may not feel or be good for victims? The answer is by focusing on the perpetrator, not on the victim nor her self-blaming stance. When we focus on blaming perpetrators, we put aside questions of whether victims or society should forgive them, asking instead whether perpetrators should forgive themselves, whether they should indeed beg for forgiveness. When a perpetrator asks to be forgiven, he acknowledges that his violations are to be resented—he, we hope, repudiates his act.[20] By expecting this acknowledgment from perpetrators we help them to focus on *their* responsibility, leaving forgiveness to be dealt with at some later time, quite possibly the very distant future.

PUNISHMENT

Blaming is one thing, punishment another. And pure retribution is unsavory because though we might want to blame a perpetrator fully and advocate his taking responsibility for his acts, we might also feel uncomfortable seeking revenge and intentionally making him suffer. Arguments against punishment for the sake of punishment (retribution) claim that first, it does not do any good; second, there is no objective way for anyone to determine what kind of punishment an offender deserves; third, there is no such thing as responsibility in the grand scheme of things; and fourth, we all are "sinners" and so are in no position to punish.[21]

Retribution is only one of three basic ways that punishment has been justified.[22] Ungracefully called retributivism, this belief claims that certain people deserve punishment regardless of whatever good it may bring about.[23] Retributivists believe that guilty people should suffer.

The second justification is utilitarian and stipulates that punishment must have beneficial effects. These beneficial effects can focus on the reform of the wrongdoer, the protection of society, the deterrence of crime, or even, and more subtly, the communication of rules to the society. But utilitarians have argued that deliberately hurting another person is wrong unless it leads to some greater good. The third justification comes from those who believe that guilty parties should suffer simply because they have committed a wrong, but also that the suffering of the punished should have beneficial effects.

Retributivism has recently become increasingly popular, undoubtedly as an assertion of power and control over the helplessness we feel when faced with growing crime rates. Retributivism may also be an expression of vengeance, pure and simple, unconcerned with reform, since the prevailing opinion now is that punishment does not deter criminals, especially not sex offenders.

But if punishment has not worked well to deter sex crimes or to reform sexual offenders, what of its other purposes? One of the strongest arguments for punishment emphasizes that it has the ability to communicate something about social values in a broad and explicit way.[24] In punishing a sexual offender or a man who batters his wife, we communicate to him, to ourselves, and to the community that what he did was wrong. Whether or not punishment changes actual perpetrator behavior, this potential to communicate several broad messages reaches beyond the area of individual improvement. In the very least, punishment defines a sexual offense as wrong. Punishment through imprisonment gives "material and symbolic expression to the spiritual separation created by the crime."[25] It allows us to believe, albeit at times hypocritically, that we as a community are separate from the wrongdoer, and that he, through his acts, has severed an important and necessary connection. Punishing also says to a sex offender that we want him to suffer the pain of remorse, and to repent.[26] It is a moral comment on a person's soul and an aim to reform the offender spiritually.[27]

The perpetrator's punishment may also communicate something to the victim, although at present it seems as if punishment and adjudication often ignore victims' injuries. The criminal justice system emphasizes an abstract injury to society and leaves victims on their own, and with considerable expense, to bring separately a civil suit for damages. Victims are usually reluctant to enter into this process because they are not thinking about their injuries in terms of money, nor do they seek repayment of any kind.[28] (And it may be that only when some incest victims began to look at their suffering in terms of "damages," bringing civil suits against their perpetrators, that groups like the False Memory Syndrome Foundation began organizing.) It is my experience that victims are primarily looking for some larger group, some human company to join them in labeling what happened to them as wrong and to acknowledge that they have been injured.

One particular case in Canada shows the court's failure to take into account the injuries of the victim. Giles Renaud, a Canadian attorney, has written about *R. v. M.,* in which a twelve-year-old boy sexually abused his sister who was six years younger than he and continued to do so for "many years" after that.[29] The victim filed a complaint some ten years after her brother had moved away from the family. The brother was initially sentenced to two years in prison, but the court changed its mind. The court saw her brother as "self-rehabilitated" because there was no evidence of any further abuse. (One wonders about his "self-rehabilitation" given that the man's own lawyers argued that he might regress and abuse again *if* he were to be punished!) The court also took into consideration how young the man was when he started abusing his sister and the fact that his wife and children were now financially dependent on him. So the court overturned a two-year prison sentence and made it a two-year "home detention" probation period.

This change in sentencing does not sound altogether unreasonable, until viewed in light of the fact that the man did not plead guilty and did not express remorse. But these facts did not seem to have an impact on the judge, who wrote in his opinion: "While he (the offender) has exhibited little remorse, the trial judge found him as a person who, despite having difficulty expressing emotions, was in fact remorseful." But if this offender were truly remorseful, why didn't he try to prevent further harm to his sister by pleading guilty and not making her go through the trial?[30]

Do legal systems make it so difficult to express remorse that a judge can only *assume* its presence? The author of the article suggests that a court who takes into account victims' points of view might allow perpetrators who confess their wrongdoing, or feel remorse, and who seek therapy and forgiveness, to escape substantial jail sentences, with the understanding that remorse of this kind would have therapeutic benefits to victims.

Punishment can communicate something important to the victim. Although it does not erase the crime nor the injury, it pronounces social opinion about her relative responsibility, proclaims that what happened to her was wrong, validates her rights, and thus allows her the luxury of not having to overstate her own rights and her own suffering. This is not to say that sex crimes are merely crimes against victims—they are also crimes against society. It is very important for society to begin to see itself as harmed by these crimes against women. And if rape, sexual abuse, and battering of women were to be considered fundamental crimes against society, we would find less ambiguity about punishing perpetrators. But there is ambiguity. Women and children are no longer seen as the property of their husbands and fathers, which of course is a good thing, but because of this change, it is sometimes hard for men to see the rape of a woman as an offense that harms them too. In my experience, it is the more conservative or sexist father who will feel the most violent rage against the perpetrator who abuses his daughter, as if he himself were personally injured. And sometimes these men will find their own harm greater than that inflicted on their daughters. Frequently men and the institutions they embody seem to find it difficult to see the *offense* in rape, abuse, or battering when it is no longer a specific offense against *them*.[31] It may be because of this distance between the lawmakers (men) and the crime that men find it difficult to conceptualize these offenses as crimes against the state; this may also explain why they sometimes are adjudicated so poorly.

Perhaps it is better not to enlist men into the victim category and to refer to these offenses as crimes against girls and women—not individuals per se, but the "class" of girls and women. Perhaps instead of trying to conceptualize these crimes in the broader context of individual rights, we grab hold of the idea that these are specific crimes against a group, in this case, women—indeed, all women who are made fearful by these crimes and whose freedoms and rights are diminished by the necessity of extra protection. It may also be important for women to have a special say in terms of what would be protective for them, what can be considered proper penance for these crimes, and what kind of repayment is necessary to individuals and to women in general.

In summary, punishment could do two things and do them well: punishment can deliver the message to perpetrator and victim that what the offender did was wrong. It could also provide an opportunity to reform the perpetrator. But for punishment to reform the wrongdoer, there has to be a chance for repentance and a chance for reparation.

Even with children, "time-outs" have little impact unless combined with supports that help children use their "time-outs" constructively.[32] Isolation does not in and of itself bring about self-reflection. The opportunity for reparation is the support missing from punishment as it is now administered, a support that acknowledges the perpetrator's actual connection to his community and attempts to reconnect him. Just as shame, when it is exposed, holds the opportunity of reconnecting to his community the shameful person who has isolated himself, making reparation offers the chance to avoid more problems that result from the isolation of imprisonment.[33] It assists in the self-reflection that underlies the act of penance.

REPENTANCE, REFORM, AND MAKING REPARATIONS

Repentance, reform, and reparation make sense on so many levels: perpetrators are often returned to the community after they have served out their prison sentences, and so few sex offenders are ever brought into the criminal justice system at all.[34] But how to achieve these three noble goals is another question. Whereas punishment on its own offers few opportunities for change within the perpetrator, rehabilitation programs look promising. Rehabilitation programs in prisons offer treatment in the form of sex education, empathy training, assertiveness training, sexism education, thought stopping, anger management, and other behavioral techniques, but the outcome of these programs is still mixed, and many directors of *juvenile* treatment programs in correctional institutions think that the best we can hope for is "to lengthen the time between offenses and reduce the seriousness of the behavior."[35] They stress "management, not cure" and the need for "long-term follow-up."[36]

Every person who treats perpetrators deals first with the issue of denial. And the perpetrators' denial and minimization of their deeds are frightening since we optimistically try to think of prison as a place for repentance and reform. But we need to find a way to provide better means for perpetrators to repent and reform. Ironically, while courts, the law, and the police seem to weigh in heavily on the side of blame, they offer perpetrators inadequate opportunities to take responsibility, become penitent, and make reparations.

How Important Is Feeling Sorry?

I have heard of several perpetrators who have admitted their wrongs to their victims in private, but have lied about and denied their offenses in the more public spheres of the courts. Somehow I find this more hopeful than the cases of perpetrators who have convinced themselves that they have done no wrong. Are these perpetrators simply avoiding punishment, or are there other ways in which the legal and criminal systems discourage the expression of guilt and remorse? Punishment should not work in such a way as to invite denial. It should invite remorse, penance, self-reflection. Without these acts and emotions, further reparation is meaningless.

Earlier I argued that remorse was cheap and easy—and alone, it is. Nigel Walker has also argued that remorse is different from repentance. In a state of remorse the wrongdoer may feel regret and shame, but the offender who repents must renounce his way of thinking and living. Walker points out that "remorse may gradually lose its *agenbite,* and eventually become no more than a remembered discomfort. Repentance must be kept up."[37]

What would be enough guilt for any particular offense, enough remorse, say, for a sex offender? Currently we get too much "shallow, easily obtained self-absolution for a horrible violation of another."[38] Michael S. Moore asks himself what it would feel like if *he* were to have smashed open the skull of another human being. Considering this image, he answers, "I would feel guilty unto death." Anything less than this would be too little.[39] Even if one were drunk at the time, or under the influence of some drug that changed one's personality, even if one were so justifiably rageful that it was difficult to control oneself, feeling guilt would be the most sane and human response. Walker adds that it is "elitist" and "condescending" not to grant wrongdoers the same responsibility you would grant yourself. If you were to believe that killing another human being would leave you feeling "guilty unto death," you must expect that same guilt in perpetrators.

But let us return to the state of mind of the offender, whose tendency to absolve himself seems especially suspect. If he committed an offense against another, and tried to make reparations for his crime, and then feels that these reparations were enough, we might judge that he does not feel sufficiently guilty. It is safe to say that the perpetrator is in no position to determine how much guilt is enough.

The irony of perpetrator remorse is that if a perpetrator actually did feel guilt very forcefully and rearranged his life so as to make reparations on a long-term basis to those whom he injured, he would have to be seen as *not* the same person who committed the original crime, and thus so changed and reformed that he need not show lifelong guilt and self-punishment. Amelie Rorty uses the phrase "character" or "agent regret" to differentiate regret over who one has become (a person who could do such a thing) from regret over one's acts (that which you, an otherwise decent person, did). Only remorse that addresses who one has become seems to truly reflect taking responsibility for one's crimes.[40]

The truly repentant person thus paradoxically "severs himself from his act" by taking full responsibility for it.[41] Responsibility is the key to rehabilitation for several reasons, the most practical of which is that offenders who do not take responsibility for their crimes, or who blame their victims, have a higher recidivism rate.[42] In the words of one imprisoned sex offender, "We come in here justifying everything we ever did wrong. But when we have to look at ourselves as perverts, rapists, and crooks, it becomes clear how ugly we really are. We get fed up with the things we have done, the way we think, the way we act. We begin to change because we can't stand to stay so messed up."[43]

Reparation is not something that happens quickly, by writing a check or making some phone calls. Rather, it is much akin to the rebuilding of character; it is done gradually and over time. The offender, who has realized whom he has actually injured, needs to take not a "law and order" perspective, but one that recognizes sexism and makes reparation to that particular group in society: women.[44]

The Undoing of Bad Character by Good Deeds

Just as children need help to become mature moral agents, so do offenders. This is not to say that they are or even resemble children, but to say that the development of morality is a process that, if gone awry, can be repeated later. It is wrong to think that an approach to punishment that emphasizes perpetrators' individual responsibility means that the offenders should be left on their own, alone with their conscience, to either rot or "self-rehabilitate." They need support, and although many people have been disappointed with the results of rehabilitation, it may be the only way for perpetrators to avoid repeating their offenses.[45]

Think of reparation as a key to rehabilitation. Reparation both embodies repentance and reconnects the offender to the community from which he alienated himself. And reparation can be specifically directed toward women as the community whose harms offenders need to take note of, the community they need to see. If society sees that women have been harmed by these crimes, we may then seek and codify ways for perpetrators to make reparation in the form of good works that benefit women directly. Hard labor used to be a sentence handed down to prisoners, as if, according to the American work ethic, this labor could make a better man out of each prisoner, or simply keep him busy—"Idle hands are the devil's work." But if prisoners were to be expected to work hard in ways that were useful to battered women's movements, to improving the lives of women and children (the very people whose lives they have harmed in a broad sense by their crimes against society), these men would reconnect not only to society and the hoped-for values of society, but also to the very people whom they have harmed. Such good work could at its best reinforce nonsexist values, provide education, and rebuild character.

Prisoners left in isolation with no opportunity to make reparations and no chance for rehabilitation would only be serving time. More important, the present prison system often leaves them alone with their behaviors and fantasies, thus recreating the "bad" parent of early years through whose neglect or abuse the child began to make those choices consistent with perpetrator behavior. Given the difficulty in changing a human being, we cannot expect that suffering, or prison, or therapy alone will work. But isolation from the community can only do more harm.

It is no wonder that, with little opportunity to self-reflect and make amends within a supportive community, many prisoners turn to God. We sometimes laugh at criminals who are "born again," thinking that religion offers an easy way to remake themselves or even absolve themselves of their crimes. But how dare we judge this turning to God so harshly when we offer no others to turn to? For some, there is no one to make reparation to except God, no one who will hear their shame and remorse, and no other way to rebuild character. If the prisoner seeks the "other's" watchful eye, the only "other" he may find is God.

Reconnecting Offenders to a Community

There need to be opportunities other than religion for offenders to make reparation, other ways for them to attempt to belong to society. Steven Schulhofer writes that the criminal justice system has rejected a model of caring and connection because there "cannot be a genuine community of interest between the public at large and the offender who resorts to violence."[46] But this cannot be true, not even for sex offenders and victims of sex crimes. The criminal justice system and women's advocates may pretend that the connection between us and perpetrators does not exist because they prefer the adversarial struggle; but women victims know all too well of the connections between the offender and his community. The offenders are, in fact, women's husbands, boyfriends, brothers, sons, friends. They are not the "stranger out there," but the men among us in a sometimes scary but very real sense.

Indeed, the rehabilitation programs that seem to work depend heavily on relationships. Group therapy has been a promising form of treatment because the relationships formed are both supportive and confrontational. In groups, offenders are not isolated; it is difficult to remain self-centered or secretive without being confronted by another group member. Interestingly enough, in one successful program, the men who graduated were asked to name what it was about the program that helped them not to reoffend. They were given choices regarding aspects of the treatment such as the sex education or the empathy training. The majority believed that their nonoffending was due more to the way they were treated in the program than to its content.[47]

Others have remarked that the "relationship an offender builds will ultimately determine the outcome of the treatment."[48] But can you force a relationship where there is none, or create a new one in the ashes of the old? This is the important question in attempting to reconnect the offender to the community of women.

The thought has been attributed to Kant that to penalize

someone is to sacrifice him to the interests of others, and that we must never treat a person as only a means to an end.[49] Although we can understand the dilemma of using one person for the benefit of another, we also see that we sacrifice some people to the interests of others regularly in our society, in acknowledged ways (through taxes) and in ways that we do not acknowledge (sacrificing the poor to the rich in capitalist countries). Women know both the oppression of being coerced to sacrifice one's own goals to the visions of others and the joy in choosing to sacrifice the self, at times, for the good of others. Sacrifice is not altogether a bad thing.

Battered women's shelters, victim assistance programs, and clinics that treat victims of men's violence at very low fees are extremely underfunded and overburdened. At one clinic, in Doylestown, Pennsylvania, the turnover rate for counselors is high. They get too little pay and supervision. Unable to see their clients more than twelve times, they are frustrated by the fact that this is rarely enough.[50]

There must be some way incarcerated sex offenders could be offered the chance to do work that would educate them about sex offenses and at the same time help these shelters and victim assistance programs. Entrepreneurs would not want to invest in prisons, privatize them, as it were, if there were not ways to use the resources there to make money. Still, labor unions have objected vociferously to the prospect of eliminating jobs for nonoffending individuals. Offenders could work for shelters and victims' services centers, where most of the work is voluntary, and thus not take jobs away from lawful citizens. This would have the added benefit of being meaningful work, since it is connected to the crimes they committed.

And who better to lead these programs and privatize prisons for sex offenders than women? Who better to educate about sexism and empathy? Some may argue that women may be the worst choice to run these programs since they are the ones who have forgiven their battering husbands and boyfriends, believed the lies of the fathers of their children, and taken on their men's crimes as their own. But so far, the men who run these citadels of reform and penitence have done a poor job of protecting women's interests. As the veteran sex offender treatment provider William Marshall concludes, "If women were in the positions of political power to decide whether or not to treat sex offenders, we would have extensive programs all over this continent and they would have been in operation for years."[51]

EPILOGUE

When faced with the question of what to do about victims' self-blame, I am tempted to say do nothing, absolutely nothing, because victims are already convinced that they need to do something to improve themselves; they already take on too much responsibility. Ironically, to advance one more piece of advice, one more talk show, or one more popular self-help book to women who have been victims is to imply that they should be taking even more responsibility.

But I also don't want to follow in the footsteps of those who oversympathize with women (seeing them as models of responsibility and caretaking), and tell them not to blame themselves. Their self-blame sometimes is healing, and in some part appropriate.

Perhaps the most important message should be directed toward those who would help and identify with victims. Victims' sense of overresponsibility, though sometimes harmful and other times pathological, should not be dismissed. At its core are real moments of responsibility, times when they made poor choices, foolish decisions. Almost every victim, except those of the most horrendous crimes, will speak of these moments. It is crucial in working with victims to tease out the accurate level of responsibility, to work away at the very odd self-destructive tendency of victims to assume more responsibility than they should.

It is also important to remember that this tendency to accuse oneself comes from two sources: the individual herself and society; victims who take on too much of the blame are reflecting the long-standing social response to victimization. But, as we as a society work on the way we see perpetrators, and focus our attention on perpetrators' responsibility for the evils they commit, victims may find some relief from overblaming themselves.

Although there is no ultimate protection from being victimized, there are certain ways of being and reacting that may be more self-protective than others. Two controversial questions, should a woman resist, and should an explicit "no" be a requirement for nonconsent of sexual intercourse, are currently being debated. The data are mixed about resistance, and the answer to the first question may actually depend on the kind of rapist, father, or husband a woman is dealing with.[1] But resistance should not be so narrowly defined as to mean only physical force. There are multiple strategies of resistance, and the more a woman is prepared to use all of them, the better her chances of protecting herself. The underlying notion for all of these strategies, however, is the belief that *this should not be happening to me.*

With regard to the second question, a law that sees a woman's silence as a lack of consent may encourage the view of women as passive and helpless—can't we even expect a simple "no" from her? But at the same time I don't support the recent Pennsylvania Supreme Court decision which claims that a woman needs to have said "no" for "it" to be rape. This would encourage male entitlement, the feeling that a man may take what he wants unless he is told no. I could use the analogy with "taking" an item from a grocery store, but I would not want to further objectify the woman in my example. A man who rapes, even on a date, has many opportunities to know that the rape is non-consensual, even if the victim does not explicitly say "no."

Who, at present, sees victimization accurately? Who among us can apportion blame correctly? Victims apportion too much to themselves; therapists too little to victims. Perpetrators assume too little blame. And we as a society blame victims and perpetrators either too much or not enough. When we blame perpetrators too little, the self-blame of victims is supported and encouraged; when we blame victims too much, perpetrators need not admit responsibility. When we blame perpetrators too much, they lose the much-needed support to help them in their process of rebuilding their character, reforming, and making reparations. When we blame victims too little, we make them too small as individuals and reinforce the passivity that was inherent in the experience of victimization.

Nietzsche argued against seeing evil: "Let us not become darker ourselves on their [criminals'] account, like all those who punish others and feel dissatisfied. Let us sooner step aside. Let us look away."[2] In *Genealogy* he writes that deserved punishment is a "title to cruelty": "It can give us the pleasure of being allowed to vent [our] power freely upon one who is powerless, the voluptuous pleasure of doing evil for the pleasure of doing it, the enjoyment of violation."[3] According to Nietzsche, our envy and jealousy of the offender for his acts are at the foundation of retribution.[4]

But we cannot look away. Seeing violence is important because it mimics the good parent, the first "other" through which the morals of the culture as well as the morals of interpersonal relationships are transmitted. Within the dialogue between parent and child, morals emerge, are first understood and reinvented. Because of the eyes of the "other," the first moral emotions arise in the form of guilt and shame and self-consciousness; indeed, without the vision of the other, self-consciousness is unattainable.

Sartre spoke of the Other as the indispensable mediator between myself and me: "I am ashamed of myself as *I appear* to the Other."[5] He describes the sadist who is confounded by the fact that his victim has seen him: "The sadist discovers his error when his victim *looks* at him; that is, when the sadist experiences the absolute alienation of his being in the Other's freedom."[6]

Looking away supports the isolation of the adolescent who first begins to offend. Harry Stack Sullivan warned us of this isolation. In isolation, what he referred to as the "lust dynamism," an antiquated term for the powerful sexual feelings a teenager can experience, remains unformed.[7] If we leave our adolescents isolated, they are likely to resolve these feelings in nonsocial, destructive, or self-destructive ways. And if we look away from adolescents' fantasies and actual offenses, we imitate the earlier "other" who isolated the youth and made the search for social guidance too difficult.

It is in this respect that our fear of sex education has disastrous consequences for youth. The problem is that sex is a social act unable to be discussed socially. For society not to take sex on as a topic of overt socialization is at once to deny the social aspect of it and also to leave youths alone with their questions and sometimes absurd ideas about it.[8] Lucky the adolescent who can in the very least exchange jokes, sexual stories, or misinformation about sexuality with his gang or her best friend. The isolated adolescent has no community at all in which to learn about or engage in dialogue about sex, except the "community" of pornography, 1-900 numbers, and other asocial or antisocial versions.

We need to recognize sexuality earlier in life and provide a place where deviant or harmful sexual impulses can be discussed. We cannot look away from the dangerous sources of misinformation, hidden and shameful sources; and we must provide alternative sources. It is not simply or only that pornography is wrong. Nor is it crucial that it be outlawed. There simply have to be other, overwhelmingly available sources of information and healthy social and delight-filled discussion of sexual impulses at an early age.

Sexually offensive impulses, once they are acted upon by a confused adolescent or another aggressive individual, may become exposed. Although exposure causes shame and is indeed the very thing that offenders avoid most, it can cure and bring relief.

Kenneth Wolpin has done research that shows a high inverse association between violence rates and the likelihood of being identified.[9] If someone is watching, you probably won't do it. But this is not particularly true with regard to date rape even though there is a high chance of being identified, and that is because the crime is not seen, sometimes not seen by the actual perpetrator because of his distortions, and often not seen by our society.

Seeing has been described as the crucial feminist statement against violence: "Women's vision may be seen as an act of resistance in its own right," a guide to "concrete resistance."[10] This extends from seeing the possibility of rape and sexual violence in the smaller acts of men around us, and rightfully being suspicious and careful, to seeing the actual violence and exploitation of the women and girls around us. Seeing is a choice.

The more a perpetrator takes on the responsibility for his acts, the less the victim will need to. And as the perpetrator assumes more responsibility, he becomes less abhorrent. But even if the offender takes on the responsibility for his harm and violence, the victim may still self-blame, and this is not always a bad thing.

Self-reflection will often lead to some self-blame. And for victims of violence in which the coercion was not so utterly total as to reduce them to mere objects, a proportion of blame could be theirs. When we rush out to stop the victim-blaming it is not useful or accurate to blame everyone *but* the victim; in so doing we thwart the very impulse of change, self-assertion, and courage that underlies recovery. But we also must remember that when we apportion some blame to the victim, this cannot diminish our holding perpetrators accountable in a realistic and full way. The capacity and willingness to look inward, to focus on one's self and to find one's acts defining of oneself is noble, but in its exaggerated sense (as in the overactive sense of victims' blame) it leaves victims with little self-respect. By contrast, this capacity would serve perpetrators well.

There is great variety in the perpetration of abuse. Not all abusers are predators who leave their brutalized victims to die in the woods. Victims themselves were coerced to varying degrees and had varied opportunities to take action. In all but situations involving extreme coercion or extreme youth we cannot completely excuse victims for their passivity, however much we would like to, for to do so would necessitate excusing the perpetrator of his impulsivity. Nor can we support a view that a victim is not responsible at all for her symptoms or any disorders that develop from the abuse or from her prior history or from the social response to her victimization. In excusing this kind of responsibility we would also be lending perpetrators a handy excuse: "I was poor," "My father abused my mother," "I was raped as a child." And we must expect of victims a good amount of resentment, for if they do not resent their victimization, their perpetrators, and society's part in it, they lend support to the perpetrators' excuses and send a message that such acts are forgivable.

My argument is largely one of balance: if we hold one side

responsible (by means of various excuses, myths, evidence, and other devices), then we need to look at the responsibility of the other side. To enhance the blaming of perpetrators and make them more accountable for their acts, we also need to look closely at victim responsibility. But those who had hoped at the beginning of this book to find the exaggerated, angry, vindictive victim-supporters getting their comeuppance may be disappointed. After a close analysis of victims and their reactions to their abuse, one sees them at times exaggerating their helplessness, symptoms, and reactions, but also at times exaggerating their responsibility and blameworthiness—taking more than their fair share of the blame. Needless to say this discussion about responsibility takes place in a context of sexism, public excusing of any behavior that can be given the name of a disorder, a willingness to see the self as easily thrown over and created anew. But the effects of context are not always unidirectional. By virtue of people's spontaneity and individuality, by the choices they make, contexts are indeed changed and shaped. It is for this part in the overall process between individuals and contexts that I hold victims responsible and blame perpetrators for their acts.

It is fashionable, under the paradigm of postmodernism, to argue that the "self" is not a constant, that it is a continuous process, a cohesion of narratives, or a foolish projection.[11] If we assume this position wholeheartedly, we are left merely with shells of people for whom insides are changeable and onto which moral standards cannot adhere. It is a premise of this book that blameworthiness requires personhood, the belief in persons as vehicles and representatives of moral values.

To hate or resent an offender is to "view him as a member of the moral community, only as one who has offended against its demands."[12] Jeffrie Murphy, following Hegel, speaks of a "right to be punished" that coincides with the right to be "regarded as a responsible agent."[13] Hatred too is a right, and a sign of a relationship with another person, quite the opposite of what we see in the novel *A Clockwork Orange* where the technique of classical conditioning is employed to make the lead character respond with revulsion to violence or violent thoughts. The problem with this technique is that, though it is successful in making the protagonist nonviolent, he can no longer enjoy his beloved Beethoven. In this behavioristic treatment, the humanity of the person and his relationship to others are ignored.[14]

C. S. Lewis, in his essay "The Humanitarian Theory of Punishment," wrote that "to be punished, however severely, because we have deserved it, because we ought to have known better, is to be treated as a human person made in God's image."[15] Perpetrators not only deserve blame but are *worthy* of it, in the fullest, most human sense of the word.

NOTES

ACKNOWLEDGMENTS

INDEX

NOTES

1 WHO IS TO BLAME?

1. In the Menendez trials, even though the judge did not leave open the possibility of acquittal (he gave the juries the choice of manslaughter, first- or second-degree murder), the two juries could not decide on a sentence, and the judge declared a mistrial.
2. It appears quite certain that Lorena Bobbitt had suffered multiple beatings and rapes by her husband over the course of their marriage. The last night that he raped her, after he had fallen asleep, in a moment of rage or panic, revenge or dissociation, she severed his penis. The jury acquitted her.
3. Tonya Harding is the Olympic figure skater who may have been part of a plan to maim her rival Nancy Kerrigan. Kerrigan was attacked and suffered an injury to her knee. Tonya had recently reconnected with her divorced husband, the person who planned the attack. He had abused her in the past, and her mother had been verbally abusive. Public sympathies were torn between the two skaters.
4. William Ryan, *Blaming the Victim* (New York: Vintage, 1971).
5. See Chapter 4 for a discussion of those people and organizations that are currently suggesting that sexual abuse is less prevalent than the public believes.
6. See an early paper by Lauretta Bender and Abram Blau, "The Reaction of Children to Sexual Relations with Adults," *American Journal of Orthopsychiatry* 7 (1937): 500–518.

7. See Philip Cushman, "Ideology Obscured: Political Uses of the Self in Daniel Stern's Infant," *American Psychologist* 46 (1991): 206–219.

8. See John Sabini and Maury Silver, "Emotions, Responsibility, and Character," in Ferdinand Schoemann, ed., *Responsibility, Character, and the Emotions* (Cambridge, England: Cambridge University Press, 1987).

9. I do turn to philosophers who have addressed more modern solutions to the combatibilist dilemma (how determinism and free will can coexist). Chief among these philosophers is Daniel Dennett, from whom I acquired the phrase I use often regarding the "kinds of" or "varieties of free will worth wanting." See Daniel D. Dennett, *Elbow Room* (Cambridge, Mass.: MIT Press, 1984).

10. Alan Wertheimer, *Coercion* (Princeton, N.J.: Princeton University Press, 1987).

11. This phrase is from Sara Smilansky, "Free Will and Being a Victim," *International Journal of Moral and Social Studies* 6 (1991): 19–32.

12. Although the defense attorneys attempted to make a case that the Menendez brothers and Lorena Bobbitt were, at the time, operating under the illusion that they were acting in self-defense, I do not think that the jurors believed this to be true. Instead, I think that they excused the defendants' behavior on the grounds that their prior abuse in some vaguer way incapacitated their free will.

13. It is tempting to treat the issue of blame simplistically, to say that, in fact, blaming is good and necessary and we should rid it of its weighty and unpleasing ambiguities. For example, we could throw out phrases such as "mutual accountability" and "taking responsibility" because they remove the sharpness of blame and deprive us of the emotion inherent in it. We could adopt the emotive language of the Far Right or the Moral Majority and speak of what is "right" and what is "wrong." For example, both groups call abortion "murder," whereas abortion rights advocates who may indeed see abortion as a kind of murder will not use that word because it uncomplicates a complicated issue. I have considered putting two bumper stickers side by side on my rear bumper, the one that states "Abortion stops a

beating heart," and the one that states "I support a woman's right to choose."

14. See June Tangney's work on the difference between guilt and shame; for example, June P. Tangney, Patricia Wagner, Carey Fletcher, and Richard Gramzow, "Shamed into Anger? The Relation of Shame and Guilt to Anger and Self-Reported Aggression," *Journal of Personality and Social Psychology* 62 (1992): 669–675.

15. Helen M. Lynd, "The Nature of Shame," in Herbert Morris, ed., *Guilt and Shame* (Belmont, Calif.: Wadsworth Publishing Co., 1971), p. 159.

16. Ibid., p. 180.

17. Richard A. Shweder, *Thinking through Cultures: Expeditions in Cultural Psychology* (Cambridge, Mass.: Harvard University Press, 1991).

18. These studies and others are summarized in Martin Seligman's popular book *Learned Optimism* (New York: Knopf, 1991).

19. Lenore Walker, *The Battered Woman Syndrome* (New York: Springer, 1984). Oddly enough, this very learned helplessness phenomenon, which explains why women might stay, does not explain their final violent act—killing their husbands. They do not look very helpless at that point.

20. E. Annie Proulx, *The Shipping News* (New York: Touchstone, 1993), p. 308.

21. But Seligman warns, of course, that these ways of thinking are *helpful* only for people who blame themselves too much and unrealistically.

22. Herbert Fingarette, *On Responsibility* (New York: Basic Books, 1967).

23. Howard Tennen and Glenn Affleck, "Blaming Others for Threatening Events," *Psychological Bulletin* 108 (1990): 209–232.

24. Fred Berlin, "Interviews with Five Rapists," *American Journal of Forensic Psychology* 5 (1987): 3–33.

25. Proulx, *The Shipping News,* pp. 217–218.

2 VICTIMS

1. See Wendy Kaminer, *I'm Dysfunctional You're Dysfunctional: The Recovery Movement and other Self-Help Fashions* (Reading, Mass.:

Addison-Wesley Publishing Company, Inc., 1992), and David Rieff, "Victims All?: Recovery, Co-dependency, and the Art of Blaming Somebody Else," *Harpers* (October 1991): 49–56.

2. Katie Roiphe's book *The Morning After: Sex, Fear, and Feminism on Campus* was published in the fall of 1993 (Boston: Little, Brown and Co.). Several critical reviews pointed out the research errors she made in stating her claims. See Katha Pollitt, "Not Just Bad Sex," *New Yorker,* October 4, 1993, pp. 220–224, and Susan Faludi, "Whose Hype?" *Newsweek,* October 25, 1993, p. 61.

3. Herbert Morris, "Introduction," in Herbert Morris, ed., *Guilt and Shame* (Belmont, Calif.: Wadsworth Publishing Company, Inc., 1971), p. 1.

4. See C. R. Snyder, Raymond L. Higgins, and Rita J. Stucky, *Excuses: Masquerades in Search of Grace* (New York: Wiley, 1983), for some excellent examples.

5. Howard Tennen and Glenn Affleck, "Blaming Others for Threatening Events," *Psychological Bulletin* 108 (1990): 209–232.

6. Ronnie Janoff-Bulman, *Shattered Assumptions: Towards a New Psychology of Trauma* (New York: The Free Press, 1992), pp. 76–77; Charles Figley, "From Victim to Survivor: Social Responsibility in the Wake of Catastrophe," in Elizabeth Waites, *Trauma and Its Wake: The Study and Treatment of Post-traumatic Stress Disorder* (New York: W. W. Norton, 1985), pp. 398–415.

7. Dale Miller and Carol Porter, "Self-blame in Victims of Violence," *Journal of Social Issues* 39 (1983): 139–152. In this article there is a note stating that information regarding the comfort a victim obtains in knowing about other people her perpetrator has abused can be found in Carol Porter, "The Interrelationship among Causal Attributions, Affect, and Coping in Battered Women," paper delivered at the Annual Meeting of the Canadian Psychological Association, Toronto, June 1981.

8. Anna Freud, *The Ego and the Mechanisms of Defense* (New York: International Universities Press, 1966).

9. Lenore Terr, *Too Scared to Cry* (New York: Basic Books, 1990). See pp. 39–251 for examples of post-traumatic play, and pp. 265–280

for examples of how the trauma is reenacted throughout the victims' lives in various ways. Freud also described such play as a mastery phenomenon in "Beyond the Pleasure Principle," in James Strachey, ed., *The Standard Edition of the Complete Psychological Works of Sigmund Freud*, vol. XVIII (London: The Hogarth Press, 1920/55).

10. Sigmund Freud, *Introductory Lectures on Psychoanalysis*, ed. James Strachey (New York: W. W. Norton, 1920–1966), p. 275.

11. Sigmund Freud, *Moses and Monotheism*, trans. Katherine Jones (New York: Knopf, 1939).

12. Melanie Klein was a psychoanalyst who wrote most powerfully of the infant's destructive wishes. In "Love, Guilt, and Reparation," found in *Love, Hate, and Reparation*, eds. Melanie Klein and Joan Riviere (New York: Norton, 1964), she describes the infant as raging against the frustrating "breast" or "mother," leading to a long-standing unconscious belief in one's badness and an equally strong unconscious desire to assuage one's guilt by making reparation.

13. Sigmund Freud, *Civilization and Its Discontents* (New York: W. W. Norton and Co., 1961).

14. Judith Herman, *Trauma and Recovery* (New York: Basic Books, 1992), p. 107; Philip Lichtenberg, personal communication, October 1993.

15. Lyn Abramson, Martin Seligman, and John Teasdale, "Learned Helplessness in Humans: Critique and Reformulation," *Journal of Abnormal Psychology* 87 (1978): 49–74; Aaron T. Beck, *Depression: Clinical, Experimental, and Theoretical Aspects* (New York: Harper and Row, 1967); and Aaron T. Beck, *Cognitive Therapy and the Emotional Disorders* (New York: International Universities Press, 1976).

16. Melvin Lerner, "The Desire for Justice and Reactions to Victims: Social Psychology Studies of Some Antecedents and Consequences," in Jacqueline Macauley and Leonard Berkowitz, eds., *Altruism and Helping Behavior* (New York: Academic Press, 1970); Melvin Lerner, *The Belief in a Just World* (New York: Plenum Press, 1980); Melvin Lerner and Dale Miller, "Just World Research and the Attributional Process: Looking Back and Ahead," *Psychological Bulletin* 85 (1978): 1030–1051.

17. Baruch Fischoff, "Hindsight = Foresight: The Effect of Outcome

Knowledge on Judgment under Uncertainty," *Journal of Experimental Psychology: Human Perception and Performance* 75: 288–299.

18. Ellen Langer, "The Illusion of Control," *Journal of Personality and Social Psychology* 32 (1975): 311–328.

19. Susan Sontag, *Aids and Its Metaphors* (New York: Farrar, Straus and Giroux, 1989).

20. Andrea Medea and Kathleen Thompson, *Against Rape* (New York: Farrar, Straus and Giroux, 1971), cited in Miller and Porter, "Self-blame in Victims of Violence."

21. Morton Bard and Dawn Sangrey, *The Crime Victim's Book* (New York: Basic Books, 1979).

22. Janoff-Bulman, *Shattered Assumptions*, p. 6. Earlier, Janoff-Bulman listed these three assumptions as (1) the belief in personal invulnerability; (2) the belief that the world is meaningful and comprehensible; and (3) the ability to view ourselves in a positive light. Ronnie Janoff-Bulman and Irene H. Frieze, "A Theoretical Perspective for Understanding Reactions to Victimization," *Journal of Social Issues* 39 (1983): 1–17, p. 3.

23. Janoff-Bulman, *Shattered Assumptions*, p. 62.

24. Tennen and Affleck, in "Blaming Others for Threatening Events," review the studies that show positive adaptations versus those that show negative ones.

25. Ronnie Janoff-Bulman and Linda Lang-Gunn, "Coping with Disease and Accidents: The Role of Self-blame Attributions," in Lyn Abramson, ed., *Social-personal Inference in Clinical Psychology* (New York: Guilford Press, 1989).

26. Patricia Frazier, "Victims' Attributions and Post-Rape Trauma," *Journal of Personality and Social Psychology* 59 (1990): 298–304.

27. Henry Murray, *Thematic Apperception Test Manual* (Cambridge, Mass.: Harvard University Press, 1943).

28. Lucy Gilbert and Paula Webster, *Bound by Love* (Boston: Beacon Press, 1982).

29. Herman, *Trauma and Recovery*, p. 69.

30. Gilbert and Webster, *Bound by Love*, p. 134.

31. Jo-Ann Kresten and Claudia Bepko, "Codependency: The Social

Reconstruction of Female Experience," in Claudia Bepko, ed., *Feminism and Addiction* (New York: The Haworth Press, 1992), pp. 49–66, quotation from p. 52.

32. The attention to women's overresponsibility can be seen in Carol Gilligan's *In a Different Voice* (Cambridge, Mass.: Harvard University Press, 1982), where this responsibility is discussed as a special characteristic of women that sometimes does not serve them well (as in the second stage she describes) if they neglect to see themselves as needing caretaking. The term "overresponsibility" comes from Kresten and Bepko's chapter on the co-dependency movement in *Feminism and Addiction* in which they attack the notion of women as "enablers" from a feminist perspective.

33. Herman, *Trauma and Recovery*, p. 103.

34. David Finkelhor, *Child Sexual Abuse: New Theory and Research* (New York: The Free Press, 1984).

35. Herman, *Trauma and Recovery*, p. 104.

36. Kim Scheppele and Pauline Bart, "Through Women's Eyes: Defining Danger in the Wake of Sexual Assault," *Journal of Social Issues* 34 (1983): 63–80.

37. Betty Bardige, "Reflective Thinking and Prosocial Awareness: Adolescents Face the Holocaust and Themselves," Ed.D. diss., Harvard Graduate School of Education, 1983.

38. Irene Frieze, "The Female Victim: Rape, Wife-beating, and Incest," in Gary VandenBos and Brenda Bryant, eds., *Cataclysms, Crises, and Catastrophes: Psychology in Action* (Washington, D.C.: American Psychological Association, 1987), pp. 109–146.

39. P. F. Strawson, *Freedom and Resentment and Other Essays* (New York: Harper and Row, 1974), pp. 2–3.

40. Finkelhor, *Child Sexual Abuse*, pp. 17–18.

41. Lenore Walker and Angela Browne, "Gender and Victimization by Intimates," *Journal of Personality* 53 (1985): 179–194.

42. Norma Costrich, J. Feinstein, Louise Kidder, Jeanne Marecek, and L. Pascale, "When Stereotypes Hurt: Three Studies of Penalties for Sex-role Reversals," *Journal of Experimental Social Psychology* 11 (1975): 520–530; Allen Israel, Pamela Raskin, Judith Libow, and

Marsha Pravader, "Gender and Sex-role Appropriateness: Bias in the Judgment of Disturbed Behavior," *Sex Roles* 4 (1978): 399–413.

43. Herman, *Trauma and Recovery*, pp. 76–95.

44. For a discussion of the defenses of Hedda, see Gloria Steinem, as quoted in R. Lacayo, "A Question of Responsibility," *Time*, February 13, 1989, p. 68, and Susan Schechter's interview in "The Hedda Conundrum," *MS.* (April 1989), pp. 54–66.

45. The Stockholm Syndrome resulted from a 1973 bank robbery in Sweden in which hostages developed a close identification with their captors and continued to express empathy even after their release. See Georges Gachnochi and N. Skurnik, "The Paradoxical Effects of Hostage-taking," *International Social Science Journal* 44 (1992): 224–235, and Irka Kuleshnyk, "The Stockholm Syndrome: Toward an Understanding," *Social Action and the Law* 10 (1984): 37–42.

46. Herman, *Trauma and Recovery*, p. 68.

47. Quoted in Elaine Hilberman, "Overview: The Wife-beater's Wife Reconsidered," *American Journal of Psychiatry* 137 (1980): 1336–1347.

48. Aristotle, *Nicomachean Ethics,* in R. M. Hutchins, ed., W. D. Ross, trans., *Great Books of the Western World,* vol. 9 (Chicago: Encyclopaedia Britannica, 1952), pp. 335–436; quotation is from p. 356.

49. Robert Nozick, *Anarchy, State, and Utopia* (New York: Basic Books, 1974).

50. This was a project headed by Carolyn Newberger on the long-term effects of childhood sexual abuse. As a postdoctoral fellow at the Family Violence Unit at Children's Hospital in Boston, I helped Dr. Newberger collect her data.

51. There are several excellent reviews of the long-term effects of child sexual abuse, beginning with Angela Browne and David Finkelhor, "Impact of Child Sexual Abuse: A Review of the Research," *Psychological Bulletin* 99 (1986): 66–77, to the more recent and comprehensive Joseph Beitchman, Kenneth Zucker, Jane Hood, Granville DaCosta, Donna Akman, and Erika Cassavia, *Child Abuse and Neglect* 16 (1992): 101–118.

52. Terr argues that PTSD needs to refer to a one-time stressor. See

Naomi Breslau and Glenn Davis, "Posttraumatic Stress Disorder: The Stressor Criterion," *Journal of Nervous and Mental Disease* 175 (1987): 255–264, and the commentaries that follow for a discussion pertaining to DSM-III; also see Jonathan Davidson and Edna Foa, "Diagnostic Issues in Posttraumatic Stress Disorder: Considerations for the DSM-IV," *Journal of Abnormal Psychology* 100 (1991): 346–355, for a more recent analysis.

53. American Psychiatric Association, *Diagnostic and Statistical Manual-III R* (Washington, D.C.: American Psychiatric Association, 1987), pp. 247–248.

54. In a study of ninety-eight physically and sexually abused children who were hospitalized, the rate of PTSD among the physically abused was 20 percent and the rate among the sexually abused was 43 percent; see Balkozar Adams, Betty Everett, and Effie O'Neal, "PTSD in Physically and Sexually Abused Psychiatrically Hospitalized Children," *Child Psychiatry and Human Development* 23 (1992): 3–8. A study of battered women at a shelter found that almost half of the thirty subjects interviewed had PTSD; see Ghole West, Adelaide Fernandez, James Hillard, Marry Schoof et al., "Psychiatric Disorders of Abused Women at a Shelter," *Psychiatric Quarterly* 61 (1990): 295–301. In a retrospective study of fifteen hundred nurses, of the fifty-four who had been sexually abused as children, only 4 percent met the criteria for PTSD; see Evan Greenwald and Harold Leitenberg, "PTSD in a Nonclinical and Nonstudent Sample of Adult Women Sexually Abused as Children," *Journal of Interpersonal Violence* 5 (1990): 217–228. A study comparing sexually abused, physically abused, and nonabused child inpatients found the rates of PTSD to be 21 percent, 7 percent, and 10 percent respectively; see Esther Deblinger, Susan McLeer, Marc Atkins, Diana Ralphe et al., "Post-traumatic Symptoms in Sexually Abused, Physically Abused, and Nonabused Children," *Child Abuse and Neglect* 13 (1989): 403–408. Finally, in a study of 295 women who had been victimized, rape victims had a lifetime prevalence of 57 percent, although only 16 percent currently suffered from PTSD, while 33 percent of those molested in childhood had PTSD at some time, and only 8 percent

were currently diagnosable. Interestingly, 28 percent of burglary victims also had had PTSD at some time in their lives, while 7 percent were currently diagnosable; see Dean Kilpatrick, Benjamin Saunders, Lois Veronen, Connie Best, and Judith Von, "Criminal Victimization: Lifetime Prevalence, Reporting to Police, and Psychological Implications," *Crime and Delinquency* 33 (1987): 479–489.

55. John S. March, "The Stressor Criterion in DSM-IV Posttraumatic Stress Disorder," in John Davidson and Edna Foa, eds., *Posttraumatic Stress Disorder in Review: Recent Research and Future Development* (Washington, D.C.: American Psychiatric Press, 1992).

56. John Wing, *Reasoning about Madness* (New York: Oxford University Press, 1978), p. 22.

57. Lawrie Reznek, *The Nature of Disease* (New York: Routledge and Kegan Paul, 1978), p. 1.

58. See the discussion in Reznek, ibid., pp. 23–25, Thomas Szasz's many writings on the subject, and Ivan Illich, *Medical Nemesis: The Expropriation of Health* (Harmondsworth: Penguin, 1976).

59. Stuart Kirk and Herb Kutchins, *The Selling of DSM: The Rhetoric of Science in Psychiatry* (New York: Aldine de Gruyter, 1992), p. 237.

60. Reznek writes of a time in American history when the reactions of slaves to slavery, for example, the wish to escape, were classified as a disorder called drapetomania. Reznek, *The Nature of Disease*, p. 17.

61. Robert Rescorla, "Variation in the Effectiveness of Reinforcement and Nonreinforcement Following Prior Inhibitory Conditioning," *Learning and Motivation* 2 (1971): 113–123.

62. Edna Foa, Richard Zinbarg, and Barbara Rothbaum, "Uncontrollability and Unpredictability in Post-traumatic Stress Disorder: An Animal Model," *Psychological Bulletin* 112 (1992): 218–238.

63. Dean Kilpatrick, Benjamin Saunders, Angelynne Amick-McMullan, Carol Best, Lois Veronen, and Heidi Resnick, "Victim and Crime Factors Associated with the Development of Crime-related Posttraumatic Stress Disorder," *Behavior Therapy* 20 (1989): 177–198.

64. This finding was presented by Linda Perloff, "Perceptions of Vulnerability to Victimization," *Journal of Social Issues* 39 (1989): 41–61, and in Susan McLeer, Esther Deblinger, Marc Atkins, Edna Foa, and

Diana Ralphe, "Post-traumatic Stress Disorder in Sexually Abused Children," *Journal of the American Academy of Child and Adolescent Psychiatry* 27 (1989): 650–654.

65. Edna Foa, Barbara Rothbaum, David Riggs, and Tamera Murdock, "Treatment of Posttraumatic Stress Disorder in Rape Victims: A Comparison between Cognitive-behavioral Procedures and Counseling," *Journal of Consulting and Clinical Psychology* 59 (1991): 715–723.

66. Elizabeth A. Waites, *Trauma and Its Wake* (New York: W. W. Norton, 1993), p. 22.

67. Bessel Van Der Kolk, *Psychological Trauma* (Washington, D.C.: American Psychiatric Press, 1987), pp. 31–62.

68. Bessel Van Der Kolk, "The Compulsion to Repeat the Trauma: Re-enactment, Revictimization, and Masochism," *Psychiatric Clinics of North America* 12 (1989): 389–411.

69. Waites, *Trauma and Its Wake,* p. 22.

70. One is reminded of the endless search to find a gene for homosexuality that appears to be supported by the gay rights movement. See the *New York Times* article of July 18, 1993, by Natalie Angier, "Study of Sex Orientation Doesn't Neatly Fit the Mold," p. C24. If homosexuality is considered to be genetically determined, gay men can feel less shame for what society considers "deviant" behavior because homosexuality is not a choice. Research has shown that when homosexuality is viewed as a choice it elicits more anger from the public. See Joseph Aguero, Laura Bloch, and Donn Byrne, "The Relationship among Sexual Beliefs, Attitudes, Experience, and Homophobia," *Journal of Homosexuality* 10 (1984): 95–107, or Bernard Whitley, "The Relationship of Heterosexuals' Attributions for the Causes of Homosexuality to Attitudes toward Lesbians and Gay Men," *Personality and Social Psychology Bulletin* 16 (1990): 369–377.

71. Daniel Dennett, *Elbow Room* (Cambridge, Mass.: MIT Press, 1984). See pp. 7–10 for a discussion of "agents who vie with us for control of our bodies."

72. Strawson, *Freedom and Resentment.*

73. Philip Hallie, *Cruelty* (Middletown, Conn.: Wesleyan University

Press, 1982). See the chapter entitled "Sade and the Music of Pain," pp. 37–63.

74. This story was told to me by a colleague, Sue Edgar-Smith, who was the group leader.

3 PERPETRATORS

1. Robert Louis Stevenson, *The Strange Case of Dr. Jekyll and Mr. Hyde* (New York: Current Literature Publishing Co., 1906).

2. A. Nicholas Groth, *Men Who Rape: The Psychology of the Offender* (New York: Plenum Press, 1979), p. 51.

3. David T. Ballard, G. D. Blair, Sterling Devereaux, Logan K. Valentine, Anne L. Horton, and Barry L. Johnson, "A Comparative Profile of the Incest Perpetrator: Background Characteristics, Abuse History, and Use of Social Skills," in Anne L. Horton, Barry L. Johnson, Lynn M. Roundy, and Doran Williams, eds., *The Incest Perpetrator: A Family Member No One Wants to Treat* (Newbury Park, Calif.: Sage, 1990).

4. C. R. Snyder, Raymond L. Higgins, and Rita J. Stucky, *Excuses: Masquerades in Search of Grace* (New York: Wiley, 1983).

5. Ibid.

6. The legal scholar Michael Corrado conceptualizes excuses for bad or criminal behavior in terms of two basic theories. In the "voluntariness theory" we excuse actors if they were in circumstances where they had no choice. In "character theory" we excuse the actors if their acts do not represent their true characters, if they were "uncharacteristic." But Corrado asserts that there is really only one reason a person uses a justification or an excuse: so that he may not be blamed. See Michael Corrado, "Notes of the Structure of a Theory of Excuses," *Journal of Criminal Law and Criminology* 82 (1992): 465–498.

7. Joan Kaufman and Edward Zigler, "Do Abused Children Become Abusive Parents?" *American Journal of Orthopsychiatry* 57 (1987): 186–192.

8. Ballard et al., "A Comparative Profile."

9. Ron Langevin, *Sexual Strands: Understanding and Treating Sexual*

Anomalies in Men (Hillsdale, N.J.: Erlbaum, 1983); Vondra Loretto Pelto, "Male Incest Offenders and Non-Offenders: A Comparison of Early Sexual History," *Dissertation Abstracts International* 42 (September 1981), section B (3): 1154.

10. Groth, *Men Who Rape;* Mary de Young, *The Sexual Victimization of Children* (Jefferson, N.C.: McFarland, 1982).

11. Ballard et al., "A Comparative Profile."

12. Kevin Epps, "The Residential Treatment of Adolescent Sex Offenders," *Issues in Criminological and Legal Psychology* 1 (1991): 58–67.

13. Ann W. Burgess, Carol R. Hartman, and Arlene McCormack, "Abused to Abuser: Antecedents of Socially Deviant Behavior," *American Journal of Psychiatry* 144 (1987): 1431–1436.

14. Michael Petrovich and Donald I. Templer, "Heterosexual Molestation of Children who Later Became Rapists," *Psychological Reports* 54 (1984): 810.

15. David Tingle et al., "Childhood and Adolescent Characteristics of Pedophiles and Rapists," *International Journal of Law and Psychiatry* 9 (1986): 103–116.

16. Frances J. Fitch and Andre Papantonio, "Men Who Batter: Some Pertinent Characteristics," *Journal of Nervous and Mental Disease* 171 (1983): 190–192.

17. Edward K. Suh and Eileen M. Abel, "The Impact of Spousal Violence on the Children of the Abused," *Journal of Independent Social Work* 4 (1990): 27–34.

18. Burgess et al., "Abused to Abuser."

19. Elaine H. Carmen, Patricia P. Rieker, and Trudy Mills, "Victims of Violence and Psychiatric Illness," *American Journal of Psychiatry* 141 (1984): 378–383.

20. But see Jerome Kagan, *The Nature of the Child* (New York: Basic Books, 1984), for a discussion on the presupposition of continuity from childhood to adulthood and the evidence that exists against it.

21. P. F. Strawson, *Freedom and Resentment* (New York: Harper and Row, 1974), p. 10.

22. Ballard et al., "A Comparative Profile."

23. Ibid.

24. The description of the behavior of the digger wasp, found in Daniel Dennett's *Elbow Room*, comes from Dean E. Wooldridge, *The Machinery of the Brain* (New York: McGraw Hill, 1963), p. 82. The term "sphexishness" was proposed by the philosopher Douglas R. Hofstadter in "Can Creativity Be Mechanized?" *Scientific American* 247 (September 1982): 18–34.

25. See chapter 3 in Michael Gottfreson and Travis Hirschi, *Understanding Crime: Current Theory and Research* (Beverly Hills: Sage Publications, 1980), for a criticism of biological theories of criminality, and see Jack Katz, *Seductions of Crime* (New York: Basic Books, 1988), for a nontraditional, phenomenological view of criminal behavior.

26. Paul Ekman, "An Argument for Basic Emotions," *Cognition and Emotion* 6 (1992): 169–200.

27. Carol Tavris, *Anger: The Misunderstood Emotion* (New York: Simon and Schuster, 1982).

28. Roy F. Baumeister, Arlene Stillwell, and Sara R. Wortman, "Victim and Perpetrator Accounts of Interpersonal Conflict: Autobiographical Narratives about Anger," *Journal of Personality and Social Psychology* 59 (1990): 994–1005.

29. This quote, found in Fay H. Knopp, *Retraining Adult Sex Offenders: Methods and Models* (Syracuse, N.Y.: Safer Society Press, 1984), p. 10, is from Richard Laws, founder of the Sexual Behavior Laboratory at Atascadero State Hospital in California.

30. A. Nicholas Groth, "Juvenile and Adult Sex Offenders: Creating a Community Response" (training lecture sponsored by the Tompkins County Sexual Abuse Task Force, Ithaca, N.Y., June 16–17, 1983); cited in Knopp, *Retraining Adult Sex Offenders*, p. 10.

31. Patricia S. Greenspan, "Unfreedom and Responsibility," in Ferdinand Schoeman, ed., *Responsibility, Character, and the Emotions: New Essays in Moral Psychology* (New York: Cambridge University Press, 1987), pp. 63–80.

32. Robert M. Adams, "Involuntary Sins," *The Philosophical Review* XCIV (1985): 3–31.

33. Greenspan, "Unfreedom and Responsibility."

34. Paradoxical therapy of this sort is described in Paul Watzlawick, John Weakland, and Richard Fisch, *Change: Principles of Problem Formation and Problem Resolution* (New York: Norton, 1974).

35. David Lisak, "Sexual Aggression, Masculinity, and Fathers," *Social Problems* 16 (1991): 238–262.

36. Vicky Phares and Bruce E. Compas, "The Role of Fathers in Child and Adolescent Psychopathology: Make Room for Daddy," *Psychological Bulletin* 111 (1992): 387–412. See also Judith A. Martin, "Neglected Fathers: Limitations in Diagnostic and Treatment Resources for Violent Men," *Child Abuse and Neglect* 8 (1984): 387–392, for a discussion of the lack of attention abusive fathers have received in the literature.

37. Nathalie Angier, "Elementary Dr. Watson: The Neurotransmitters Did It," *New York Times,* January 23, 1994, p. C1. Dr. Evan Balaban, a neurobiologist from Harvard University, was quoted as saying, "There's a constant up-and-down roller-coaster ride, between when we like to hear things are complicated and when we want to hear things are simple. . . . Right now, people want to hear that maybe everything is simple."

38. There are several popular books on temperament that talk about the "difficult child" or the "spirited child."

39. Judith N. Shklar, *Ordinary Vices* (Cambridge, Mass.: Harvard University Press, 1984), p. 43.

40. Philip N. Johnson-Laird and Keith Oatley, "The Meaning of Emotions: Analysis of a Semantic Field," *Cognition and Emotion* 3 (1989): 81–123.

41. Philip N. Johnson-Laird and Keith Oatley, "Basic Emotions, Rationality, and Folk Theory," *Cognition and Emotion* 6 (1992): 201–223.

42. Robert W. Levenson, Paul Ekman, and Wallace Y. Friesen, "Voluntary Facial Action Generates Emotion-Specific Autonomic System Activity," *Psychophysiology* 27 (1990): 363–384.

43. Cited in Anne Wierzbicka, "Talking about Emotions: Semantics, Culture, and Cognition," *Emotions and Cognition* 6 (1992): 285–313. The information comes from Catherine Lutz's chapter "Goals, Events, and Understanding in Ifaluk Emotion Theory," in Dorothy

Holland and Naomi Quinn, eds., *Cultural Models in Language and Thought* (Cambridge, England: Cambridge University Press, 1987), pp. 290–312.

44. Cited in Wierzbicka, "Talking about Emotions." The word was discussed in Michelle Z. Rosaldo, *Knowledge and Passion: Ilongot Notions of Self and Social Life* (Cambridge, England: Cambridge University Press, 1980).

45. Wierzbicka, "Talking about Emotions."

46. Ibid., p. 307.

47. Dennett, *Elbow Room.*

48. Rachel T. Hare-Mustin, "Discourses in the Mirrored Room: A Postmodern Analysis of Therapy," *Family Process* 33 (1994): 19–35; and Wendy Hollway, "Gender Difference and the Production of Subjectivity," in Julian Henriques, Wendy Hollway, Cathy Urwin, Couze Venn, and Valerie Walkerdine, eds., *Changing the Subject: Psychology, Social Regulation, and Subjectivity* (New York: Methuen, 1984), pp. 227–263.

49. Stanton Peele, *The Diseasing of America: Addiction Treatment out of Control* (Lexington, Mass.: Lexington Books, 1989).

50. One study puts the number of sex addicts who were themselves abused as children at 36 percent, although 56 percent report having been neglected as children. Patrick J. Carnes, "Sexual Addiction," in Horton, Johnson, Roundy, and Williams, eds., *The Incest Perpetrator.*

51. Ballard et al., "A Comparative Profile."

52. Deborah C. Richardson and Jennifer L. Campbell, "Alcohol and Wife Abuse: The Effect of Alcohol on Attributions of Blame for Wife Abuse," *Personality and Social Psychology* 6 (1980): 51–56.

53. Craig MacAndrew and Robert B. Edgerton, *Drunken Comportment: A Social Explanation* (Chicago: Aldine Publishing Co., 1969).

54. Ibid.

55. Alan R. Lang, Daniel J. Goeckner, Vincent J. Adesso, and G. Alan Marlatt, "Effects of Alcohol on Aggression in Male Social Drinkers," *Journal of Abnormal Psychology* 84 (1975): 508–518. See also Stanton Peele, "The Cultural Context of Psychological Approaches to Alcoholism: Can We Control the Effects of Alcohol?" *American Psycholo-*

gist 39 (1984): 1337–1351, for a review of the effects of beliefs and expectations on drinking behavior.

56. Katz, *Seductions of Crime.*

57. Katz is referring to a phrase found in David Matza's *Becoming Deviant* (Englewood Cliffs, N.J.: Prentice-Hall, 1969).

58. I am reminded of the former president of Catholic University who was arrested for making obscene phone calls, sometimes terrifying and disturbing to recipients. He is currently on a lecture tour in which he describes his childhood experiences of sexual abuse and draws connections to his adult behaviors, which he also describes as a compulsion. There seems to be a large gap between the view of himself as a sufferer who is compelled to bring more suffering to others, and what Katz has called the "sneaky thrills" that are part and parcel of the obscene caller's repertoire!

59. Kathleen C. Faller, "Sexual Abuse by Paternal Caretakers: A Comparison of Abusers Who Are Biological Fathers in Intact Families, Stepfathers, and Noncustodial Fathers," in Horton et al., *The Incest Perpetrator.*

60. Duncan Chappel and J. James, "Victim Selection and Apprehension from the Rapist's Perspective: A Preliminary Investigation," unpublished paper presented at the Second International Symposium on Victimology (Boston, Mass.: September 1976), cited in Robert Alan Prentky, Ann Wolbert Burgess, and Daniel Lee Carter, "Victim Responses by Rapist Type: An Empirical and Clinical Analysis," *Journal of Interpersonal Violence* 1 (1986): 73–98. This study suggests that fighting back angers a rapist. However, Prentky and the other authors also cite studies that suggest that fighting back thwarts a rape attempt: P. B. Bart and P. O'Brien, "Stopping Rape: Effective Avoidance Strategies," *Signs* 10 (1984): 83–101; J. J. McIntyre, Y. Myint, and L. A. Curtis, *Sexual Assault: Alternative Outcomes,* Final Report to the National Institute of Mental Health, Grant no. RO1 MH29045; W. B. Sanders, *Rape and Women's Identity* (Beverly Hills: Sage, 1980).

61. Ellen Berscheid and Elaine Walster, "When Does a Harm-Doer Compensate a Victim?" *Journal of Personality and Social Psychology* 6 (1969): 435–441.

62. Kenneth A. Dodge and Daniel R. Somberg, "Hostile Attributional Biases among Aggressive Boys are Exacerbated under Conditions of Threats to the Self," *Child Development* 58 (1987): 213–224.
63. Guest on *The Oprah Winfrey Show,* September 17, 1993.
64. John Gottman, "The Roles of Conflict Engagement, Escalation, and Avoidance in Marital Interaction: A Longitudinal View of Five Types of Couples," *Journal of Consulting and Clinical Psychology* 6 (1993): 6–15.
65. Sandra L. Ingersoll and Susan O. Patton, *Treating Perpetrators of Sexual Abuse* (Lexington, Mass.: Lexington Books, 1990).
66. Adams, "Involuntary Sins," p. 26.
67. Dennett, *Elbow Room,* p. 33.
68. Philip Hallie, *Cruelty* (Middletown, Conn.: Wesleyan University Press, 1982), p. 13.
69. Ibid., p. 24.
70. Richard Seely, of Minnesota Security Hospital, as quoted in Knopp, *Retraining Adult Sex Offenders,* p. 16.
71. Ballard et al., "A Comparative Profile." Groth, *Men Who Rape,* quotes one perpetrator as saying, "You know what you are doing is wrong, and it's not too late to stop" (p. 59).
72. Janet Landman, *Regret* (New York: Oxford University Press, 1993).
73. Quoted in Scott Sleek, "Sexual Deviancy a Disorder, Not an Evil," *APA Monitor* 25(1) (January 1994), p. 32.
74. John Kekes, *Facing Evil* (Princeton, N.J.: Princeton University Press, 1990), p. 5.
75. Ibid., p. 100.
76. Ibid. This view is put forth in several chapters of the book.

4 ONLOOKERS

1. Judith Shklar, *Ordinary Vices* (Cambridge, Mass.: Harvard University Press, 1984), p. 17.
2. Jenny Kitzinger, "Defending Innocence: Ideologies of Childhood," *Feminist Review* 28 (1988): 78–79.
3. Marilyn D. McShane, M. D., and Frank P. Williams, III, "Radical

Victimology: A Critique of the Concept of Victim in Traditional Victimology," *Crime and Delinquency* 38 (1992): 258–271.

4. We can see this tendency particularly in the research on sexual abuse survivors' amnesia. For example, Jon R. Conte and John Briere researched a large sample of adult women survivors of sexual abuse. They asked the women whether they at any time did not remember their abuse, and they came up with 59 percent who had "amnesia." They worded the question in such a way as to include any kind of "forgetting," however, from amnesia to simply not having thought about the abuse for a while. (See John Briere and Jon R. Conte, "Self-Reported Amnesia for Abuse in Adults Molested as Children," *Journal of Traumatic Stress* 6 (1993): 21–31.) In the current atmosphere of victim defense, one would also wonder whether victims might reframe their "putting it out of their minds" or their "simply not thinking about it" as amnesia. This is not to say that there are no true cases of amnesia as a result of the abuse a victim has suffered, but that many more cases are included in this category because of the dramatic sense of the term "amnesia."

5. This idea is expressed by McShane and Williams, "Radical Victimology."

6. This excerpt from a trial was presented in Richard Green, *Sexual Science and the Law* (Cambridge, Mass.: Harvard University Press, 1992).

7. Fritz Heider, *The Psychology of Interpersonal Relations* (New York: Wiley, 1958); Edward E. Jones and Ricard E. Nisbett, "The Actor and the Observer: Divergent Perceptions of the Causes of Behavior," in Edward E. Jones, David E. Kanouse, Harold H. Kelley, Ricard E. Nisbett, S. Valins, and Barnard Weiner, eds., *Attributions: Perceiving the Causes of Behavior* (Morristown, N.J.: General Learning Press, 1972).

8. Kelly G. Shaver, "Defensive Attribution: Effects of Severity and Relevance on the Responsibility Assigned for an Accident," *Journal of Personality and Social Psychology* 14 (1970): 101–113.

9. The summarized research comes from the following studies as well as others too numerous to cite: Sheila Bietz and Lynne Byrnes,

"Attributions of Responsibility for Sexual Assault: The Influence of Observer Empathy and Defendant Occupation and Attractiveness," *Journal of Psychology* 108 (1981): 17–29; Lynne Hillier and Margaret Foddy, "The Role of Observer Attitudes in Judgments of Blame in Cases of Wife Assault," *Sex Roles* 29 (1993): 629–645; Judith A. Howard, "Societal Influences on Attributions: Blaming Some Victims More Than Others," *Journal of Personality and Social Psychology* 47 (1984): 494–505; Suresh Kanekar and Laura Vaz, "Attribution of Causal and Moral Responsibility to a Victim of Rape," *Applied Psychology* 37 (1988): 35–49; Judith E. Krulewitz and Janet E. Nash, "Effects of Rape Victim Resistance, Assault Outcome, and Sex of Observer on Attributions of Rape," *Journal of Personality* 47 (1979): 557–574; Travis Langley, Greg Beaty, Elizabeth A. Yost, Edgar C. O'Neal et al., "How Behavioral Cues in a Date-Rape Scenario Influence Judgments Regarding Victim and Perpetrator," *Forensic Reports* 4 (Special Section: Psychology and Tort Law) (1991): 355–358; Kevin D. McCaul, Lois G. Veltum, Vivian Boyechko, and Jacqueline J. Crawford, "Understanding Attributions of Victim Blame for Rape: Sex, Violence, and Forseeability," *Journal of Applied Social Psychology* 20 (1990): 1–26; Richard M. Ryckman, Linda M. Kaczor, and Bill Thornton, "Traditional and Non-Traditional Women's Attributions of Responsibility to Physically Resistive and Nonresistive Rape Victims," *Journal of Applied Social Psychology* 22 (1992): 1453–1463; Deborah G. Schult and Lawrence J. Schneider, "The Role of Sexual Provocativeness, Rape History, and Observer Gender in Perceptions of Blame in Sexual Assault," *Journal of Interpersonal Violence* 6 (1991): 94–101; A. Daniel Yarmey, "Older and Younger Adults' Attributions of Responsibility toward Rape Victims and Rapists," *Canadian Journal of Behavioral Science* 17 (1985): 327–338.

10. For research on date-rape attributions, refer to the following studies: R. Lance Shotland and Lynne Goodstein, "Sexual Precedence Reduces the Perceived Legitimacy of Sexual Refusal: An Examination of Attributions Concerning Date Rape and Consensual Sex," *Person-*

ality and Social Psychology Bulletin 18 (1992): 756–764; Megan J. Jenkins and Faye H. Dambrot, "The Attribution of Date Rape: Observer's Attitudes and Sexual Experiences and the Dating Situation," *Journal of Applied Social Psychology* 17 (1987): 875–895; Mary P. Koss, T. E. Dinero, Cynthia A. Seibel, and Susan L. Cox, "Stranger and Acquaintance Rape: Are There Differences in the Victims' Experience?" *Psychology of Women Quarterly* 12 (1988): 1–24; Charlene L. Muehlenhard, D. E. Friedman, and C. E. Thomas, "Is Date Rape Justifiable?: The Effects of Dating Activity, Who Initiated, Who Paid, and Men's Attitudes toward Women," *Psychology of Women Quarterly* 9 (1985): 297–309.

11. Caroline K. Waterman and Deborah Foss-Goodman, "Child Molesting: Variables Relating to Attribution of Fault to Victims, Offenders, and Nonparticipating Parents," *Journal of Sex Research* 20 (1984): 329–349.

12. Steven J. Collings and Merrilee F. Payne, "Attribution of Causal and Moral Responsibility to Victims of Father-Daughter Incest: An Exploratory Examination of Five Factors," *Child Abuse and Neglect* 15 (1991): 513–521. See also S. D. Broussard and W. G. Wagner, "Child Sexual Abuse: Who Is to Blame?" *Child Abuse and Neglect* 12 (1988): 563–569.

13. D. L. Doughty and H. G. Schneider, "Attribution of Blame in Incest among Mental Health Professionals," *Psychological Reports* 60 (1987): 1159–1165; M. W. Morris, "Five-Factor Construct for the Attribution of Incest Blame: Differential Blame as a Function of Age and / or Respondent Characteristics" (Ph.D. diss., University of Utah, 1988), *Dissertation Abstracts International* 49 (1989): 4017b.

14. Donald G. Dutton, "Wife Assaulters' Explanations for Assault: The Neutralization of Self-Punishment," *Canadian Journal of Behavioural Science* 18 (1986): 381–390. While 79 percent used these excuses, the other 21 percent gave even more disturbing excuses. They excused their assaults completely by saying the abuse was not their responsibility.

15. Connie M. Kristiansen and Rita Giulietti, "Perceptions of Wife

Abuse: Effects of Gender, Attitudes toward Women, and Just-World Beliefs among College Students," *Psychology of Women Quarterly* 14 (1990): 177–189.

16. David B. Sugarman and Ellen S. Cohn, "Origin and Solution Attributions of Responsibility for Wife Abuse: Effects of Outcome Severity, Prior History, and Sex of Subject," *Violence and Victims* 1 (1986): 291–303.

17. B. Corenblum, "Reactions to Alcohol-Related Marital Violence: Effects of One's Own Abuse Experience and Alcohol Problems on Causal Attributions," *Journal of Studies on Alcoholism* 44 (1983): 665–674.

18. Stephen T. Skiffington, James B. Parker, Deborah Richardson, and James F. Calhoun, "The Applicability of the Empathic Set Effect to Modify Perceptions of Domestic Violence," *Social Behavior and Personality* 12 (1984): 39–43.

19. Gertrude Summers and Nina S. Feldman, "Blaming the Victim vs. Blaming the Perpetrator: An Attributional Analysis of Spouse Abuse," *Journal of Social and Clinical Psychology* 2 (1984): 339–347.

20. Howard, "Societal Influences on Attributions."

21. Mary Douglas, *Risk and Blame: Essays in Cultural Theory* (London: Routledge, 1992), p. 278.

22. Richard A. Gardner, *Sex Abuse Hysteria: Salem Witch Trials Revisited* (Cresskill, N.J.: Creative Therapeutics, 1991). Elizabeth Loftus, a professor at the University of Washington, and Stephen Ceci, a professor at Cornell University, have also referred to the Salem Witch trials and discussed the current concern about sexual abuse as a "national hysteria." See Elizabeth Loftus's book *Witness for the Defense*, written with K. Ketcham (New York: St. Martin's Press, 1991).

23. Anne Llewellyn Barstow, *Witchcraze: A New History of the European Witch Hunts* (New York: Pandora / Harper Collins, 1994).

24. One research study sets the number of fictitious original reports of sexual abuse between 4 and 8 percent. This is M. D. Everson and B. W. Boat, "False Allegations of Sexual Abuse by Children and Adolescents," *Journal of the American Academy of Child and Adolescent Psychiatry* 28 (1989): 230–235. Another research study found that

only 2 percent of recalled allegations were false. Linda Meyer Williams, "Recall of Childhood Trauma: A Prospective Study of Women's Memories of Child Sexual Abuse," *Journal of Consulting and Clinical Psychology* 62 (1994): 1167–1176.

25. Ellen Gray, *Unequal Justice: The Prosecution of Child Sexual Abuse* (New York: The Free Press, 1993).

26. L. J. Hlady and E. J. Gunter, "Alleged Child Abuse in Custody Access Disputes," *Child Abuse and Neglect* 14 (1990): 591–593.

27. Kathleen C. Faller, "Possible Explanations for Child Sexual Abuse Allegations in Divorce," *American Journal of Orthopsychiatry* 61 (1991): 86–91.

28. Nancy Thoennes and Patricia G. Tjaden, "The Extent, Nature, and Validity of Sexual Abuse Allegations in Custody / Visitation Disputes," *Child Abuse and Neglect* 14 (1990): 151–163.

29. Frank Bruni, "Twisted Love," *Philadelphia Inquirer Magazine*, December 8, 1991, pp. 18–26.

30. David Finkelhor, *Public Welfare* 48 (Winter 1990): 22–29, p. 26.

31. Gail S. Goodman, Elizabeth P. Taub, David P. Jones, Patricia England et al., "Testifying in Criminal Court: Emotional Effects on Child Sexual Assault Victims," *Society for Research in Child Development* (Chicago: University of Chicago Press, 1992).

32. Linda Meyer Williams, "Recall of Childhood Trauma: A Prospective Study of Women's Memories of Child Sexual Abuse," *Journal of Consulting and Clinical Psychology* 62 (1994): 1167–1176.

33. Roland C. Summit, "Displaced Attention to Delayed Memory," *Advisor* 5 (1992): 21.

34. Green, *Sexual Science and the Law.*

35. Faller, "Possible Explanations for Child Sexual Abuse Allegations"; Jones and Seig, "Child Sexual Abuse Allegations in Custody or Visitation Disputes"; Thoennes and Tjaden, "The Extent, Nature, and Validity of Sexual Abuse Allegations."

36. Elizabeth Loftus, "The Malleability of Memory," *Advisor* 5 (1992): 9.

37. Gail Goodman and C. Aman, "Children's Use of Anatomically Detailed Dolls to Recount an Event," Society for Research in Child

Development, Baltimore, April 1987; Gail Goodman and A. Clarke-Stewart, "Suggestibility in Children's Testimony: Implications for Sexual Abuse Investigations," in J. Doris, ed., *The Suggestibility of Children's Recollections: Implications for Eyewitness Testimony* (Washington, D.C.: American Psychological Association, 1991); Karen Saywitz, Gail Goodman, E. Nicholas, and S. F. Moan, "Children's Memories of Physical Examinations involving Genital Touch: Implications for Reports of Child Sexual Abuse," *Journal of Consulting and Clinical Psychology* 59 (1991): 682–691.

38. Margaret S. Steward, "Preliminary Findings from the University of California, Davis, Child Memory Study: Development and Testing of Interview Protocols for Young Children," *Advisor* 5 (1992): 11–13. J. Clare Wilson and Margaret Ellen Pipe, "The Effects of Cues on Young Children's Recall of Real Events," *New Zealand Journal of Psychology* 18 (1989): 65–70.

39. Kay Bussey, "Adult Influences on Children's Eyewitness Testimony," in Stephen Ceci (Chair), *Do Children Lie? Narrowing the Uncertainties*, Biennial Meeting of the American Psychology-Law Society, Williamsburg, Va. (as cited in N. W. Perry, "How Children Remember and Why They Forget," *Advisor* 5 (1992); Gail S. Goodman and Vicki S. Helgeson, "Child Sexual Assault: Children's Memory and the Law," *University of Miami Law Review* 40 (1985): 181–208; Gail S. Goodman and Rebecca S. Reed, "Age Differences in Eyewitness Testimony," *Law and Human Behavior* 10 (1986): 317–332; Douglas P. Peters, "Confrontational Stress and Children's Testimony: Some Experimental Findings," in Ceci, *Do Children Lie?*

40. Gail S. Goodman, Jodi E. Hirschman, Debra Hepps, and Leslie Rudy, "Children's Memory for Stressful Events," *Merrill-Palmer Quarterly* 37 (1991): 109–157. A. Warren-Leubecker, C. Bradley, and I. D. Hinton, "Scripts and Development of Flash-Bulb Memories" (paper presented at the Conference of Human Development, Charleston, S.C., March 1988), as cited in Perry, "How Children Remember."

41. Steward, "Preliminary Finding from the University of California, Davis, Child Memory Study," p. 12.

42. Katie Roiphe, *The Morning After: Sex, Fear, and Feminism on Campus* (Boston: Little, Brown and Co., 1993), p. 11.

43. Ibid., p. 45.

44. Wendy Kaminer, "What Is This Thing Called Rape?" *New York Times Book Review,* September 19, 1993, p. 1.

45. Linda Gordon, *Heroes of Their Own Lives: The Politics and History of Family Violence* (New York: Viking, 1988).

46. Neil Gilbert, "Realities and Mythologies of Rape," *Society* 29 (1992): 4–10. See also Mary Koss's response to Gilbert's and others' misuse of the statistics and misunderstanding about date-rape research methodology: Mary P. Koss, "Defending Date Rape," *Journal of Interpersonal Violence* 7, (1992): 122–126.

47. Murray A. Straus, Richard J. Gelles, and Suzanne K. Steinmetz, *Behind Closed Doors: Violence in the American Family* (New York: Doubleday / Anchor, 1980), and Susan Steinmetz, "The Battered Husband Syndrome," *Victimology: An International Journal* 2 (1977–1978): 499–509.

48. Murray A. Straus and Richard A. Gelles, "Societal Change and Change in Family Violence from 1975 to 1985 as Revealed by Two National Surveys," *Journal of Marriage and the Family* 48 (1986): 465–479.

49. Daniel G. Saunders, "Wife Abuse, Husband Abuse, or Mutual Combat? A Feminist Perspective on the Empirical Findings," in Kersti Yllo and Michele Bograd, eds., *Feminist Perspectives on Wife Abuse* (Beverly Hills, Calif.: Sage, 1988).

50. Steinmetz, in "The Battered Husband Syndrome," used the term "battered husband syndrome" whereas Elizabeth Pleck, Joseph H. Pleck, McKee Grossman, and Pauline B. Bart argued that these claims were wild projections made from very little data in "The Battered Data Syndrome: A Comment on Steinmetz's Article," *Victimology: An International Journal* 2 (1977–1978): 680–684. It is also interesting to note that this kind of backlash occurred in the area of sexual abuse, with some backlash researchers arguing that women sexually abuse children as often as men do. Mary MacLeod and Esther Saraga, however, point out that this occurrence is rare, and

studies show incest by mother perpetrators to constitute 1 percent of all incest ("Challenging the Orthodoxy: Toward a Feminist Theory and Practice," *Feminist Review* 28 (1988): 16–55).

51. R. Emerson Dobash and Russell P. Dobash, *Violence against Wives: A Case against the Patriarchy* (New York: The Free Press, 1979); Pleck, Pleck, Grossman, and Bart, "The Battered Data Syndrome"; and Susan Schechter, *Women and Male Violence: The Visions and Struggles of the Battered Women's Movement* (Boston: South End Press, 1982).

52. Richard A. Berk, Sarah Berk, Donileen R. Loseke, and David Rauma, "Mutual Combat and Other Family Violence Myths," in David Finkelhor, Richard J. Gelles, Gerald T. Hotaling, and Murray A. Straus, eds., *The Dark Side of Families: Current Family Violence Research* (Newbury Park, Calif.: Sage, 1981), pp. 197–212.

53. Ibid., p. 107.

54. See Daniel G. Saunders, "Wife Abuse, Husband Abuse," pp. 91–94, for a discussion of feminist viewpoints of science and the influence on research on battered women.

55. Susan Schechter, personal communication.

56. Duncan Lindsey and Cheryl Regehr, "Protecting Severely Abused Children: Clarifying the Roles of Criminal Justice and Child Welfare," *American Journal of Orthopsychiatry* 63 (1993): 509–517; and David Besharov, "Doing Something about Child Abuse," *Harvard Journal of Law and Public Policy* 8 (1985): 539–589.

57. Florence Rush, *The Best-Kept Secret: Sexual Abuse of Children* (Englewood Cliffs, N.J.: Prentice-Hall, 1980); Erna Olafson, David L. Corwin, and Roland C. Summit, "Modern History of Child Sexual Abuse Awareness: Cycles of Discovery and Suppression," *Child Abuse and Neglect* 17 (1993): 7–24; Linda Gordon, *Heroes*.

58. Olafson et al., "Modern History of Child Sexual Abuse Awareness," pp. 12–13. It is of course fascinating to think of the underlying motives of J. Edgar Hoover in his pursuit of sexual deviancy. Recent revelations regarding his own cross-dressing would lead a psychologist to ponder whether his taking the lead in defining the boundaries of deviancy calmed his own anxieties regarding how deviant his own behavior may have been. (He may have said to himself, "Well, at

least I don't prey on small children; at least I am not violent," and so forth.) However, this is just conjecture.

59. Ibid., p. 14.

60. Estelle B. Freedman, "Uncontrolled Desires: The Response to the Sexual Psychopath, 1920–1960," *Journal of American History* 74 (1987): 83–106, p. 84.

61. Ibid.

62. Olafson et al., "Modern History of Child Sexual Abuse Awareness."

63. Alette Olin Hill, *Mother Tongue, Father Time: A Decade of Linguistic Revolt* (Indianapolis: Indiana University Press, 1986); Ursula K. Le Guin, *Dancing at the Edge of the World: Thoughts on Words, Women, Places* (New York: Harper and Row, 1989), pp. 147–160; Adrienne C. Rich, *On Lies, Secrets, and Silence: Selected Prose, 1966–1978* (New York: Norton, 1979).

64. Julia Penelope, *Speaking Freely: Unlearning the Lies of the Fathers' Tongues* (New York: Pergamon Press, 1990); Dale Spender, *Man Made Language* (London: Routledge and Kegan Paul, 1980); Barrie Thorne, Cheris Kramarae, and Nancy Henley, "Language, Gender, and Society: Opening a Second Decade of Research," in Barrie Thorne, Cheris Kramarae, and Nancy Henley, eds., *Language, Gender, and Society* (New York: Harper and Row, 1983).

65. Penelope, "Speaking Freely," p. xiv.

66. Ibid.

67. Nancy Henley, Michelle Miller, and Jo Anne Beazley, "Syntax, Semantics, and Violence in the Print Media" (paper presented at the Society of Experimental Social Psychology Meetings, Santa Barbara, Calif., October 1993).

68. Found in Penelope, "Speaking Freely"; the quote is from Sonia Johnson, "Telling the Truth," *Trivia* (Fall 1986): 19.

69. Nancy Henley, Michelle Miller, and Jo Anne Beazley, "Use of Passive Voice in Reports of Violence against Women," (paper presented at the Western Psychological Association Meeting, Phoenix, Ariz., April 1993).

70. Penelope, "Speaking Freely," pp. 151–155.

71. Ibid., p. 144.

72. Sharon Lamb and Susan Keon, "Blaming the Perpetrator: Language That Distorts Reality in Newspaper Articles on Men Battering Women," *Psychology of Women Quarterly* 19 (1995): 209–220.

73. Ann Jones, *Next Time She'll Be Dead: Battering and How to Stop It* (Boston: Beacon Press, 1994). This is why battered women often do not see themselves as being battered: because physical injury is only a small part of the whole relationship of control and intimidation.

74. Mary McIntosh, "Introduction to an Issue: Family Secrets as Public Drama," *Feminist Review* 28 (1988): 6–15.

75. Donald D. Jackson, "Family Rules: Marital Quid Pro Quos," *Archives of General Psychiatry* 12 (1965): 589–594.

76. Robert Lilienfeld, *The Rise of Systems Theory: An Ideological Analysis* (New York: Wiley, 1978). All of these criticisms are mentioned by Lilienfeld in this work but are also presented by several family therapists.

77. Michael Nichols and Richard Schwartz, *Family Therapy: Concepts and Methods* (Boston: Allyn and Bacon, 1991), p. 147.

78. Virginia Goldner, "Feminism and Family Therapy," *Family Process* 24 (1985): 31–47. K. James and Laurie MacKinnon, "The 'Incestuous Family' Revisited: A Critical Analysis of Family Therapy Myths," *Journal of Marital and Family Therapy* 16 (1990): 71–88; Nicola Gavey, Joy Florence, Sue Pezaro, and Jan Tan, "Mother-Blaming, the Perfect Alibi: Family Therapy and the Mothers of Incest Survivors," *Journal of Feminist Family Therapy* 2 (1990): 1–25.

79. See the following references for ways feminists have integrated their understanding of male violence into a family approach. Virginia Goldner, Peggy Penn, Marcia Sheinberg, and Gillian Walker, "Love and Violence: Gender Paradoxes in Volatile Attachments," *Family Process* 29 (1990): 343–364; Mary Jo Barrett, Terry Trepper, and Linda Stone Fish, "Feminist-Informed Family Therapy for the Treatment of Intrafamily Child Sexual Abuse," *Journal of Family Psychology* 4 (1990): 151–166; Anne Bernstein, "Profile of Rhea Almeida," *AFTA Newsletter* (Spring 1994): 38–42.

80. Karen H. Coleman, "Conjugal Violence: What Thirty-Three Men

Report," *Journal of Marital and Family Therapy* 6 (1980): 207–214. In this report 55 percent saw their violence as retaliation; 24 percent saw it as a result of chronic dissatisfaction with their wives as wives or mothers; 18 percent saw it as a result of jealousy of their partners' past or present relationships with other men.

81. Lola B. Buckley, Donna Miller, and Thomas A. Rolfe, "Treatment Groups for Violent Men: A Windsor Model," *Social Work with Groups* 6 (1983): 189–195, p. 189, cited in Liane V. Davis, "Battered Women: The Transformation of a Social Problem," *Social Work* 32 (1987): 306–311.

82. Mary Maynard, "Violence toward Women," in Diane Richardson and Victoria Robinson, eds., *Thinking Feminist: Key Concepts in Women's Studies* (New York: Guilford, 1993), pp. 99–122.

83. MacLeod and Saraga, "Challenging the Orthodoxy."

84. Linda Gordon, "The Politics of Child Sexual Abuse: Notes from American History," *Feminist Review* 28 (1988): 56–64.

85. Michele Bograd, "Family Systems Approaches to Wife Battering: A Feminist Critique," *American Journal of Orthopsychiatry* 54 (1984): 558–568; Vincent Fish, "Introducing Causality and Power into Family Therapy Theory: A Correction to the Systemic Paradigm," *Journal of Marital and Family Therapy* 16 (1990): 21–37; Rachel T. Hare-Mustin, "A Feminist Approach to Family Therapy," *Family Process* 12 (1978): 181–194; Kerrie James and Deborah McIntyre, "The Reproduction of Families: The Social Role of Family Therapy?" *Journal of Marital and Family Therapy* 9 (1983): 119–129; Laurie K. MacKinnon and Dusty Miller, "The New Epistemology and the Milan Approach: Feminist and Sociopolitical Consideration," *Journal of Marital and Family Therapy* 13 (1987): 139–155; Morris Taggart, "The Feminist Critique in Epistemological Perspective: Questions of Context in Family Therapy," *Journal of Marital and Family Therapy* 11 (1985): 113–126.

86. Bograd, "Family Systems Approaches," p. 560.

87. MacLeod and Saraga, "Challenging the Orthodoxy."

88. Wendy Lesser, *Pictures at an Execution* (Cambridge, Mass.: Harvard University Press, 1993).

89. Helen Benedict, *Virgin or Vamp* (New York: Oxford University Press, 1992).

90. Michel Foucault, *The History of Sexuality*, vol. 1 (New York: Pantheon, 1978).

91. Robert Elias, *The Politics of Victimization: Victims, Victimology, and Human Rights* (New York: Oxford University Press, 1986), p. 19.

92. Ibid., p. 23.

93. Stuart Oskamp, *Applied Social Psychology* (Englewood Cliffs, N.J.: Prentice-Hall, 1984).

94. Neil Postman, *Conscientious Objections: Stirring Up Trouble about Language, Technology, and Education* (New York: Knopf, 1988), p. 156.

95. One might argue here that many times it is not possible to prevent oneself from being a victim. I refer the reader to Jane Campion's recent movie *The Piano*, in which the heroine turns each victimization into a triumph, every oppressive offense against her into an act, not of courage and coping on her part, but of choice and self-assertion. The proposed coerced sex she transforms by choice into an expression of her formerly subdued desire. Even the rope that threatens to pull her and keep her under the sea she emerges from unfettered.

96. McShane and Williams, "Radical Victimology," remark that there was a modification of the victim's role from one "who has been harmed in some way" to one "who provides emotional credibility to the prosecution," and in this modification, "real harm" has been subordinated to "legal harm" (p. 260).

5 THE MAKING OF PERPETRATORS AND VICTIMS

1. Richard A. Shweder, "Anthropology's Romantic Rebellion against the Enlightenment, or There's More to Thinking Than Reason and Evidence," in Richard A. Shweder and Robert A. LeVine, eds., *Culture Theory: Essays on Mind, Self, and Emotion* (Cambridge: Cambridge University Press, 1984), pp. 56–57.

2. Stephen J. Morse, "Psychology, Determinism, and Legal Responsibility," *Nebraska Symposium on Motivation* 33 (1985): 35–85.

3. Rollo May, "Contributions of Existential Psychotherapy," in Rollo May, Ernest Angel, and Henri F. Ellengerger, eds., *Existence: A New Dimension in Psychiatry and Psychology* (New York: Basic Books, 1958), pp. 59–60. Found in C. R. Snyder, Raymond L. Higgins, and Rita J. Stucky, *Excuses: Masquerades in Search of Grace* (New York: Wiley, 1983).

4. Observations of early childhood morality have been documented by Martin Hoffman, "The Development of Prosocial Motivation: Empathy and Guilt," in Nancy Eisenberg, ed., *The Development of Prosocial Behavior* (New York: Academic Press, 1982); Carolyn Zahn-Waxler and Marian Radke-Yarrow, "The Development of Altruism: Alternate Research Strategies," in Eisenberg, *The Development of Prosocial Behavior;* Sharon Lamb, "First Moral Sense: An Examination of the Appearance of Morally Related Behaviors in the Second Year of Life," *Journal of Moral Education* 22 (1993): 97–109; Judy Dunn, "The Beginnings of Moral Understanding: Development in the Second Year," in Jerome Kagan and Sharon Lamb, eds., *The Emergence of Morality in Young Children* (Chicago: University of Chicago Press, 1987); and Jerome Kagan, *The Nature of the Child* (New York: Basic Books, 1985).

5. The study of adolescent mothers has not been published as of yet, but middle-class American toddlers have been studied by Lamb, "First Moral Sense," as well as by Zahn-Waxler and Radke-Yarrow, "The Development of Altruism."

6. Eliot Turiel and his colleagues have worked for some two decades on this idea, that morality is socially constructed in a way that takes advantage of the child's individual development but also the natural consequences to wrongs committed. His theory discusses two domains of morality, one conventional, in which rules are arbitrary, contextual, and can easily be changed, the other moral, in which rules are seen as universal and unalterable.

7. See Jerome Kagan's *The Second Year,* in which he documents the

emergence of the self in the second year of life (Cambridge, Mass.: Harvard University Press, 1981).

8. Snyder, Higgins, Stucky, *Excuses*.

9. This was overheard on one of our local Philadelphia news broadcasts in reference to a man who had allegedly kidnapped several women from shopping malls and stolen their cars. Snyder, Higgins, and Stucky, in *Excuses*, write about how parents foster excuse-making by supplying excuses for their children when their children fail to provide them for their behavior. They say that parents comfort crying children with excusing phrases such as "You didn't mean to."

10. Snyder et al., *Excuses*, p. 170.

11. Martin Hoffman, "Moral Internalization, Parental Power, and the Nature of the Parent-Child Interaction," *Developmental Psychology* 5 (1967): 45–57; Martin Hoffman and H. D. Saltzstein, "Parent Discipline and the Child's Moral Development," *Journal of Personality and Social Psychology* 5 (1967): 45–47.

12. Justin M. Aronfreed, *Conduct and Conscience: The Socialization of Internalized Control over Behavior* (New York: Academic Press, 1968).

13. Emmy E. Werner and Ruth S. Smith, *Overcoming the Odds: High-Risk Children from Birth to Adulthood* (Ithaca: Cornell University Press, 1992).

14. Nancy Eisenberg, Mark Schaller, Richard A. Fabes, Denise Bustamante, Robin M. Mathy, Rita Shell, and K. Rhodes, "Differentiation of Personal Distress and Sympathy in Children and Adults," *Developmental Psychology* 24 (1988): 766–775; Richard A. Fabes, Nancy Eisenberg, and Lisa Eisenbud, "Behavioral and Physiological Correlates of Children's Reactions to Others in Distress," *Developmental Psychology* 29 (1993): 655–663.

15. Mary Main and Carol George, "Responses of Abused and Disadvantaged Toddlers to Distress in Agemates: A Study in the Daycare Setting," *Developmental Psychology* 21 (1985): 407–412.

16. Susan Shott, "Emotion and Social Life: A Symbolic Interactionist Analysis," *American Journal of Sociology* 84 (1979): 1317–1334.

17. Silvan S. Tomkins, *Affect, Imagery, Consciousness, Vol. II: The Negative Affects* (New York: Springer, 1963), p. 185.

18. Mary W. Nicholas, *The Mystery of Goodness* (New York: W. W. Norton, 1994), p. 144.

19. Helen B. Lewis, *Shame and Guilt in Neurosis* (New York: International Universities Press, 1971).

20. F. W. Wicker, G. C. Payne, and R. D. Morgan, "Participant Descriptions of Guilt and Shame," *Motivation and Emotion* 7 (1983): 25–39.

21. June P. Tangney, Patricia E. Wagner, Deborah Hill Barlow, Donna E. Marschall, Jennifer Sanftner, Tim Mohr, and Richard Gramzow, "The Relation of Shame and Guilt to Constructive vs. Destructive Responses to Anger across the Lifespan," (unpublished manuscript).

22. Ibid.

23. Diana Scully, "Convicted Rapists' Perceptions of Self and Victim: Role Taking and Emotions," *Gender and Society* 2 (1988): 200–213.

24. William D. Pithers, Janice K. Marques, C. C. Gibat, and G. Alan Marlatt, "Relapse Prevention with Sexual Aggressives: A Self-Control Model of Treatment and Maintenance of Change," in Joanne G. Greer and Irving R. Stuart, eds., *The Sexual Aggressor: Current Perspectives on Treatment* (New York: Van Nostrand Reinhold Co., 1983).

25. Melanie Klein, "Notes on Some Schizoid Mechanisms," in M. Klein, *Envy and Gratitude and Other Works, 1946–1963* (New York: Delacorte Press, 1946 / 1975).

26. Susan Nolen-Hoeksema, "Sex Differences in Unipolar Depression: Evidence and Theory," *Psychological Bulletin* 101 (1987): 259–282.

27. Arlie Russell Hochschild, *The Managed Heart: Commercialization of Human Feeling* (Berkeley: University of California Press, 1988).

28. Richard J. Davidson, "Prolegomenon to the Structure of Emotion: Gleanings from Neuropsychology," in Nancy L. Stein and Keith Oatley, *Basic Emotions* (Hillsdale, N.J.: Erlbaum, 1992), pp. 245–268.

29. Xu Jun-mian, "Some Issues in the Diagnosis of Depression in China," *Canadian Journal of Psychiatry* 32 (1987): 368–370; Kathleen S. Crittenden, Stephen S. Fugita, Hyunjung Bae, Corazon B. Lamug et al., "A Cross-Cultural Study of Self-Report Depressive Symptoms among College Students," *Journal of Cross-Cultural Psychology* 23 (1992): 163–178.

30. David B. Mumford, "Somatization: A Transcultural Perspective," *International Review of Psychiatry* 5 (1993): 231–242.

31. Arlie Hochschild, "Ideology and Emotion Management: A Perspective and Path for Future Research," in Theodore D. Kemper, ed., *Research Agendas in the Sociology of Emotion* (Albany, N.Y.: State University of New York Press, 1990), pp. 117–142, p. 121.

32. Catherine A. Lutz, "Engendered Emotion: Gender, Power, and the Rhetoric of Emotional Control in American Discourse," in Catherine A. Lutz and Lila Abu-Lughod, eds., *Language and the Politics of Emotion* (Cambridge, England: Cambridge University Press, 1990), p. 73.

33. Michelle Z. Rosaldo, "Toward an Anthropology of Self and Feeling," in Richard Shweder and Robert A. LeVine, eds., *Culture Theory: Essays on Mind, Self, and Emotion* (Cambridge, England: Cambridge University Press, 1984), pp. 137–157.

34. James R. Averill, *Anger and Aggression: An Essay on Emotion* (New York: Springer-Verlag, 1982).

35. Hochschild, *The Managed Heart.*

36. Averill, *Anger and Aggression.*

37. Stuart R. Garrison and Arnold L. Stolberg, "Modification of Anger in Children by Affective Imagery Training," *Journal of Abnormal Child Psychology* 11 (1990): 115–129.

38. E. Mark Cummings, Dena Vogel, Jennifer S. Cummings, and Mona El-sheikh, "Children's Responses to Different Forms of Expression of Anger between Adults," *Child Development* 60 (1989): 1392–1404.

39. Candace Clark, "Emotions and Micropolitics in Everyday Life: Some Patterns and Paradoxes of 'Place,'" in Kemper, *Research Agendas,* pp. 305–333.

40. John A. Martin, "A Longitudinal Study of the Consequences of Early Mother-Infant Interaction: A Microanalytic Approach," *Monographs of the Society for Research in Child Development* 46 (1981): 1–59.

41. Hochschild, *The Managed Heart,* p. 129.

42. Peggy A. Thoits, "Emotional Deviance: Research Agendas," in Kemper, *Research Agendas,* pp. 180–203.

43. Sigmund Freud, "Some Character Types Met with in Psychoanalytic

Work," trans. James Strachey (London: Hogarth Press, 1916 / 1953), Standard Edition, 14: 309–336.

44. Heinz Kohut, "Creativeness, Charisma, Group Psychology," *Psychological Issues* 34 / 35 (1976): 379–425.

45. Hildy Ross, Caroline Tesla, Brenda Kenyon, and Susan Lollis, "Maternal Intervention in Peer Conflict: The Socialization of Principles of Justice," *Developmental Psychology* 26 (1990): 994–1003.

46. Hochschild, *The Managed Heart*.

47. Jean Berko Gleason, "Sex Differences in Parent-Child Interaction," in Susan U. Philips, Susan Steele, and Christine Tanz, eds., *Language, Gender, and Sex in Comparative Perspective* (Cambridge, England: Cambridge University Press, 1987), pp. 189–199.

48. H. Charles Fishman, "Diagnosis and Assessment in Family Therapy, III: Reflections on Assessment in Structural Family Therapy," *Family Therapy Collections* 4 (1983): 63–81.

49. Mark J. Blechner, "Entitlement and Narcissism: Paradise Sought," *Contemporary Psychoanalysis* 23 (1987): 244–255.

50. P. J. Watson and Ronald J. Morris, "Narcissism, Empathy, and Social Desirability," *Personality and Individual Differences* 12 (1991): 575–579.

51. Judith Herman, "Real Incest and Real Survivors: Readers Respond," *New York Times Book Review* 98 (February 14, 1993), p. 34. Also see Dorothy Gibbens, Philip Lichtenberg, and Janneke van Beusekom, "Working with Victims: Being Empathic Helpers," *Clinical Social Work Journal* 22 (1994): 211–222.

52. John Rowan, "How I Gave up Pornography," in Victor J. Seidler, ed., *Men, Sex, and Relationships: Writings from Achilles Heel* (London: Routledge, 1992), p. 86.

53. Selma Kramer, "A Contribution to the Concept 'The Exception' as a Developmental Phenomenon" (special issue), *Child Abuse and Neglect* 11 (1987): 367–370.

54. Naomi G. Rotter and George S. Rotter, "Sex Differences in the Encoding and Decoding of Negative Facial Emotions," *Journal of Nonverbal Behavior* 12 (1988): 139–148.

55. Carol Z. Malatesta and C. Lamb, "Emotion Socialization during the

Second Year" (paper presented at the annual meeting of the American Psychological Association, New York, August 1987), cited in A. S. R. Manstead, "Gender Differences in Emotion," in Anthony Gale and Michael W. Eysenck, *Handbook of Individual Differences: Biological Perspectives* (New York: John Wiley and Sons, 1992), pp. 355–387; Beverly I. Fagot and Richard Hagan, "Assertive Behavior in Toddlers," *Sex Roles* 21 (1985): 34–351.

56. Florence Laura Goodenough, *Anger in Young Children* (Minneapolis, Minn.: University of Minnesota Press, 1931); Fagot and Hagan, "Assertive Behavior in Toddlers."

57. Marion K. Underwood, John D. Coie, and Cheryl R. Herbsman, "Display Rules for Anger and Aggression in School-Age Children," *Child Development* 63 (1992): 366–380.

58. Malatesta and Lamb, "Emotional Socialization during the First Year."

59. Richard A. Shweder, "Menstrual Pollution, Soul Loss, and the Comparative Study of Emotions," in Arthur Kleinman and Byron Good, eds., *Culture and Depression* (Berkeley: University of California Press, 1985), pp. 182–215.

60. Thomas G. Power and Ross D. Parke, "Patterns of Early Socialization: Mother- and Father-Infant Interaction in the Home," *International Journal of Behavioral Development* 9 (1986): 331–341.

61. Rosemary S. L. Mills and Kenneth H. Rubin, "A Longitudinal Study of Maternal Beliefs about Children's Social Behaviors," *Merrill-Palmer Quarterly* 38 (1992): 494–512.

62. Norma D. Feshbach and Seymour Feshbach, "Affective Processes and Academic Achievement," Special Issue: Schools and Development, *Child Development* 58 (1987): 1335–1347.

63. Leonard D. Eron, "Gender Differences in Violence: Biology and / or Socialization," in Kaj Bjorkqvist and Pirkko Niemela, eds., *Of Mice and Women: Aspects of Female Aggression* (San Diego: Academic Press, 1992), pp. 89–97.

64. L. Rowell Huesmann and Leonard D. Eron, "Individual Differences and the Trait of Aggression," Special Issue: Personality and Aggression, *European Journal of Personality* 3 (1989): 95–106.

65. Eron, "Gender Differences in Violence."

66. L. Rowell Huesmann, Leonard D. Eron, Monroe M. Lefkowitz, and Leopold O. Walder, "Stability of Aggression over Time and Generations," *Developmental Psychology* 20 (1984): 1120–1134; Lea Pulkkinen and Matti Pitkanen, "Continuities in Aggressive Behavior from Childhood to Adulthood," *Aggressive Behavior* 19 (1993): 249–263; J. D. Roff, "Childhood Aggression, Peer Status, and Social Class as Predictors of Delinquency," *Psychological Reports* 70 (1992): 31–34.

67. Kenneth A. Dodge, Gregory S. Pettit, Cynthia L. McClaskey, and Melissa M. Brown, "Social Competence in Children," *Monographs of the Society for Research in Child Development* 51 (1986): 1–85.

68. David G. Perry, Louise C. Perry, and Paul Rasmussen, "Cognitive Social Learning Mediators of Aggression," *Child Development* 57 (1986): 700–711.

69. Janet P. Boldizar, David G. Perry, and Louise C. Perry, "Outcome Values and Aggression," *Child Development* 69 (1989): 571–579.

70. Ibid.

71. David G. Perry, Louise C. Perry, and Robert J. Weiss, "Sex Differences in the Consequences that Children Anticipate for Aggression," *Developmental Psychology* 25 (1989): 312–319.

72. L. Rowell Heusmann, Nancy G. Guerra, Arnaldo Zelli, and Laurie Miller, "Differing Normative Beliefs about Aggression for Boys and Girls," in Bjorkqvist and Niemela, eds., *Of Mice and Women*.

73. Daphna Oyserman and Hazel Marcus, "Possible Selves in Balance: Implications for Delinquency," *Journal of Social Issues* 46 (1990): 141–157.

74. Ronald G. Slaby and Nancy G. Guerra, "Cognitive Mediators of Aggression in Adolescent Offenders: I. Assessment," *Developmental Psychology* 24 (1988): 580–588.

75. Averill, *Anger and Aggression*.

76. Ronald de Sousa, "The Rationality of Emotions," in Amelie O. Rorty, ed., *Explaining Emotions* (Berkeley: University of California Press, 1980), pp. 127–152.

77. Averill, *Anger and Aggression*.

78. Heusmann et al., "Differing Normative Beliefs about Aggression."
79. Barrie Thorne and Zella Luria, "Sexuality and Gender in Children's Daily Worlds," *Social Problems* 33 (1986): 176–190.
80. Ruth G. Goodenough, "Situational Stress and Sexist Behavior among Young Children," in Peggy R. Sanday and Ruth G. Goodenough, eds., *Beyond the Second Sex: New Directions in the Anthropology of Gender* (Philadelphia: University of Pennsylvania Press, 1990).
81. Beverly I. Fagot, "Beyond the Reinforcement Principle: Another Step toward Understanding Sex Role Development," *Developmental Psychology* 21 (1985): 1097–1104.

6 FORGIVENESS AND PUNISHMENT

1. Jeffrie G. Murphy, "The Retributive Emotions," in Jeffrie G. Murphy and Jean Hampton, *Forgiveness and Mercy* (Cambridge, England: Cambridge University Press, 1988), pp. 1–9, p. 4.
2. Jeffrie G. Murphy, "Forgiveness and Resentment," in Murphy and Hampton, *Forgiveness and Mercy*, pp. 14–35, p. 30.
3. Nigel Walker, *Why Punish?* (Oxford: Oxford University Press, 1991), p. 114.
4. Donald Hope, "The Healing Paradox of Forgiveness," *Psychotherapy* 24 (1987): 240–244.
5. Richard B. Shekelle, Meryl Gale, Adrian Ostfeld, and Paul Oglesby, "Hostility, Risk of Coronary Disease, and Mortality," *Psychosomatic Medicine* 45 (1983): 109–114.
6. Carol Tavris, *Anger: The Misunderstood Emotion* (New York: Simon and Schuster, 1982).
7. Richard Fitzgibbons, "The Cognitive and Emotive Uses of Forgiveness in the Treatment of Anger," *Psychotherapy* 23 (1986): 629–633.
8. Murphy, "The Retributive Emotions," p. 9.
9. As cited in Murphy and Hampton (p. 18 and p. 31), Friedrich Nietzsche, *On the Genealogy of Morals*, trans. Walter Kaufman (New York: Vintage, 1969), essay I, section 10.
10. Murphy, "Forgiveness and Resentment," p. 16.

11. P. F. Strawson, *Freedom and Resentment and Other Essays* (London: Methuen & Co., 1974).

12. Bonnie Burstow, *Radical Feminist Therapy: Working in the Context of Violence* (Newbury Park: Sage, 1992).

13. Ibid., p. 140.

14. Lenore Walker, *The Battered Woman Syndrome* (New York: Springer, 1984).

15. Joram Graf Haber, *Forgiveness* (Savage, Md.: Rowman & Littlefield Publishers, 1991). Haber writes of a poignant tale by Simon Wiesenthal in which a Nazi on his deathbed confesses and begs him for forgiveness, which he refuses to grant on the grounds that he cannot speak for the Nazi's victims; only a victim may grant forgiveness. This same issue occurs in *The Brothers Karamazov*, notes Haber, where Dostoevsky writes that God lacks standing to forgive another's misconduct.

16. This quote was also found in Haber, *Forgiveness*.

17. Ibid., p. 11 and p. 39.

18. Ibid.; also see Jeffrie G. Murphy, "Forgiveness and Resentment," *Midwestern Studies in Philosophy* 7 (1982): 503–556, p. 505.

19. Haber, *Forgiveness*, p. 60.

20. Strawson, *Freedom and Resentment*, p. 6.

21. Michael S. Moore, "The Moral Worth of Retribution," in Ferdinand Schoeman, ed., *Responsibility, Character, and the Emotions: New Essays in Moral Psychology* (Cambridge, England: Cambridge University Press, 1987), pp. 179–219, p. 188.

22. These particular three were spoken of by Robin Antony Duff, *Trials and Punishments* (Cambridge, England: Cambridge University Press, 1986), but are dealt with by virtually all philosophers currently writing on the issue of punishment.

23. Richard Burgh, "Guilt, Punishment, and Desert," in Schoeman, ed., *Responsibility, Character, and the Emotions*, pp. 316–337; Moore, "The Moral Worth."

24. The general idea of punishment as communicative is developed by Duff, *Trials and Punishments*, but also expressed by Hegel; see David

G. Cooper, "Hegel's Theory of Punishment," in Z. A. Pelczynski, ed., *Hegel's Political Philosophy: Problems and Perspectives* (Cambridge, England: Cambridge University Press, 1971). Walker, *Why Punish?*, also writes of punishment as a message from people whose values are assumed to be correct. Joel Feinberg, "The Expressive Function of Punishment," *The Monist* 49 (1965): 397–408, also speaks of the symbolic significance of punishment.

25. This may seem as if I am contradicting myself since I earlier claimed that it is wrong for us to see ourselves as so very separate from perpetrators. Still, imprisonment communicates the choice they themselves have made to separate themselves; later in this chapter I advocate the very important reconnecting support that must be there during imprisonment, a support that speaks to the connections between "us" and "them." The quote is from Duff, *Trials and Punishments*, p. 260.

26. These four communications of punishment were outlined by Duff, *Trials and Punishments*.

27. Ibid., p. 261.

28. Jeffrie G. Murphy, "Getting Even: The Role of the Victim," in Ellen Paul, Fred Miller, and Jeffrey Paul, eds., *Crime, Culpability, and Remedy* (New York: Basil Blackwell, 1990).

29. Giles Renaud, "Sentencing of Stale Sexual Offences: An Overview," *Criminal Law Quarterly* 36 (1994): 241–256.

30. Ibid., p. 252.

31. Unfortunately, one of the only ways to get through to perpetrators of rape and sexual abuse is to ask them to imagine if someone did this to their sister, their mother. See Naomi Scheman's piece on "Rape" for the *Encyclopedia of Ethics*, Lawrence C. Becker, ed. (New York: Garland Press, 1992). In it she describes the origin of the word "rape" in carrying off property, and describes the way rape gradually took on sexual meaning when applied to a "particular sort of quasi-property, namely women" (p. 1060).

32. This idea was conveyed by Myrna Shure in a talk she gave to the Human Development Department at Bryn Mawr College. Dr. Shure has devised ways for preschool children to develop skills for dealing

with interpersonal problems; some of these skill-building techniques are used during "time-outs."

33. See John Braithwaite's idea about "reintegrative shaming," in *Crime, Shame and Reintegration* (Cambridge, England: Cambridge University Press, 1989).

34. Daniel D. French, "Distortion and Lying as Defensive Processes in the Adolescent Child Molester," *Journal of Offender Counseling, Services, and Rehabilitation* 13 (1988): 27–37.

35. Allen D. Sapp and Michael Vaughn, "Juvenile Sex Offender Treatment at State-Operated Correctional Institutions," *International Journal of Offender Therapy and Comparative Criminology* 34 (1990): 131–146. See also Lita Furby, Mark Weinrott, and Lyn Blackshaw, "Sex Offender Recidivism: A Review," *Psychological Bulletin* 105 (1989): 3–30, although this review has had many critics. For reviews that emphasize the positive see Judith V. Becker and John A. Hunter, "Evaluation of Treatment Outcome for Adult Perpetrators of Child Sexual Abuse," *Criminal Justice and Behavior* 19 (1992): 74–92, and William Marshall, R. Jones, T. Ward, P. Johnson, and Howard E. Barbaree, "Treatment Outcome with Sex Offenders," *Clinical Psychology Review* 11 (1991): 465–485.

36. Sapp and Vaughn, "Juvenile Sex Offender Treatment," and Robert Freeman-Longo and Fay Honey Knopp, "State-of-the-Art Sex Offender Treatment: Outcome and Issues," *Annals of Sex Research* 5 (1992): 141–160.

37. Walker, *Why Punish?* p. 111.

38. Moore, "The Moral Worth," p. 213.

39. Ibid.

40. Amelie O. Rorty, *Explaining Emotions* (Berkeley, Calif.: University of California Press, 1980), found in Janet Landman, *Regret* (Oxford: Oxford University Press, 1994).

41. Murphy, *Forgiveness and Mercy*, p. 25.

42. Timothy Kahn and Heather J. Chambers, "Assessing Reoffense Risk with Juvenile Sexual Offenders," *Child Welfare* 70 (1991): 333–345.

43. Joe is a four-year veteran of a program at Meynard Psychiatric Center

in Southern Illinois. Quoted in Scott W. Darnell, "No More Vicitms: Alternative Treatment Methods for the Incarcerated Sex Offender," *Prison Journal* LXVIX (1989): 83–87.

44. See Lawrence Kohlberg's theories of moral development in which reasoning in Stage 4 is said to take a law and order perspective, one in which a person tries to do good by obeying and identifying with the institutions of the culture. Lawrence Kohlberg, *Essays on Moral Development*, vol. 1 (San Francisco: Harper and Row, 1981).

45. Amitai Etzioni, "Incorrigible," *Atlantic Monthly* (July 1994): 14–16.

46. Steven J. Schulhofer, "The Gender Question in Criminal Law," in Paul, Miller, and Paul, eds., *Crime, Culpability, and Remedy*, p. 124.

47. Janis F. Bremer, "Serious Juvenile Sex Offenders: Treatment and Long-Term Follow-Up," *Psychiatric Annals* 22 (1992): 326–332.

48. Ibid.

49. Walker, *Why Punish?* See Chapter 6, "Human Sacrifice," for his discussion of Kant's *Rechtslehre*, pp. 53–60.

50. I once served as a consultant to this clinic (Network of Victim Assistance) in Doylestown, Pennsylvania, where counselors did all kinds of tricks to stretch the upper limit of twelve sessions per client.

51. Personal communication of William Marshall (January 20, 1992) to authors Freeman-Longo and Knopp, cited in "State-of-the-Art Sex Offender Treatment," p. 153.

EPILOGUE

1. Robert A. Prentky, Ann Burgess, and D. L. Carter, "Victim Responses by Rapist Type: An Empirical and Clinical Analysis," *Journal of Interpersonal Violence* 1 (1986): 73–98, is a study of 389 victims of 108 convicted rapists which showed that the effects of resistance depended on rapist type. Gary Kleck and Susan Sayles, "Rape and Resistance," *Social Problems* 37 (1990): 149–162, studied 378 rapes and found that rapes of victims who resisted were less likely to have been completed, and that most forms of resistance were not associated with greater injury.

2. Friedrich Nietzsche, *The Gay Science*, trans. Walter Kaufman (New

York: Vintage, 1974), p. 254. This reference and the following references to Nietzsche were brought to my attention by Michael S. Moore, "The Moral Worth of Retribution," in Ferdinand Schoeman, ed., *Responsibility, Character, and the Emotions: New Essays in Moral Psychology* (Cambridge, England: Cambridge University Press, 1987), pp. 179–219.

3. Friedrich Nietzsche, *On the Genealogy of Morals*, trans. Walter Kaufman (New York: Vintage, 1969), p. 65.

4. Friedrich Nietzsche, *Thus Spoke Zarathustra*, in Walter Kaufman, ed., *The Portable Nietzsche* (New York: Viking, 1954), p. 213.

5. Jean-Paul Sartre, *Being and Nothingness: An Essay on Phenomenological Ontology*, trans. Hazel E. Barnes (New York: Philosophical Library), p. 222.

6. Ibid., p. 405.

7. Harry Stack Sullivan, *The Interpersonal Theory of Psychiatry* (New York: Norton, 1953).

8. The dismissal of Joycelyn Elders, the United States Surgeon General, for her suggestion that sex education might include open acknowledgment of masturbation is the most recent example of our country's avoidance of straight talk about sex with children and adolescents.

9. Kenneth I. Wolpin, "An Economic Analysis of Crime and Punishment in England and Wales, 1894–1967," *Journal of Political Economy* 86 (1978): 815–840.

10. Bonnie Burstow, *Radical Feminist Therapy: Working in the Context of Violence* (Beverly Hills: Sage, 1992), p. 18 and p. 19.

11. Joram Graf Haber, *Forgiveness* (Savage, Md.: Rowman and Littlefield Publishers, 1991).

12. P. F. Strawson, *Freedom and Resentment and Other Essays* (London: Methuen and Co., 1974), p. 22.

13. Jeffrie G. Murphy, *Retribution, Justice, and Therapy: Essays in the Philosophy of the Law* (Boston: D. Reidel Publishing Co., 1979), p. 134. See also G. W. F. Hegel, *The Philosophy of Right*, trans. T. M. Knox (London: Oxford University Press, 1969), sec. 100.

14. In Murphy, *Retribution, Justice, and Therapy*, p. 163.

15. In Walker, *Why Punish?* p. 61.

ACKNOWLEDGMENTS

I would first like to thank Rachel Hare-Mustin, loving mentor and friend, who encouraged me to write this book, provided valuable insights and straightforward criticism on the manuscript itself, and allowed me my differences. Philip Lichtenberg, an intellectual soul mate at Bryn Mawr, commented on the manuscript and helped me to stay connected to helping others when anger or callousness emerged in my writing. My students asked important questions and contributed greatly to my thinking through discussions about the issues of victimization and blame. My clients taught me much about responsibility and bravery.

I also wish to thank Jerome Kagan, the scientist who taught me most deeply to distrust science through his discussions of "referents" for ideas and his emphasis on the cultural contexts in which certain ideas in psychology are born and take hold. Earlier help and influences came from Catherine Snow, who has been so generous professionally and intellectually, Carol Gilligan, Rick Shweder, Kay Davis, Barbara Pillinger, old friends at the Pumping Station, and friends and supervisors at Massachusetts General Hospital and Children's Hospital in Boston. Barbara Torpie believed in me from start to finish. Steve Heims read chapters and helped me through the early, influential loan of Philip Hallie's book *Cruelty.* Katherine Dahlsgaard provided research help, editing, and an unmatched enthusiasm for my ideas. My in-laws, Doris and Shelley Orgel, were very involved with the whole process of writing the book and provided important feedback at crucial times. On a very practical level, I could not have completed this book without the warm and generous help of my day-care provider, Germaine Fountain.

Nancy Keyes is, and has been for a long time, my most internalized source of support; Mimi Rabinovitch is both internalized and a constant external support. Without the loyal and loving friendships of Mimi, Sarah Sappington, Diane Anstadt, and Kate Schenck, I would be lost.

I must also acknowledge three institutions for their help and support: the wonderful teachers at Lawrence University in Appleton, Wisconsin, first introduced nonfiction reading to me; the Harvard Graduate School of Education with its emphasis on theory-building and its broad-minded view of what constitutes research and the field of psychology deserves thanks; and I am grateful to Bryn Mawr College for my junior-leave year and to those people who encouraged me to pursue work that is most meaningful to me. The Bryn Mawr College library was my intellectual home for the year, and thanks are due Anne Denlinger, Florence Goff, Chuck Burke, Andrew Patterson, Maggie Nerz, Joan Staples, Judy Regueiro, and many others for rolling out the red carpet whenever I walked in.

At Harvard University Press Angela von der Lippe was steadfastly encouraging, and Christine Thorsteinsson edited the manuscript with enthusiasm, care, and insight into the importance of the language chosen.

Finally, my husband, Paul Orgel, gave practical help in the form of "right" words for my "wrong" ones; our discussions at home helped me to understand issues of blame and responsibility much more personally. My two sons, Willy and Julian, supported and interfered with the writing of this book in complex ways, but their presence and love make this work worth doing.

INDEX

Abramson, Lyn, 15–16

Absolution, 21, 164–165, 172

Abuse: reactions to, 2, 7–8, 9, 11, 43–46, 53, 70, 184, 185; effects of, 40, 46, 47, 52, 90, 101, 124, 184, 185; cycle of, 54, 57, 60–67; commonality of, 60–61. *See also* Sexual abuse

Academia, 87, 114–116, 121–123, 124–125

Accountability, 8

Actor-observer divergence, 92

Adams, Robert, 71, 82

Addiction, 51, 56, 57, 60, 76

Aggression, 142; and children, 132, 133, 153–154, 155, 157

Alcohol and alcoholism, 14, 17, 34, 51, 57, 58, 60, 77–78, 94

Anger: and blame, 18–19, 43; and gender, 33, 34, 72–73, 80, 145, 147–148, 150, 151–152, 154, 155; victims', 28, 53, 123, 131, 158; and addiction, 60; and biological inevitability, 60, 69, 73–75; and impulse, 69–72, 82, 146–147; long-standing, 72–73; and children, 72–73, 134, 152, 155, 157; and cultural and social training, 74–75, 146–147; and aggression, 69, 80, 132, 140, 153, 154; and depression, 145, 146, 154; and entitlement, 150, 154; and forgiveness, 161, 162, 163; and guilt, 170

Anger-control training, 72

Anxiety, 7, 47, 101, 138, 145

Aristotle, 10, 43

Aronfreed, Justin, 138

"Attributional egotism," 58

Attributions, 24–25, 91–96; cognitive, 15–18

Backlash movements, 7, 24, 96–105, 106–113, 116, 122

Badness, 36, 84, 148

Bandura, Albert, 65

Barstow, Anne Llewellyn, 98

Bateson, Gregory, 117

Battered Woman's Syndrome, 16, 40, 164

Battered women who kill, 5–6